SAINTE-MÈRE-ÉGLISE

AN AMERICAN SANCTUARY IN NORMANDY

1944-1948

From the **D-Day** battles
to the creation of American temporary military cemeteries

Antonin DEHAYS

SAINTE-MÈRE-ÉGLISE
AN AMERICAN SANCTUARY IN NORMANDY
1944-1948

From the **D-Day** battles
to the creation of American temporary military cemeteries

Translated from the French by John Bro

OREP
EDITIONS

ACKNOWLEDGEMENTS

This work is the fruit of several years of research during which witnesses, historians, archivists and enthusiasts have given me their support and their ever precious help. I would like to thank first of all those who have given me permission to share their recollections and their personal archives. A great thanks to Madeleine Valognes, Geneviève Pasquette, Jacques and Raymonde Pignot, Jean-Baptiste Feuillye, Yves De La Rüe, Léon Mignot, André Levesque, Henri-Jean Renaud and Fred B. Morgan.

This undertaking would have been impossible without the financial support of the *Mémorial de Caen* and the *Airborne Museum* of Sainte-Mère-Église. These research grants, attributed within the framework of the production of a doctoral thesis entitled *"Death and the Battle of Normandy"* (under the direction of Professors Jean Quellien and François Rouquet) have enabled me to visit different archival centers around the world ranging from Washington DC to Berlin and London, and to collect a great number of sources relative to the village of Sainte-Mère-Église.

Furthermore, I address my gratitude to the employees of the National Archives and Records Administration (NARA) based in College Park (Maryland) – where the author of these lines resides – and, particularly, to Eric Van Slander and Joshua Fennell. My thanks also go to Hans-Hermann Söchtig, director of the WASt, (Berlin) and to Ludwig Norz for their help in guiding me through the German sources.

At the local level, I sincerely thank the departmental archives of La Manche, but also, and above all, the museums of *Utah Beach* and Sainte-Mère-Église for having opened their ever so rich and precious archives to me. My thanks go to the members of the scientific branch of the *Mémorial de Caen* and particularly to Stéphane Simonnet and Marie-Claude Berthelot.

This book partially owes the diversity of its documentation to Fréderic Le Goupil, Constant Lebastard, Michaël Simon, Richard Johnson, Stéphane Lamache, Eric Belloc, Julien Paquin, and to the D-Day Paratroopers Historical Center (Saint-Côme-du-Mont). Also, I thank those who agreed to share their collection of objects from the battlefield: Jérémy Arnould, Michel Quilez, Michael Rosiers, Gil Bourdeaux, Michel De Trez and Eric Dorr.

Finally, I extend my heartfelt thanks to my wife, Lisa, and to my parents, Hubert and Maryse, for their attentive and exacting reading as well as their unfailing support in my projects.

I would like to express my gratitude to all concerned.

To Mary,

In Memory of an amazing
journey spent together in Normandy.

A. Delaroque

Jan 29th, 2016.

Oh ! Silvered ray of the moon
Which descends like a dove
To fix itself on the young tombs
And softly illuminate them…

Simone Renaud,
Norman writer and poet

Offered by a young Norman girl to an American during the summer of 1944, this flower and its ribbon come miraculously to us. They personify emblematically the wind of liberty that blew across the four corners of Normandy. Private collection

FOREWORD

It is in visiting military cemeteries that one measures the price paid for peace and liberty.

The first place freed at the dawn of June 6, 1944, by the American paratroopers, the ground at Sainte-Mère-Église, would rapidly become a shroud for tens, then hundreds, then thousands of young men coming from across the Atlantic. The multitude of tombs, spread over three provisional cemeteries, would profoundly and durably mark the spirit and the memories of the inhabitants of our region.

Men doffed their hats, women bowed at the passage of an ambulance rolling slowly toward its charge's final resting place. These dead had become our own. People came with family, as a sign of respect, to visit the cemeteries and to put flowers on the tombs. Overwhelmed by the immensity of the sacrifice, they preserve and pass on forever the memory and the spirit of gratitude toward their liberators.

Our land had become their land and the decision to return these coffins to their native country, or to regroup them at the cemetery of Colleville-sur-Mer was felt by the whole population as a real wrenching, a new separation.

Today, only three stone monuments exist at their place of origin. Each June 6, we gather before these markers in their memory and that of their bereaved families.

Our thanks go to Antonin Dehays for this work, well documented and enriched by the testimony of the participants in this period. He brings us back to the memory of this episode, today forgotten and unrecognized, of the temporary cemeteries of Sainte-Mère-Église. He thus pays tribute to all those who by their sacrifice allow us to live today in peace and in liberty.

Marc LEFÈVRE
President of the Airborne Museum
Former-Mayor of Sainte-Mère-Église
Vice-President of the General Council

PREFACE

If war is made by the living and not by the dead, it is often made by the living in the name of the dead. Nothing seems more true, looking at Sainte-Mère-Église, amid the temporary cemeteries installed by the American army between 1944 and 1948.

Every year, around June 6, a ceremony is organized at the commemorative monument dedicated to the American temporary cemetery n° 1 of Sainte-Mère-Église. The moment is solemn, for all those present know the history of this place which has been returned to civilian life for a very long time. We find a soccer field and various other things in its place. In sum, there is nothing left here that returns us to the cemetery's rows of white crosses, with the exception of this simple stone. At the time of this writing, the sixty-ninth anniversary of D-Day has just taken place. As it must be, no one has chosen to depart from this duty to memory. This is the corollary of the boundless recognition toward the thousands of young men, come from across the Atlantic, and who, in June 1944, fell on our soil. Each of us can remember more intensely why they lived, and died. Sunday, June 9, 2013, among the officials and other participants, there were a few of the old ones. Their gaze was inevitably different from ours, for they knew these places immediately after the war, and several had done a lot more than just frequent them. Antonin Dehays will tell the full story of these witnesses and rare actors of the former cemeteries in his work consecrated to the temporary cemeteries. His work, in the framework of his thesis, has brought

him to sort through masses of French and American archives and to correlate them with the testimonies of the survivors of the period. Knowing as I do the seriousness and the interest of his research, he had no need of a preface. He has already understood the notion that the History of the Present is necessarily ephemeral, oblivion closing our consciousness inexorably as generations disappear. And thus, in most humble manner, will I permit myself to sketch that which I find in this work that is important and, moreover, new from the historical point of view.

The Second World War represents, without contest, a major conflict in the history of humanity. In any case, it was, by the number of victims it produced, an extremely deadly period. In the past, numerous historians have highlighted its horrifying consequences with regard to the losses both military and civilian. No fewer than fifty million human beings died – and this is merely an estimate, likely to be increased. In this abyss of destruction, the landings of June 6, 1944 and the Battle of Normandy which followed only represent one bloody episode, among so many others. And doubtless not the worst, one might add. From this battle, which lasted one hundred days, Antonin Dehays has retained only the first four, so essential, for the success of the allied invasion. And, in this short lapse, he has chosen to highlight the very hard battles fought by the American *82nd* and *101st Airborne Divisions*: beginning on June 6th, 1944, fighting in the county of Sainte-Mère-Église lasted all of four days

An image so symbolic, taken in 1947 inside the temporary cemetery n° 2 of Sainte-Mère-Église. The picture illustrates the homage of Normandy toward its liberators. Collection Airborne Museum

and three nights. The eminently strategic location of this village of La Manche and its surroundings explain the fierceness of the two camps to take it. On both sides, losses were terrible. The American shock troops took it finally from a combative German army of occupation. Plunged, despite themselves, into the tumult, the inhabitants of the county also paid a heavy tribute to the war. Finally, the storm past, were they able to dress their wounds in an atmosphere both of gravity, and of happiness at their recovered liberty.

However, these same inhabitants had not yet finished with the war, far from it. In most of

the communes around Sainte-Mère-Église, soldiers, fallen so recently, lay on the ground. For Antonin Dehays, their story, if we can call it such, then began. They would never take an active part in this story. For the soldiers who were killed on this portion of Norman land, just like those who had preceded them in this war, were no longer masters of their destiny. And so, others would have to take their place.

How to proceed, and the time it would take, were now the business of the living, starting with their comrades who had survived. What the author shows perfectly is that thanks to detailed military reports and to testimonies of all sorts, we know the circumstances in which such and such an American paratrooper fell at such a place. Although such an assertion cannot be generalized, it underscores immediately the difference of status between Liberators and Occupiers. The latter mostly joined a nothingness synonymous with anonymity the moment they were killed. In any case, on the American side, the result is a sort of individualization of death, in contrast with the murderous excesses of the war. Let us note that this somewhat isolated aspect can be explained, in part, by the brevity of the engagement of the aforesaid divisions on a tiny geographic perimeter. That said, the question asked by the author goes well beyond this consideration: what becomes of all these soldiers left dead on the field? In the first days that followed the Landings, many were buried in haste, and at the place where they had died. It was in these fields, under their rich bloom, that they found their "first last resting place", in this late spring, 1944. It was only a little later that the American Army chose to dig them up in order to rebury them in a place provided for the purpose. One after the other, the bodies of these soldiers, scattered around the country, were thus discovered. They ended up rejoining three new places situated in and around Sainte-Mère-Église. Where yesterday they rested in isolated fields, these brothers-in-arms found themselves now reunited in military cemeteries worthy of the name. This process of gathering, very characteristic of military organizations, did not go unnoticed in the region. One can even say that it caused a sociological shock as unexpected as it was lasting on the part of certain natives.

Practices linked to the presence of these cemeteries sprang up and became established quite quickly as inescapable rituals. The strength of the author is to have restored the individual and collective reactions of a community confronting an exceptional situation. This explains, perhaps, the character, just as exceptional, of their attachment to the cemeteries.

The temporary cemetery n°.1 of Sainte-Mère-Église, photographed in 1946. NARA

Finally, avoiding all morbidity, this strange story plunges us into a universe where passion meets with the strict application of military regulations. After seventy years, its denouement has something of the Greek tragedies. Closing this preface without further delay, I leave to the reader the pleasure of discovery.

Stéphane LAMACHE
Doctor of Contemporary History

INTRODUCTION

Rare are the places in our memories which, at their mention, resonate as much as Sainte-Mère-Église, a village of the Cotentin, in Normandy. In a conversation – from Europe to the United States – you will suddenly see your partner raise eyebrows when you talk about the now legendary story of an American paratrooper hanging from the church steeple, one evening of June 1944. The story of this modest village of La Manche has gone well beyond its frontiers. The reasons for this memorial influence are not solely connected to the military operations of D-Day itself, but clearly with the days after the combats, supported by the many soldiers killed in the battle and the creation of three large cemeteries in the district of Sainte-Mère-Église. A close bond between America and the inhabitants of the county was generated and then consolidated unlike anywhere else in the European theater of operations. It is this special story, fascinating and moving, that is evoked in the present work. The reader is invited to understand the multiple facets of the slow process of sanctuarization of this incomparable site. In other words, when the sacred made this corner of Normandy an untouchable monument in the collective memory.

The village of Sainte-Mère-Église was not born on June 6th, 1944 when General Dwight D. Eisenhower and the Allied High Command chose it as the keystone of the landing sector coded for the occasion "Utah Beach". Here was an ordinary village with a past both dense and moving. From the Roman presence to the combats of June 1940, by the Vikings' presence in the 10th century, not forgetting the ravages of the Hundred Years' War, there is no doubt about the richness of the past of Sainte-Mère-Église.[1]

Came D-Day, June 6, 1944. After four years of German occupation, the village and its county found themselves in the front row of military operations. The two American airborne divisions, 13,110 paratroopers of the *82nd* and *101st Airborne Divisions*, were to jump – theoretically – around Sainte-Mère-Église with the mission to gain control of the roads and bridges in the interior of the country. The capture of these axes of communications was supposed to facilitate the amphibious landing planned for the first light of June 6 at 6:30. This strategic crossroads was intended to serve as the American forces' launch pad with the directive of cutting the Cotentin peninsula in two. Finally, after having surrounded the German *709th Infantry Division* scattered around the north of the Cotentin, three American infantry divisions were supposed, at whatever the cost, to take the deep water port of Cherbourg.

As early as 0:16[2] D-Day, the first paratroopers were unfortunately dropped beyond their defined areas.[3] The people of Sainte-Mère-Église witnessed these unfortunate drops. Certain Sainte-Mère-Églisians were coincidentally not forced to stay at home that night.[4] Those who lived near the village square were exceptionally authorized to participate in fighting a fire which had started accidentally at Ms Pommier's. Civilians, men and women, were given a show that they would never have imagined: waves of airplanes swept overhead, and suddenly, men jumped. The first American

Two American soldiers, belonging to the military police (4th Infantry Division), share their C-rations with an inhabitant of Sainte-Mère-Église at the intersection of the road to Ravenoville. NARA

paratroopers were killed on or near the village square. After a few hours of sporadic encounter, around 4:30 a.m., an American flag flew over the town hall of Sainte-Mère-Église. We were only at the beginnings of the liberation of the country.

Although the liberation was real, it was fragile, since it was threatened several times during the hours and days after the Allied landings. Far from the outpourings of joy and the waving of flags along the roads, the village and its environs began a cohabitation with death as unexpected as it was traumatic. The war, inherently destructive, created a climate of incomprehensible and unimaginable fright for those who had not lived it. A climate dominated by the fear of dying, a climate

where everyone's senses were put to the test. The dead were there, everywhere. The odor of death added to this macabre vision that takes you by the nose, an odor you never get used to. The month of June 1944 and the macabre atmosphere that came with it have forever marked a break in the history of this Norman village.

The victims were more numerous every day. To deal with this situation, special units of the American Army were charged with gathering, identifying and burying the dead.

To accomplish this thankless and titanic task, the American graves services created three temporary military cemeteries in the county of Sainte-Mère-Église. Thousands of white crosses appeared in the earth. Two military cemeteries were set up in Sainte-Mère-Église itself. A third, a little to the south, was opened in the commune of Carquebut and named incorrectly "*Blosville*". The locals then had to become familiar with these young tombs that all told the same story: that of a life broken too early, thousands of miles from home. An almost intimate relationship became established between the families of these soldiers fallen in Normandy and Sainte-Mère-Église. In what form was this exclusive and special bond with the United States made?

These great cemeteries were the origin of some surprising cultural practices. Some unusual attitudes and behaviors were adopted within them. They made the inhabitants of the county feel as if they were in another country. It was America! A little bit of America, it's true, but such splendor, and so solemn! "These were our soldiers, our cemeteries…" the inhabitants will tell you. Those of Sainte-Mère-Église were the first witnesses of this grandeur, nonetheless "temporaire". What became of the temporary cemeteries, when their very name implied their disappearance in the short or long term? When the question was posed regarding the impermanence of the sites – for that is how it was for the American Army – what did the locals think? What was the form of the outcry attempting to save the American cemeteries?

The decades have passed since 1944, and the process of sanctuarization which was generated by the presence of temporary cemeteries, is now embodied through an immaterial thing judged to be so precious, the memory of D-Day and its victims. The memory comes from the sacred insofar as it crystallizes the past which pleases many of our contemporaries who enjoy rituals. What is more reassuring than the dummy of John Steele hanging from the

steeple for eternity? He is there, immobile, embodying in himself an event linked with the parachute drops of June 6, 1944. Beware of those who would revisit the virtually sealed contours of this grand sanctuary of history. It is never very easy to touch the sacred, whence comes the difficulty for the historian to apply a scientific procedure which, in essence, must revise and nuance those facts generally committed to memory. The intention here is not to undertake in a pretentious way the slightest demystification of the history of Sainte-Mère-Église, that same story that historians and witnesses have allowed us to write until today. On the contrary, it is indeed another look – anthropological, this time – that one wishes to offer to the reader. Based on a corpus of sources both varied and new, we offer a new approach toward an often treated subject, with a constant theme: death in battle and the men's attitudes toward the victims of war.

The documentation presented in these pages comes from public institutions such as the American National Archives, based in College Park (Maryland) or the unexplored bases of the WASt[5] in Berlin. On the local scale, the departmental archives of La Manche in Saint-Lô have given us some great discoveries. Private institutions have also contributed to the elaboration of the body of sources. Several museums of the Lower Normandy region, such as the Mémorial de Caen, the Airborne Museum of Sainte-Mère-Église, the D-Day paratroopers Historical Center of Saint-Côme-du-Mont, and not forgetting the Utah Beach Museum of Sainte-Marie-du-Mont, have shared their collections with us. Finally, the inhabitants of the county of Sainte-Mère-Église, the "anciens", those who lived in proximity to the military cemeteries, have contributed a great deal to this undertaking.

The abundant documentation produced by them, makes, without doubt, the value of this work. It has been necessary to make this documentary wealth intelligible, clear and living, so that the history of each of these actors might finally be brought to light.

The village of Sainte-Mère-Église and its inhabitants were plunged, despite themselves, into the heart of the combat of June 1944. Later, the locality was chosen to accept several temporary American military cemeteries. Through the careful study of these two great events, we will see in what measure they contributed to the construction of the unparalleled myth that is today Sainte-Mère-Église. How could a society – on the scale of a county – learn to live next to some 13,996 military tombs? For an entire village and its county, what was so rightly considered unthinkable, has become unforgettable.

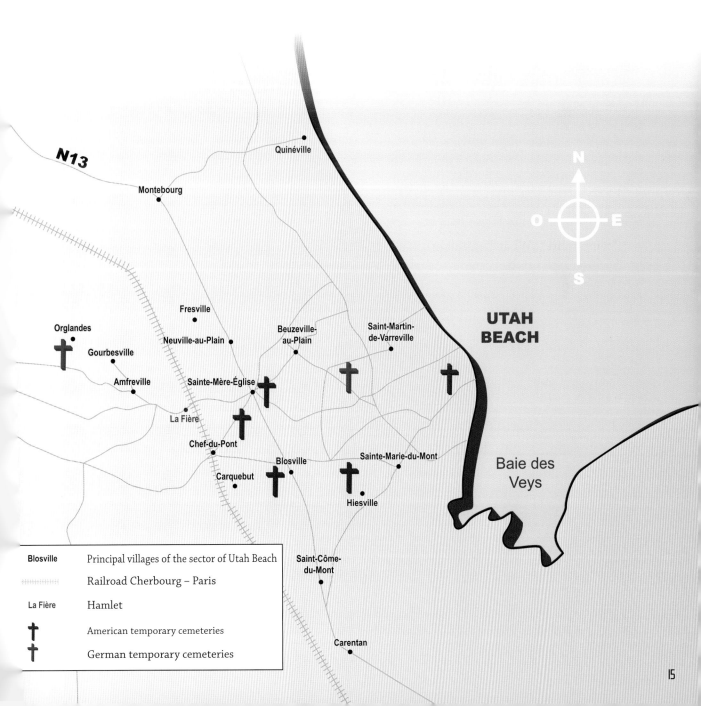

Blosville	Principal villages of the sector of Utah Beach
┼┼┼┼┼┼┼┼	Railroad Cherbourg – Paris
La Fière	Hamlet
†	American temporary cemeteries
†	German temporary cemeteries

Captain Anthony H. Stefanich, commander of C Company – *505th* PIR, photographed in England near the aerodrome of Spanhoe, a few hours before he was dropped in Normandy. He landed north of Sainte-Mère-Église, near Baudienville, on June 6, 1944. He then participated in the battle to secure the bridge of La Fière. He was photographed here by the soldier Joseph C. Fitt who described him in these terms "a damned good guy in spite of a few of the lieutenants". He was seriously wounded on D-Day when an enemy bullet went through a smoke grenade attached to his belt. Although he survived the Battle of Normandy, he was killed in action on September 18, 1944 in Holland.

© Gil Bourdeaux

OBJECTIVE "BROOKLYN"

The Capture of Sainte-Mère-Église

A VILLAGE OF THE COTENTIN UNDER THE GERMAN JACKBOOT

Well before being coded "Brooklyn" for the Allies, or even "Bochum" for the Germans, Sainte-Mère-Église was a peaceful village on the eve of the Second World War. In the heart of the Cotentin peninsula, in this wonderfully fertile region called Le Plain, between marshes and farmland, the village was situated barely ten kilometers from the coast. In those days, orchards covered a large part of the land, dividing it into thousands of parcels, sometimes very narrow, and bordered by centuries-old hedges. The soil, like everywhere else in the peninsula, is particularly generous. Three hundred sixty-five days a year, it produces grass, green and rich, so appreciated by the local breeds of cattle. But the pride of the people here was the horse. Horse breeding activity in Sainte-Mère-Église was an offshoot of the celebrated stud farms of Saint-Lô. André Levesque, a boy of five in 1944, lived in the stud farm of Sigosville, to the north of Sainte-Mère-Église. In his memoires, he remembers these local activities fondly: "but what made the success of Sainte-Mère was its thoroughbreds and especially its trotters. The undoubted star of the area was named Javari [...], he had won the Prix d'Amérique in 1936 at the rate of 1 minute 24.8 seconds per kilometer."[6] It was not unusual to see stallions from Sainte-Mère-Église on the greatest racetracks. On the village square, the 12th century church and its bell tower (known as "saddle-back") had been witness every Thursday since 1889 to a major livestock market. This market was famous well beyond the boundaries of the county. Farmers would come from the four corners of the peninsula to buy their calves.

These picturesque daily events were not much disturbed by the beginning of hostilities on September 3rd, 1939, when France and England declared war on Nazi Germany - a war which everyone thought would be short, and which in any case, was taking place hundreds of miles away. People worried all the same about the ninety-two soldiers of the county of Sainte-Mère-Église headed off to the front[7]. A front that wasn't really one, until May 10, 1940 and the German breakthrough at Sedan. June 14 saw the German troops enter Paris. The war was coming closer so quickly that on June 18, 1940, the day the Germans arrived in Sainte-Mère-Église, very few inhabitants even saw General Erwin Rommel's *7th Armored Division*. "The phantom division" - the nickname given because of its speed – had bypassed the town with a view to capturing Cherbourg and to slowing down the reorganization of the French troops. The occupation of villages was not on the agenda and it was not until July 6, 1940, that the arrival and installation of elements of the German *216th Infantry Division* took place. During the 1,487 days that followed, the village and its county would learn to live, for better or worse, with the German soldiers whose job was to progressively control the rural areas.

Germans take the town hall of Sainte-Mère-Église during the summer of 1940. Collection H.-J. Renaud

Picture taken during the summer of 1940 in what is now called impasse Robert Murphy. The German soldier who lived at Mme. Morin's washes a few of his clothes while M. Hébert watches. Collection H.-J. Renaud

A present-day view of the Impasse Robert Murphy. Photo by the author.

Thus began a long cohabitation marked on a daily basis by a variety of constraints and restrictions. In his memoirs, Alexandre Renaud, pharmacist and member of the town council, tells of the arrival of the occupier: "The Germans occupied the houses immediately, leaving only a minimum of space to the inhabitants."[8] He adds: "On the town hall's square, an immense flag flew with a swastika. On the walls, the Ortskommandantur splashed the first notices, in German and French, naming for execution those patriots who were guilty of compromising the security of the occupier's army." The scene was set. Nothing would be the same, and the feeling of injustice for some, of humiliation for others, only added to the growing difficulties of daily life. Jacques Pignot was 14 in 1941. He recalls these difficult times: "My father was a police officer in Isigny-le-Buat. He died in 1941. I had an aunt who lived in Sainte-Mère-Église. My mother, my sister and I had left the South Manche and we arrived in this house situated on a dead-end not far from the church. Life was especially hard under the Occupation. It was misery: I had to work from an early age. I became the mailman for Sainte-Mère-Église."[9]

The occupation changed regularly; movements of troops were frequent and the density of soldiers was always high, particularly after March 23, 1942, when Adolf Hitler published his directive

ID of Jacques Pignot, the young mailman of Sainte-Mère-Église. In 1941, accompanied by his mother and his sister, he moved into the house at the end of a dead-end street. Collection J. Pignot

September 1940, review of troops for this company of the 216th German infantry division at the place called "La garde à Feuardent", on the site of the current museum. Collection H.-J. Renaud

Churchill on the BBC concerning an allied landing in the fall of 1943 had been broken, and some people felt beaten. The fact that the war remained distant became a source of anxiety, as Alexandre Renaud explains: "We only felt the war by its echoes that arrived from time to time, allied bombardments on the airports of Cherbourg or in the vicinity of Valognes."[10] In parallel, the relationship between occupiers and occupied was still as distant, generally speaking. It is true that events that could appear insignificant, like the expulsion of old folks from the hospice to Carquebut in 1941, did not ease relations with the German army. These relations were made even more complex by the fact that they were based on the principle of submission inherent in any military occupation.

n° 40 announcing the policy of great works of fortification from the coast of Norway down to the north of Spain. The construction of the Atlantic Wall and the need for labor was one of the principal factors in the requisitioning of men and beasts.

With the winter of 1943-1944 the Occupation grew heavier each day. The promise of Winston

Hope would have to come from the sky. The battlefield, the only one, was placed above people's heads. Given the proximity of Britain, aerial combat and other reconnaissance flights in this part of France were frequent. From the ground, the show was exciting, as Jacques Pignot explains: "A few months before the Invasion, while our football team was on its way to Carentan, we saw two P-47 fighters at the top of the hill at Fauville, going from east to west – that same pair of Thunderbolts that we would supposedly see fly over the square of Sainte-Mère, the evening of June 5, 1944, toward 9.00 p.m. (solar time)."[11]

In March 1944, a unit of the *Flak* – German anti-aircraft defense – was set up in Sainte-Mère-Église. Arriving without any canons, the "*Flak*", as they were known to some, were Austrians, most of them old and of fairly poor combat value, much like the unit's commander, a lover of good wines and other local spirits.

The latter had installed himself in the house of the Parc de la Haule at Dr. Pelletier's. In the days that followed, this new unit was followed by

September 1940: two German soldiers near Julia Pommier's barn, from which fire accidentally struck the evening of June 5, 1944. Collection H.-J. Renaud

These soldiers of the army of occupation pose at the opening of the Rue du General-de-Gaulle. Collection H.-J. Renaud

Germans on the church square in 1940. Collection H.-J. Renaud

another German battalion, a little sharper than the preceding one this time, who set themselves up in the nearby hamlets of Gambosville, Fauville, and La Coquerie. This was a more disciplined unit that was placed under the orders of a German officer, here described by Alexandre Renaud, who had become temporary mayor following Louis Leroux's health problems: "A certain Lieutenant Zitt, a badly constructed giant, was named commandant of the place. He called me to Gambosville to tell me in five words what he wanted from me. What he wanted was absolute obedience to every word."[12] Thus followed multiple threats – of death at times – toward M. Renaud when he refused to transfer the wireless sets stored in the mayor's offices to the command post of Lieutenant Zitt in Gambosville.

A veritable war of nerves went on between these two protagonists, one displaying the arrogance and superiority of a victorious army, the other, as a mediator, trying to square the aspirations of his citizens with those of an occupier whose requirements were often impossible.

To the surprise of the people of Sainte-Mère-Église, on May 10, 1944, Lieutenant Zitt and his unit were sent to the other side of the Cotentin, to Vauville, to the great relief of the new mayor of the commune. On May 16, 1944, the city council elected Alexandre Renaud mayor following the death of Louis Leroux. This pharmacist, veteran of the Great War, had married Simone Cornière in 1923. Father of three boys, Paul, Henri-Jean, and Maurice, this cultured community leader enjoyed the greatest respect of his townspeople.

The soccer team of Sainte-Mère-Église in 1941. Jacques Pignot, standing (2nd from the left). Raymond Paris (2nd from the right) was forced to leave the village from January until June 1944, having chosen to flee the obligatory work service. He hid for six months in a farm in Les Deux-Sevres department. A member of the Resistance (OCM group), he returned to Sainte-Mère-Église June 3, 1944. Collection J. Pignot

There were new troop movements at the end of May 1944 in Sainte-Mère-Église. Gunners were set up in Gambosville immediately securing all access to the village. Howitzers were placed along the roads to La Fière, Cap-de-Laine, Ravenoville and Carentan. It was a battalion comprising men enlisted from the four corners of the *Reich*, as the new mayor at the time underlines: "Mongols, with gallows jaws, wander around town in the evening."[13] The Osttruppen (the troops from the East) were quickly transferred to Saint-Côme-du-Mont a few days before the allied landings. This was tremendous luck for the paratroopers of the 82nd Airborne Division whose job would be to capture and secure Sainte-Mère-Église on June 6, 1944.

During the night of 28 to 29 May, around sixty Lancaster bombers pulverized the installations of the German batteries code-named "1/II/1261 H.K.A.R.", situated in Saint-Martin-de-Varreville. The vibrations of this bombardment were felt all the way to Sainte-Mère-Église. It was "a day of violent light, bluish and uniform" according to Alexandre Renaud. The Germans of the area were put on alert, fearing an attempted landing. The degree of nervousness among some of these men was extreme: "The owner of the Manor of Fauville, Mrs Chapey whose husband had been a lawyer in Valognes and was killed in Verdun in 1917, went out into her park. A German soldier, taking her for a paratrooper, shot her dead, making her the first victim of this tragic week."[14] It was a premonition of the great battle that would follow a week later in which death would not spare civilians, on the

Winter 1943: German soldiers and civilians, photographed at the intersection of Cap-de-Laine street, and the road to Ravenoville.

Collection F. Le Goupil

The home rented by Dr. Pelletier in the park of la Haule, facing the church, just on the edge of the square. This served as the command post to the successive German units after March 1943. During the combats of June 6, 1944, several shell fragments and other projectiles of all sorts damaged the gate in the foreground. Photo by the author

contrary. A surprising fact: "planes flew over the road to Ravenoville, near the new houses, and twenty or so paratroopers jumped out from east to west above the town hall and went to land toward the road to La Fière. Meanwhile, they were doused with tracer bullets by the machine guns in the steeple."[15]

Alexandre Renaud's memoirs are complemented by those of another young man who was seventeen in 1944, Yves De La Rüe, from Carquebut: "A few days before the invasion, a soldier dressed in German gear came to stay with us, alone. He took a bedroom upstairs. He didn't say a word. We were surprised when he asked my father for a wireless. He wanted to hear the BBC. The next day he was gone, early in the morning, leaving behind a little French flag. We thought he was probably a soldier of the allies ..."[16] It would appear, after these reports, that allied high command had decided to send several reconnaissance missions to the county of Sainte-Mère-Église no doubt to

evaluate the state of alert of the German troops installed in the sector, but also to gauge the state of mind of the civilians on the eve of military operations in Normandy.

Jacques Pignot remembers a similar phenomenon: "The Sunday evening before D-Day, I was walking in town with my friends. Arriving in front of the Dubost bakery, I saw a piece of cigarette pack on the ground, Camels, in good enough shape that I could recognize it. [...] They must have dropped sikkies [little dummies dressed like paratroopers] to create a diversion, to mask a drop of real paratroopers. I can still see this German holding one of those dolls in his hands. I think a careless fellow, just parachuted, could have left his package on the sidewalk..."[17] A few days before the Landing, Jacques Pignot, once again, was asked to rub shoulders with a soldier of the occupying army. Even if all friendly relations with the enemy were banned, the Germans had ended up by gaining a little empathy with the French.

"Rudolph Brauning occupied a requisitioned bedroom at our neighbor's, Mme Morin's. His family had a furniture business near Mannheim, destroyed in a bombardment at the end of May, 1944. But his family survived. He got permission to see them. On his return, his company it seems had moved to Pont-l'Abbé. He had zero morale. We spoke with him in English, which he knew rather well. He asked me if he could shave, which he did in the kitchen, and then he left. At the Liberation, that resulted in the arrest of my mother one evening of July or August 1944, by some people, probably intelligence, after she was denounced by the so-called resistants of the area."[18] Before leaving, Brauning left a bit of paper with Jacques Pignot on which he had written a name and an address, hoping perhaps to get some news once the war was over. Except that the German never saw the end of the conflict. He was killed June 20, 1944, during the battle of Saint-Sauveur-le-Vicomte. He lies in the German military cemetery in Orglandes.

The intensity of these first days of June began to seriously worry the occupier. The long-awaited Landing was imminent, and this information was confirmed by the local Resistance, the OCM network (Organisation Civile et Militaire) commanded by Mr Maury. The young clerk of the notary, Raymond Paris, was shaken when he heard on the BBC, thanks to a little crystal radio he had constructed, the following message: "The dice are on the mat". A message with heavy consequences but above all full of hope. It was addressed to the different groups of the Resistance of the north-west coast of France and indicated that the D-Day operation would take place within the next forty-eight hours.

Alexandre Renaud, center, elected mayor of Sainte-Mère-Église on May 16, 1944, accompanied by members of the city council and some mayors of the county. Collection H.-J. Renaud

SAINTE-MÈRE-ÉGLISE: "KEYSTONE" OF THE UTAH BEACH SECTOR

On the other side of the Channel, in the ports and airports of southern England, the machine of war was running. For several months, the nervous men had been waiting patiently for D-Day. The opening of a new front in western Europe answered the repeated demands of Stalin, who wanted to see the German army crumble over a territory so broad that their exhaustion would be inevitable. Even though another front had been opened by the allies in Italy with the landing in Sicily in July of 1943, the principal effort – the shock so hoped for – would take place in Normandy, along the coasts of La Manche and Calvados.

The American, Canadian and British divisions, placed under the command of the American General Dwight D. Eisenhower, had to land in Europe and create a bridgehead as solid as possible with the aim of landing vast quantities of soldiers and equipment. In the vanguard of this undertaking, three allied airborne divisions had to be dropped around the five sectors of beach dedicated to the amphibious landings. In the east, the British *6th Airborne Division* was charged with capturing two bridges across the Orne River, to the north of the city of Caen, to block any German counter-attack coming from the east. Further west, in the Cotentin peninsula, the *82nd* and *101st Airborne* Divisions had the mission of jumping onto the American sector code-named *Utah Beach* in order to secure all the axes of communication leading to the beach of La Madeleine and thus to facilitate the amphibious landing that was to occur at dawn on June 6, 1944. Military operations were placed under the command of the *VIIth US Corps* (Gen. Joseph Lawton Collins). The principal mission consisted of capturing, as quickly as possible, the deep water port of Cherbourg in order to be able to land even more men and material in the days and months to come.

The *101st Airborne Division*, commanded by Maj. Gen. Maxwell D. Taylor, was to be parachuted on the east side of the National Road 13, over three theoretical zones. The "Screaming Eagles" were supposed to control four roads that overlooked the wetlands which had been flooded by the Germans since November 1942, capture two bridges to the south on the Douve river, and take the lock of La Barquette near Carentan with a view to blocking any German counter-attacks in the first hours of D-Day.

The mission to take Sainte-Mère-Église fell to the *82nd Airborne Division*. Close to 6,600 paratroopers, under the orders of Generals Matthew Ridgway and James Gavin, were to take the bridges on the Douve and on the Merderet Rivers, to the west of this village coded for the occasion "Brooklyn". The barriers installed at each communication point were supposed to contain the expected German offensives while awaiting the link-up with the *4th Infantry Division* which had landed at *Utah Beach*. Up until May 15, 1944, the Allies had planned for an air drop to the west of Saint-Sauveur-le-Vicomte. However, with the arrival and installation of Germany's *91st Luftland Infantry Division* in the sector around the first of the month, it became preferable to concentrate air assaults around Sainte-Mère-Église in order to consolidate rapidly the American foothold near Utah Beach. Once these last-minute modifications were in place, the conquest of Sainte-Mère-Église, in the first hours, became the keystone of the assault. The village was now considered by the allied high command to be the most important point of communications in the Cotentin Peninsula. It had to be held, in consequence, by the paratroopers of the *82nd Airborne Division*.

C COMPANY
505TH PIR, CAMP QUORN (ENGLAND)

The soldier Joseph C. Fitt, with his little Zeiss Ikon camera, recently acquired in a game of cards, immortalizes some of his comrades-in-arms from C Company, *505th PIR*, attempting to relax during the last 48 hours before the invasion. Death is still only a game for some. Still, this naive vision of war turned out to be only too real for the principal protagonist of this scene. The soldier who is shown bayoneting his comrade, the soldier Robert E. Blackmore, is PFC Orell G. Hollande, nicknamed for the occasion "Horrible Hollande". He would be engaged in the terrible combats in La Fière of 6 and 7 June 1944 before the first battalion was relieved. On June 8, he was the target of a sniper. Succumbing to his wounds, he was buried, temporarily, at the military cemetery of Blosville.

The soldier Francis McDewitt, C Company – 505th PIR, writes a final letter, a few hours before taking part in the airborne assault on Normandy
© Gil Bourdeaux

© Gil Bourdeaux

Two paratroopers of C Company relax before the big jump. Their combat outfit is away being reinforced by regimental "tailors". Beside "Tommy" Loren Thompson (left) is an unknown soldier who was not afraid to cut his hair like the Mohawks. When the old warrior symbols come to the front... © Gil Bourdeaux

Portrait of 1st Lt Richard Brownlee, C Company. Dropped near Baudienville, the night of June 6, Brownlee broke both ankles landing and was among the first patients of Maj. Dan McIlvoy, the chief doctor of the 505th PIR. Collection J. Arnould

It should have been, secondly, the American infantry's starting point toward Carentan, Barneville-Carteret and, finally, Cherbourg. The site offered a significant strategic position to the allied troops, the village being built on a slight hill. The stone houses offered the paratroopers a first-class fortification while they were awaiting the arrival of the infantry coming from the sea.

For the VIIth US Corps, Sainte-Mère-Église, alias "Brooklyn", had become objective number one. To accomplish this mission, General Ridgway selected the 82nd Airborne Division's most experienced regiments. The *505th Parachute Infantry Regiment (505th PIR)* had experienced fire several times. Colonel William E. Ekman, commander of the *505th PIR*, in a report to the historical service of the American Army, written in July 1944, recalls the principal missions assigned to the three battalions that constituted the regiment, in a few lines:

"*505th* PIR: During and after the drop.
(This is from a statement by Colonel William E. Ekman, regimental commander throughout the operation. Colonel Ekman came down midway in the valley between Fresville and Neuville la Plant [au Plain], and the CP [Commanding Post] was established within three and a half hours and collected its command elements within three and a half hours). [...]

10. Our particular drop zone which was in the area to the North West of Sainte-Mère-Église between the main highway running north approximately north and south of the river [Merderet], was practically devoid of enemy. The elements of the regiment which landed in the designated drop zone, comprised 1000 men out of 2200, most of the remainder were distributed in the vicinity and to the north and east. But in general, they collected quite rapidly throughout D-Day, and reported to their respective unit commanders. Other smaller groups which did not report on D-Day engaged in active combat with the enemy wherever encountered

thereby greatly aiding not only the regiment but the *101st Division* along its boundary.

11. The mission of the 1st Bn, under Major Frederick Augustus Kellam, was to seize and secure the crossings of the Merderet River, approximately 2.25 miles west of Ste Mère Eglise and Chef du Pont which is southwest of Ste Mère Eglise. It further was charged to assist in the capture of Sainte-Mère-Église, if such help was necessary, and to install road blocks and demolitions within its sector in order to secure the LZ [Landing Zone] for later glider landings, and to furnish continual security for the regimental CP.

12. The 2nd Bn, under Lt Colonel Benjamin H. Vandervoort, had the mission of holding a general line running approximately east and west from Baudienville through Neuville au Plain and patrolling to the west thereof. They were to establish road blocks along this northern flank of the VII Corps area, clear the regimental area within its sector, and to maintain and establish contact with the *101st Division* at a point between Baudienville and Foucarville.

13. The 3rd Bn, under Lt Colonel Edward C. Krause, was to capture and hold Sainte-Mère-Église, to clear the regimental area within its sector, and establish road blocks generally to the south and east of Sainte-Mère-Église.

14. Regimental Headquarters had the mission to establish a CP in an orchard approximately a mile west of Sainte-Mère-Église. (Regimental Headquarters Company was under the command of Captain Talton W. Long)." [19]

The 3rd battalion of the *505th PIR* was thus chosen to take Sainte-Mère-Église in the night of D-Day. This experienced unit had come out stronger from the operations of Sicily and Italy in 1943: an experience of fire which would be precious in the combats of Normandy. On the evening of

June 5, 1944, on the blacktop of Cottesmore airport, England, Lt. Col. Edward Krause addressed his men in these terms a few hours before the C-47s took off: "We all know what is ahead of us. I have no fancy speech to make to you. I want to tell you that I expect you to do your job, not as a bunch of supermen, but as soldiers. We have here the flag which you raised as the first American flag to fly over the city of Naples. I want it to be the first flag to fly over a liberated town in France. The mission is that we got to put it over Ste-Mère-Église before dawn. You will fight with me wherever you land and when you will get to Ste-Mère-Église, I will be there.."[20]

Greenham Common Airport, England. On the evening of June 5, 1944, Dwight D. Eisenhower visits the paratroopers of the 2nd battalion – *502nd PIR, 101st Airborne Division*, knowing full well the losses will be high. NARA.

Eisenhower returning to Normandy in 1964. This time, coming back as former President of the USA. CBS

ANTICIPATING DEATH

The airborne operation over the Cotentin, and by consequence, the capture of Sainte-Mère-Église was a high-risk operation. Dumping men at night, behind enemy lines, was in principle not the simplest of missions, quite the opposite. No doubt, the Allied High Command had a few hesitations regarding the launch of this vast airborne operation. Judging from estimates, the losses would have to be heavy. Dwight D. Eisenhower, Commander in Chief of the Allied forces was confronted with a dilemma that he recalls in his report on July 13, 1945[21]: "For the operation against the neck of the Cotentin to be successful, it was believed that two airborne divisions should be employed in support of the troops assaulting the Varreville beaches, still leaving one airborne division to hold vital bridges in the Orne-Dives rivers area to the northeast of Caen. Field Marshal Montgomery and Admiral Ramsay were in agreement on this point, but Air Chief Marshal Leigh-Mallory saw technical difficulties which it was necessary to consider closely. It was his feeling, both then and subsequently, that the employment of airborne divisions against the south Cotentin would result in landing losses to aircraft and personnel as high as 75% - 80%. In the face of this estimate, however, I was still convinced in the absolute necessity of quickly overrunning the peninsula and attaining the port of Cherbourg, vital to the support and maintenance of our land forces. [...] Support by the airborne troops was essential, and I ultimately took upon myself the heavy responsibility of deciding that the airborne operation against the Cotentin be carried out."[22]

In order to deal with the potential for high losses, the VIIth Corps put in place a program to deal with military victims. In a document dated May 18, 1944, entitled Administrative Order no.1 [23], addressed to the 82nd and 101st Airborne Divisions as well as the 4th Infantry Division, the question of evacuating the bodies of the dead was raised.

June 1944: Officers and men of the 508th PIR (82nd Airborne Division) attend a last religious ceremony in a hangar at Saltby in England. NARA

For the D-Day airborne operations, the medical units 307th and 326th Airborne Medical Co. were charged with installing collection points on the edges of the dropping zones. Another important piece of information furnished by this document was the fact that a site suitable for holding a military cemetery was preselected before the assault. Referred to simply by its six digit number, "365-937", this location indicated the Carrefour des Forges, straddling the villages of Blosville and Carquebut, 3km south of Sainte-Mère-Église. The site was judged favorable to the creation of a cemetery dedicated, in principle, to the victims of the two airborne divisions. Regarding the 4th Infantry Division, the unit landing on Utah Beach, the Administrative Order n° 1 specified that the men of the 1st Engineer Special Brigade had the mission to take charge of victims of the infantry and to create a military cemetery "near the beach". Everything leads us to believe that the operation "Neptune" – the airborne and amphibious assault on June 6, 1944 – was planned out to the last detail. An operation of such size had to be planned up front, like the military cemeteries.

Sgt. Elbert E. "Bert" Legg in 1945, member of the 4th Platoon (603rd QM GRC). Collection Legg via Yves De La Rüe

Two months before the Landings in Normandy, the services corps of the American army had taken the trouble of integrating into each division of the VIIth US Corps a specially trained platoon

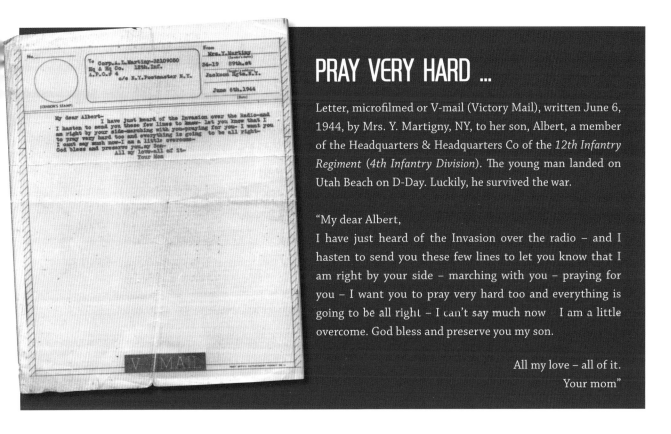

PRAY VERY HARD ...

Letter, microfilmed or V-mail (Victory Mail), written June 6, 1944, by Mrs. Y. Martigny, NY, to her son, Albert, a member of the Headquarters & Headquarters Co of the *12th Infantry Regiment (4th Infantry Division)*. The young man landed on Utah Beach on D-Day. Luckily, he survived the war.

"My dear Albert,
I have just heard of the Invasion over the radio – and I hasten to send you these few lines to let you know that I am right by your side – marching with you – praying for you – I want you to pray very hard too and everything is going to be all right – I can't say much now   I am a little overcome. God bless and preserve you my son.

All my love – all of it.
Your mom"

(22 men and an officer) to handle the inevitable losses, allied and enemy. The American general staff had planned for the *Utah Beach* sector to have the *603rd Quartermaster Graves Registration Company* arrive by sea between 6 and 9 June, 1944. The company consisted of 158 soldiers, subdivided into four platoons. The 1st Platoon was attached to the *4th Infantry Division*, the same which had taken part in the first wave of assault on the beach La Madeleine at Sainte-Marie-du-Mont on June 6. The *2nd Platoon* would follow the 9th Infantry Division during the cutting off of the Cotentin until the capture of Cherbourg. The *3rd Platoon* was, for its part, attached to the *90th Infantry Division*. And finally, the *4th Platoon* of 1st Lt. Erwin Miller would follow in the steps of the 82nd Airborne.[24] Among the men of the *4th Platoon*, Sergeant Elbert E. Legg, called "Bert", had volunteered to follow his division as early as June 6. He arrived on Norman soil, in a glider, on the evening of D-Day. Note that within the *82nd Airborne*, the *407th Airborne*

Quartermaster Company was a little group commanded by 1st Lt. James M. Fraim, the officer of the Graves Registration Service of the division. James Fraim tells us: "On June 6, before going to Normandy, France, by glider, Sergeant Elbert E. Legg, a member of the *603rd Quartermaster* (Graves Registration) Company, was attached to the division for the purpose of assisting in the establishment of a division cemetery pending the arrival of the graves registration platoon [*4th Platoon, 603rd QM GRC*]"[25]

The 101st Airborne Division was not equipped with a platoon of the Graves Registration Service. Each soldier, consequently, had the potential responsibility for a brother-in-arms fallen in combat as shown by the series of documents that follow. Addressed to the s*oldiers of the 502nd Parachute Infantry Regiment*, they highlight, some time before the Landing, the responsibilities and duties of each man regarding the protocol to follow in case of death.

(S-1) 20 May 1944

OPERATIONAL MEMORANDUM NUMBER 5

BATTLEFIELD BURIALS AND GRAVES REGISTRATION

1. COLLECTION AND EVACUATION OF THE DEAD:

a. System

The collecting point system outlined in "b" below will be used to evacuate all dead when possible. When it is impossible to evacuate the dead by this system, burials will be performed by burial parties detailed by the commanding officer of the unit concerned. (See paragraph 6)

b. Responsibility

The evacuation of American, Allied, and Enemy dead is the responsibility of all echelons of command within their zones of action.

1. Platoon Leaders, Company, Battery, or similar unit commanders are responsible for marking and reporting the location of the deceased's helmet on a rifle or stick stuck in the ground beside the body.

2. Battalion Commanders are responsible for the collection and evacuation of all dead within their areas from subordinate units to a collection point adjacent to the Battalion Aid Station.

3. The Regimental Graves Registration Officer is responsible for the collection and evacuation of all the dead within the Regimental area to collecting points established by Division. To assist the GRS Officer in this collection and evacuation, the various units of this command will supply details as and when requested by this headquarters.

c. Organization

1. Companies and Batteries - Details will be appointed as required to mark and report the location of all dead within their area.

2. Battalion - Details will be appointed as required to collect and evacuate all bodies within the battalion area to the battalion collecting point.

3. Details to be appointed as required will, under the supervision of the Regimental GRS officer, evacuate the dead from the battalion collecting points to the Division collection point.

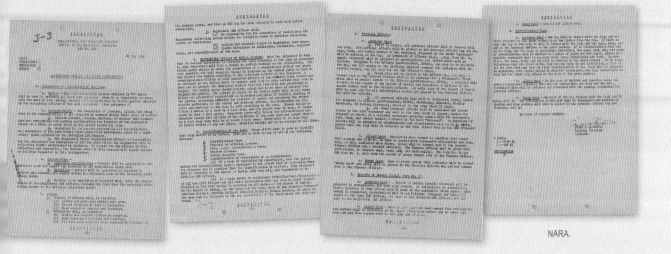

NARA.

d. Duties

1. Company or Battery will, as required:

(a) Locate and mark dead within unit area.

(b) Report location of dead to battalion.

(c) Keep record of reports and location.

2. Battalions will, as required:

(a) Locate and evacuate bodies as reported.

(b) Make searches for bodies not reported.

(c) See that each body has been examined by a member of the Medical Corps, and that an EMT tag has been attached to each body before evacuation.

3. Regimental GRS Officer will:

(a) Be responsible for the evacuation of bodies from the Regimental collecting points within the battalion areas to Division collecting points or cemeteries.

(b) Collect and evacuate bodies in Regimental rear areas.

(c) Assist battalions in collection, evacuation, registration, and identification of the dead.

2. BATTLEFIELD BURIALS BY BURIAL PARTIES:

When the situation is such that is become impossible to evacuate the dead according to the plan in paragraph 1, unit commanders will form a detail to perform burials on the battlefield. The burial party should be under the supervision of a commissioned officer and whenever possible the unit chaplain should be included in the burial party so that he may conduct the burial according to the religious beliefs of the deceased. A noncommissioned officer or well qualified private of the Medical Corps should also be included in the Burial Party to examine each body to make certain that each is dead and to prepare the Emergency Medical Tags for each body not previously so tagged. The burial party should include enough men to be used as laborers for digging the graves. The person in charge of the burial party will in all cases follow the prescribed regulations as to manner and place of burials, marking of the graves, preparing sketches for location of graves and preparing the proper reports pertaining to the burial and personal effects, and forwarding the reports and sketchbooks to the G.R.S. unit operating in the area. Graves should be 6 feet 6 inches by 2 feet by 5 feet deep, and are placed side by side, 12 inches apart in rows 3 feet apart. Temporary grave will follow the aforementioned dimensions except that if time or the condition of the soil does not permit them to be 5 feet deep they will be at least 3 feet deep. There will be no less than 12 bodies buried at any one place. Isolated burials are to be avoided at all times.

3. IDENTIFICATION OF THE DEAD.

Every effort must be made to identify each body before it is buried. This may be done by any or all of the following methods:
1. Identification Tags
2. Personal or official letters.
3. W.D., A.G.O. Identification cards.
4. Drivers license.
5. Social Security Card.
6. Identification by observation of an acquaintance. [...]

4. LES EFFETS PERSONNELS :

a. American Dead:
   1. Prior to burial, all personal effects will be removed from the body. The personal effects will be placed in the personal effects bag and the name, rank, and serial number of the deceased, followed by the words "Deceased" will be written on the bag. An inventory of effects (W.D., A.G.O. Form No. 54, sample attached) will be prepared in quintuplicate [...]

   2. Money will not be placed in the Effects Bag, but will be turned over to the nearest Finance Officer in exchange for a Treasurer's Check which will be mailed direct to the Effects Quartermaster, ETOUSA. [...]

   3. All personal effects bags will be collected, boxed, marked for shipment to Effects Quartermaster, ETOUSA, Warehouse, Division, Stanley Warehouse, US Forces, Liverpool, and sent to the Army Class 11 Depot. [...]

b. Allied Dead:
   Handled in same manner as American dead except that package and Form No. 54 will be marked with deceased's nationality and Army, Navy, or RAF, indicated when known. [...]

c. Enemy Dead:
   Same as above except that container will be marked "Enemy Dead" and money will be placed in the Personal Effects Bag and not turned over to the Finance Officer.

5. REPORTS OF BURIAL (G.R.S. FORM NO. 1).

a. American Dead

A Report of Burial (Sample attached) will be prepared in sextuplicate for each body buried.

If information is unavailable, then a notation to that effect will be made in the applicable blank space. When burial is completed, distribution will be as follows: Original and three (3) copies to the Army GRS Officer, one copy to the Division GRS Officer, and one copy to the Regimental GRS Officer.

b. Allied Dead

Same as for American dead except that nationality and service will be indicated in the upper right hand corner and an extra copy made out and five copies sent to the Army GRS Officer.

c. Enemy Dead

Same as for Allied dead.

6. IDENTIFICATION TAGS:

a. American Dead

One tag will be buried with the body and the other attached to the grave marker about two inches from the top. If there is only one tag on the body it will be buried with the body and the name, rank, and ASN of the deceased written on the grave marker. If no Identification Tags are on the body, but the body is positively identified, the name, rank, ASN, and means of identification will be written on a piece of paper and the paper, placed in a suitable container such as an empty shell case, buried with the body. In addition, the name, rank, and ASN will be written in the Grave Marker. If no identification tags are found on the body and the body is not identified, a list of all the data that may lead to later identification of the body will be prepared in duplicate, both copies placed in suitable containers, one copy buried with the body and the other copy placed at the foot of the grave marker.

b. Allied Dead

In the case of British and Canadian dead, the green (octagonal) identity disc will be buried with the body and the Red, (circular) disc will be detached and forwarded with the package containing the personal effects.

c. Enemy Dead

One-half of the tag remains with the body and is buried with it. The information on the half will be translated and written in English and this portion will then be placed in the personal effects bag and forwarded with it.

By order of Colonel MOSELEY:

EVANS C. THORNTON

Captain, Infantry Adjutant.[26]

A four-leaf clover, the Bible and photo of the fiancée of an American soldier killed on June 6, 1944, at Sainte-Mère-Église. Collection Airborne Museum

Dog-tags and charms belonging to Frances A. Petrowski (Nurse) Collection Airborne Museum

I AM A CATHOLIC
If I am seriously injured, please call for the nearest Catholic Priest. If I am unconscious and dangerously hurt or ill and there is no possible hope of obtaining any priest to come quickly, please whisper in my ear telling me that I may die and ask me to remember the words: "May God have mercy on me."

These two documents belonging to the soldier John P. Slusarz, illustrate the spiritual fervor in time of war. In addition to these pious images and little cult objects, there are instructions to follow in case the soldier were gravely wounded: "[...] please whisper in my ear telling that I may die and ask me to remember the words: MAY GOD HAVE MERCY ON ME." Collection Airborne Museum

In the mind of each soldier getting ready to take part in this great assault, the anguish of death, that terrible gnawing fear that had marked the interminable period of training in England, curiously gave way to a kind of relief. The time of action was come. The assault liberates. But for how long? The soldiers fled the anguish of death and the ultimate fear of not being identifiable if the worst happened, and marked their personal affairs and their military material almost systematically. They generally indicated the first initial of their surname, followed by the four final digits of their army serial number; first because this was required, but also because they needed to avoid the problem of loss of identity. Some would show great imagination to distinguish themselves in the heart of this incredible war machine.

They tried to reassure themselves by thinking of the life insurance policy taken out when they signed up, that paid $10,000 to their next of kin in case of death.

Then there was the rumor mill; an irrational rumor most often reassures, for an irrational rumor encourages hope. Deep within themselves, the soldiers imagined all sorts of prophecies of immediate protection, as explains Thomas Blakey of A Company – *505th PIR*: "In England, I slipped my New Testament in the pocket of my jacket, against my chest... I was sure that would help me avoid a damned accident". More than ever, the men took their lucky charms with them. Superstition grows as death approaches. This time, the charms appear as standard behavior, natural in a mad world under the reign of death.

THE DROPS OF JUNE 6, 1944

On the evening of June 5, 1944, in the airports of the south of England, 13,110 paratroopers of the *82nd* and *101st Airborne Divisions* went to their respective planes. They climbed, one after the other, with difficulty sometimes, into their C-47s. "Of course, we were scared!" exclaims Fred B. Morgan Jr, a medic of the 1st batallion – *505th PIR*, when you ask him whether he had experienced any apprehension before leaving for Normandy. "I had fought in North Africa, in Sicily and then in Italy. I knew what was waiting for us. That's why I wasn't really personally reassured. You looked at the guy next to you, and you knew he could buy it, just like you. The men of my stick were all looking serious that night."[27]

For some of them, that evening, the war began a few hours early, before any of the planes had even left the British soil. Colonel Ekman, commander of the *505th PIR explains*: "Regimental Headquarters and the 1st Bn got in the planes, and just about five or six minutes prior to taking off, a huge explosion occurred. Someone had set off a Gammon Grenade which, in turn, set off all the ammunition. I was initiated into combat that way. I saw a lot of dead bodies lying around after the explosion."[28] Among the luckless victims of this accident were the soldiers Robert L. Leakey (HQ/1 – *505th PIR*) and Kenneth A. Vaught (HQ/1 – *505th PIR*). Their bodies lie side by side today in the military cemetery in Cambridge, England. The date of their deaths, 5 June 1944, engraved in marble, reminds us that they were the first victims of D-Day.

The gigantic aerial armada composed of 821 C-47s (including twenty groups of Pathfinders) were on their way to the coast of France. Brigadier General James Gavin, second commander of the *82nd*

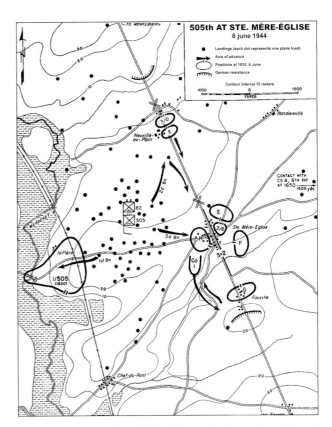

June 6: The drops of the *505th PIR* over the Drop Zone "O" west of Sainte-Mère-Église. Each point indicates the place, more or less exact, where a group of 16 to 19 paratroopers were dropped. NARA

Airborne flew on board the C-47 n° 43-30641. He recalls his flight over the Channel in an interview from the month of July, 1944: "The serial after leaving England was in good shape – tight formation – all ships apparently present. The flight, as well as it could be observed from the plane, was excellent. Some flak came up from the Channel Islands. Tracers were seen falling quite short. Shortly after crossing the west coast, the first check point was seen which I had figured would be Bricquebec. We then entered dense clouds. There were no ships in sight. A river appeared in the distance turning to the west, which I estimated to be either the Douve or the upper reaches of the Merderet. The green light went on at about the instant several ships appeared out of the fog, closing in on us. After about a three second delay, we went out. Small arms fire was coming up from the ground when

JAMES M. GAVIN (1907-1990)

Brigadier General James M. Gavin, second in command of the 82nd Airborne Division from October 1943, was from Brooklyn (New York). At 37, he was the youngest general in the American army. Graduating from West Point in 1929, he participated actively in setting up a new corps of the Army with his book *Tactics and Techniques of Airborne Troops* in 1941, a theoretical work highlighting the role of paratroopers in contemporary conflicts. On June 6, 1944, "Slim Jim" was placed at the head of Force A including the three regiments of paratroopers of the *82nd Airborne Division* as well as several detachments. He was promoted to Major General (as shown in the picture) in August, 1944, thus becoming commander in chief of the *82nd Airborne Division* at the request of Matthew Ridgway, the exiting general.

Collection of Utah Beach Museum.

the chute opened, just general shooting all over the area. Off to the right of the line of flight, there was considerable apparent gunfire and flak. I figured it probably was in the vicinity of Etienville where there were supposed to be located the only known heavy anti-aircraft installations in the area. A lot of firing was seen straight in the line of flight, tracers going into the air several miles away. I landed in an orchard, joined my aide, who landed nearby (Lt. Hugo V. Olsen), and proceeded to "roll up the stick" as per plan, arriving on the edge of a wide swamp where I found the remaining men of my stick who were endeavoring to retrieve equipment bundles from the deep mud and marsh."[29]

Although the drops were fairly inaccurate on all of the sectors attributed to the two airborne divisions, those of Drop Zone "O", assigned to the *505th PIR*, were generally speaking fairly precise. Lt. Col. Edward Krause, in charge of the 3rd Battalion - *505th PIR*, was dropped in the heart of this theoretical drop zone after a more chaotic flight: "The trip was very uneventful on the way over. As we crossed the coast of France, I talked to

my pilot on the interphone, and said, "It looks like a good deal". I looked back and saw my ships behind me. Just about that time we hit the soup, (fog or cloud), and we started to see fires on the ground, a little "ack-ack" and we had some fighters come in on us and fire at us. An element of three ships was directly under us and not more than thirty feet below. One came up from under and passed miraculously between my ship and the left wing ship. I would say that in the next three minutes I came as close to being crashed in the air as I ever hope to. We tried to keep our formation, but ships constantly over ran each other. The pilot called for evasive action and we split up. Some went high, some went lower, others right and left. This split our formation and we were well spread. Just about two or three minutes before drop time we saw this green T.[30] It was a Godsend and I felt that I had found the Holy Grail. I would say that I dropped from over 2,000 feet. It was the longest ride I have had in over fifty jumps, and while descending, four ships passed under me and I really sweated that out. Just after I landed, a mine bundle hit about 80 yards away from me without a parachute

KENNETH RUSSELL

Kenneth Russell, the "other" paratrooper of the church of Sainte-Mère-Église. Member of F Company – *505th PIR*, he finished his jump on the roof of the northern transept of the building. His valuable testimony tells of the intensity of the combats that took place on the village square, in the early hours of June 6, 1944.

Collection K. Russell.

and exploded. We tried to orient ourselves very quickly, and ran upon a conical shaped field, which I remembered as the conical shaped field that we had studied during our pre-invasion briefing." [31]

In the village of Sainte-Mère-Église, the inhabitants were required, like every evening, to stay home, curfew at 9:00 p.m. However, inside their homes, the excitement was palpable. It was still light, this evening of June 5, when a fire accidentally broke out near the park of La Haule at Julia Pommier's. A little girl of 9½ at the time, Geneviève Pasquette, tells the story of this agitated evening: "Towards 11:00 that evening [1:00 a.m. allied time], Mr Feuillie, the police lieutenant, came to tap at the door and told my father, "Marcel! Come quick! There's a fire at Ms. Pommier's and your woodshed is burning!" My father went to sound the alarm and, during that time, we heard a continuous roar. Mr Drieux shouted "I think it's the Invasion!" With the perspective of children, we understood nothing of what was going on. The noise was horrible, and we hung on to

A piece of parachute picked up by the father of Geneviève Pasquette on the square of Sainte-Mère-Église after the drops of June 6, 1944.
Private Collection

our mother's skirt. My father came back and that's when he told us he had seen a paratrooper land in the burning house." [32]

As early as 1:00 a.m., after dropping the groups of Pathfinders (three groups for each theoretical drop zone) that had begun at 0:16, several waves of planes carrying the paratroopers of the 101st Airborne Division flew over the town of Sainte-Mère-Église. Two of the three drop zones of this division were west of the village. Some of the men of the *502nd* and *506th PIR*, dropped too soon and landed in the gardens and orchards around the area. They were the first to touch the ground in this village of the Cotentin. Once they arrived on the ground, the paratroopers tried to get rid of a large part of their equipment, thinking only of getting out of this inhospitable place that wasn't even part of their initial mission. A little after 2:00 a.m., the men of the *82nd Airborne* were dropped as well. For the Drop Zone "O", situated west of the village, a handful of planes from the west dropped their loads a little late, terrible seconds late, given the proximity of the drop zone to the center of Sainte-Mère-Église. In his memoirs, bazookaman Kenneth Russell, of the *2nd platoon*, F Company, *505th PIR*, recalls the consequences of these bad drops: "after my parachute deployed, I saw something I never want to see in my life. I looked to my right, I saw a guy, and instantaneously, there was just an empty parachute coming down. A shell of some kind must have hit one of his Gammon grenades. He was blown away. I was trying to

JOHN M. STEELE

Born on November 29, 1912 in Metropolis, Illinois, John Marvin Steele was the son of a captain who navigated aboard steamboats on the Mississippi. "Marvin" had six brothers and sisters. With two of his brothers, he fought his way through the Second World War. Norman Steele was killed in action, in Germany, two weeks before the end of hostilities. In June, 1944, John Steele was 32, making him the oldest member of F Company – *505th PIR*. Popular with everybody, he had put his expertise as a barber to the service of his unit.

During the drops of June 6, his stick (a group of 13 – 19 paratroopers composing the team of a C-47 plane) were unfortunately dropped over the square of Sainte-Mère-Église. The green light, the one that signaled the drop, had gone off 10 seconds or so late. Jumping at about 150 yards, the chute of John Steele drifted toward the church and got caught on the north-west side of the bell tower, the opposite side of the building from the house that was on fire. At the same time, Kenneth Russell was caught on the north transept, while John Ray slipped along the roof and made a fall of several yards. He was severely wounded by a bullet to the stomach just after killing the German who had shot him, and had threatened the two hanging from the church.

The alarm sounding, John Steele tried to reach the knife to cut the straps of his parachute but unfortunately dropped it, and it fell near a German soldier. Taken in his sights, Steele was shot in the left foot and played dead for two or three hours until he was cut down and made prisoner by Rudolph May, the German positioned in the bell tower during the fighting. Seriously wounded, John Steele left the village in the company of its occupiers toward 4:00 a.m. His captivity lasted

Private John M. Steele
company F, *505th PIR*
Collection Airborne Museum

hide behind my reserve chute, because you could hear the shells hitting. We were all sitting ducks coming down. The pilot dropped us in the middle of the town of Ste-Mère-Église. A house on fire was lighting the square. I landed on the roof of the church hanging from my parachute. Luckily, I wasn't stuck on the side facing the square and the house on fire, but on the opposite side in a narrow street. While I reached for my boot knife in order to cut loose, John Steele hit the church steeple and was hanging there too, not far away from me, canopy and shroud lines wrapped around a gargoyle. A German came around of the church and shot John Ray in the stomach and called on Steele and me, both hanging up there. Ray got out his .45 and shot the German. I finally got my knife out of my boot and cut myself loose from

my parachute. I fell to the ground from fairly high, hurting my back in the process. I then called John to check whether he was alive but he was already gone.[33] If there was a hero that night in Normandy, it was John Ray! I got rid of as much equipment as I could and tried to hide it and ran to take cover behind the statue on the square. I thought I was hidden real good but bullets still kept coming from all directions. I made a dash across the square and it seemed to me the whole German Army was shooting at me. I then went to check if my other men were still alive. Next to the church were three telephone poles. Our Platoon Leader, Lt. Cadish, hit the first one and was killed instantly. Talapa hung dead from the second. June 6 was his 21st birthday; he lived it about one hour! On the third pole was my buddy H.T. Bryant. Van Holsbeck, also between two and three days while he was guarded with other prisoners in a stable in Ecoquenéauville. When the fighting got dangerously close, the German sentinel apparently ran and the prisoners freed themselves. After his short stay hanging from the steeple of Sainte-Mère-Église, John Steele suffered from severe problems of deafness for several weeks.

Steele was sent back to England for care. After Sicily, Italy and Normandy, he made his fourth jump in Holland on September 17, 1944. After the war, he returned to Sainte-Mère-Église and was interviewed, among others, by Cornelius Ryan, American journalist and writer. His story, briefly mentioned in the book *The Longest Day* was popularized by the film of the same name, produced by Darryl Zanuck in 1962. John Steele died at the age of 56, in 1969, of cancer of the throat. He was buried in Metropolis, his home town.

Another current of thought is worth noting, that of the civilian witnesses present on June 6, who cast doubt on the story told above. Actually, not a single inhabitant of Sainte-Mère-Église recalls having seen one or multiple American paratroopers hanging from the church. Several hypotheses could justify this historical confusion. The scene concerning the two paratroopers hanging from the church took place at exactly the opposite side of the church from the house afire, where the people of the village were concentrated. Note, too, that civilians fleeing the battles remained for only minutes on the square. Finally, the precious testimony of paratrooper Kenneth Russell and the German Rudolph May (what interest would the latter have in providing a false testimony?) are to this day the principal sources which validate this extraordinary story.

Monument of the grave of John Steele, in the cemetery of Metropolis, IL.
Photo Terence Moore

jumping from the same plane, had just joined the outfit two months before. He landed in the fire. The lack of oxygen generated by the intense heat had attracted his nylon canopy like a magnet. Charles Blankenship was hanging from a tree. He had been shot by the enemy right after landing. Penrose Shearer got stuck in a tree as well. Blanchard landed close to Blankenship and cut one of his fingers while trying to get out of his chute. He didn't notice it until a few hours later. Cliff Maughan landed in the back yard of a brick house at the corner of the square and his canopy went over the chimney. He could see the ground but could not reach his M2 knife to cut himself loose. Instead of going down, he felt like he was going up! He finally realized someone was hauling him through the window."[34]

The people of Sainte-Mère-Église living around the square were authorized by the occupier to come out

The church of Sainte-Mère-Église in June of 1944. This picture shows the north facade of the building where the paratroopers John Steele and Kenneth Russell landed on D-Day. NARA

DEFEND BROOKLYN

Message dated June 6, 1944, and sent at 6:50 a.m. by General Ridgway (by the intermediary of a lieutenant colonel) destined for General Collins, commander of the *VIIth US Corps*: "Sainte-Mère-Église occupied at 0600 and organized for defense. Signed Ridgway." NARA

In the first hours following the drops, problems with communications for the *505th PIR* were such that Col. Ekman decided to send the 2nd battalion, at the time in reserve at DZ "O", to support the defense of Sainte-Mère-Église. This message, dated June 6, was intended for Col. Krause: "Urgent [...] *2nd Bn* moving from regimental command post toward you to aid in the defense of Brooklyn [Sainte-Mère-Église]. Will arrive as soon as possible. You will coordinate the defense of the village." NARA

of their homes to fight the fire. Mystified, they observed the airdrops and Raymond Paris, 20 at the time, recalls with emotion: "With some of my buddies, we went to look for a pump for the fire. Fifty some people were on the square to put out the fire. Then, a first wave passed over our heads, followed closely by a second one, just as low. I can assure you that the water stopped! The buckets hung on the ends of arms, and everyone looked up, believing that bombs would fall on them. There were thirty Germans with us. They were charged with surveying us. They emptied their machine guns on the planes without much effect. The chain started up again, but in the two minutes that followed a third wave had arrived. We saw men jump and their parachutes open. I raised my arms to the sky and shouted "It's the Invasion!" We only stayed a minute on the square. We had to find cover. As I ran home, I saw in an impasse the lifeless body of an American paratrooper. I covered the body of this poor guy. The next day, the

parachute was still there, but the body was gone." [35] Jacques Pignot, 17, another young man living on the edge of the square, recalls this evening of June 5, 1944: "The bombardment of Saint-Martin-de-Varreville was spectacular. Jacques Muller and I wanted to see the results of the bombing. Such precision! But June 5, the Germans put back their canons in the middle of the debris. We saw them shoot. Then we went back to Sainte-Mère-Église toward 8:00 p.m. [10:00 p.m. allied time]; the curfew was at 9:00 p.m. I saw at that moment, the two P-47s flying at low altitude just over the village. Toward 11:00 p.m. [1:00 a.m. allied time] the house of Ms Pommier was on fire. I went out and got in the chain. I saw the mayor, M. Renaud, and Raymond Paris. There was a young German, 22, he was all trembling when the first paratroopers landed. One guy landed near us and M. Renaud told the soldier, in German, not to shoot, and he didn't. "[36]

On the other side of the square, Juliette Brault, 17, was preparing to celebrate her wedding in June 1944. She still has an anguished memory of this battle: "It was horrible! My parents were hairdressers in the village. We were scared. My parents, my three brothers and I took cover under a little staircase. We recited our prayers. We could hear the two German soldiers crouched in the corners of my parent's shop. They shot all night, without stopping. Men went running in every direction. We left for Vaulaville, the nearby hamlet."[37] The wedding of Juliette and Georges Brault was finally celebrated on June 22, 1944 in the garage – transformed into a chapel – of the Auvray farm, in the presence of American soldiers.

An M2 helmet, found west of Sainte-Mère-Église. The impact seen on its top allows us to imagine a tragic end to its original owner, a paratrooper of the *82nd Airborne Division*. Collection Erik L. Dorr

On the German side, no one wanted to believe that the great day had come. The persistent rumors these past few weeks about a possible landing on the coast of France were finally true. Except that no one wished to be in the initial assault zone, the one that would take the invasion full force. The few soldiers in the square and its surroundings would naturally resist purely to stay alive. Rudi Escher, 20, was among the German soldiers present on the square of Sainte-Mère-Église: "I was part of the *91. Infanterie Division*. The soldiers of my company got around on bicycles: "Strabscompany" of the 1058th Regiment. During the whole month of May, we bivouacked near the village. I was a corporal with six men under my orders. We had occupied the bell tower of the church since June 2, 1944. It served as a room when we were off duty and we slept there at night. At the beginning of the drops on Sainte-Mère-Église, during the night of 5 to 6 June, there was a young soldier in my group, Rudolph May, who was only 17. Alfred Jakl, another soldier of my group, was killed on the square. He is buried in the German cemetery of Orglandes." [38]

Rudolph May, for his part, gives us a valuable account: "We had our quarters in the bell tower of Sainte-Mère-Église. We spent the end of the day, June 5, racing bikes around the church. We felt good; we were happy. [...] The bells started ringing when a fire broke out near the square. My comrades were awakened. The fire illuminated the view around us. Then, they arrived, waves of planes dumping their paratroopers who darkened the full moon sky. They landed on the roofs, in the streets, in the chestnut trees and on the square. [...] More and more paratroopers jumping from the planes. My comrade and I got on our knees in the bell tower and watched the scene. Suddenly, it got darker, and someone flew over us. We saw the suspension lines of a parachute through the balustrade. There was a man hanging from it. He hung from the bell tower as if he had been killed, but after a while he moved. We heard him make little noises. My comrade took his rifle to kill him, which was natural in our situation. But I brushed his rifle aside and said '"Are you crazy? If someone sees us here, we won't have a chance of getting out! I was incapable of getting him up, so by cutting a few straps the paratrooper finally passed to the side of the bell tower. [...] As we were leaving the village, we arrived on the road to Carentan. Dead paratroopers were laid out in the road, run over by one of our trucks that had already left. It was a horrible sight."[39]

At the south entry of Sainte-Mère-Église, far from the commotion on the square, the inhabitants had absolutely no idea what was happening. An eyewitness, Léon Mignot, was 16: "That night we heard a lot of noise on account of the airplanes, the fire alarm... From where I lived, I could see a plane coming down in flames. It crashed into the site of the current hotel. The plane burned all night. Around our place, paratroopers were hanging from some of the trees. With the curfew, I didn't go to the square that evening of the 5th. I didn't know what was going on up there. The night was fairly clear.

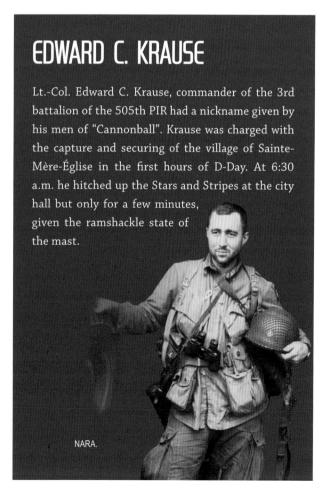

EDWARD C. KRAUSE

Lt.-Col. Edward C. Krause, commander of the 3rd battalion of the 505th PIR had a nickname given by his men of "Cannonball". Krause was charged with the capture and securing of the village of Sainte-Mère-Église in the first hours of D-Day. At 6:30 a.m. he hitched up the Stars and Stripes at the city hall but only for a few minutes, given the ramshackle state of the mast.

NARA.

We could see tracer rounds. The next day we understood it was the Americans. Then the Germans took potshots at us so we didn't go out. The first day we saw anything was June 7. Before that, the German batteries were constantly shooting at us."[40]

Less than a kilometer north-west of there, in the drop zone coded "O" where Lt. Col. Edward Krause had landed with his soldiers of the *505th PIR*, 180 paratroopers of the 3rd battalion had assembled in the first 90 minutes. The grouping operated in silence, Krause's men having no crickets to act as a disguised rallying signal. The colonel tells us: "One of my officers had landed in Sainte-Mère-Église. As he left town, he saw a group of German soldiers, and witnessed the capture of several paras, and the execution of some of them."[41] A French civilian, a bit tipsy and the worse for wear, was interrogated about the path to follow and the German forces in the sector of Sainte-Mère-Église. During the night, around 4:00 a.m., Edward Krause ordered his men to begin moving toward the town. Made up of H, G, and HQ/3 Companies, the group marched behind the French civilian. Going along either side of the main path[42] that crossed the valley of the Misère, the group of paras met no Germans until they arrived at the north entrance of the town. Other men, from various other groups, turned up and accompanied Krause's group. Progress along the street of Cap-de-Laine, toward the center of town, was made with the greatest vigilance. Sporadic shots were heard coming from the center of town. There was little or no fighting in the street at the arrival of Lt. Col. Krause's men. The Germans had backed off to the hamlet of Fauville, better known to the paratroopers of the *82nd Airborne Division* as "hill 20".

Making it to the main crossroads, the rue Cap-de-Laine and the road to Ravenoville, Edward

Krause himself cut a telephone cable – known to the allied forces – that connected Sainte-Mère-Église to Cherbourg.

From this same crossroads, several detachments were dispatched east and west to set up the roadblocks that would secure "Brooklyn". At 5:00 a.m., Krause wrote a message destined for the command post of the *82nd Airborne Division* in which he said he was in Sainte-Mère-Église. At 6:22 a.m. a new message said: "Now in Sainte-Mère-Église with about 150 men." Colonel William Ekman, commander of the *505th PIR* never received these messages, which caused some doubts in the general staff of the division. Still, the second message did arrive in the hands of Gen. Ridgway, commander of the *82nd Airborne*. He sent it on immediately to the *VIIth US Corps* in a message written at 6:50 a.m.

As promised in his speech at the airbase of Spanhoe in England, Lt. Col. Krause hoisted the American flag at city hall in Sainte-Mère-Église. It was 6:30. A strong symbol, but one that only lasted a few minutes, as Krause decided to take it down because of the defective pole. It almost fell, which might have been another symbol, one going the other way this time. But it was nothing of the sort. Lt. Col. Krause had kept his promise. But the worst was still to come. The liberation of the town was far from accomplished.

At 9:00 a.m., three hundred and sixty paratroopers of the 3rd battalion – *505th PIR* held Sainte-Mère-Église. It was time, now, to consider the defense of the village by reinforcing the seven roadblocks situated at the principal entrances. By that time, thirty German soldiers had been captured and 10 others killed. Thirty minutes later, three hundred soldiers of the 2nd battalion – *505th PIR*, commanded by Lt. Col. Benjamin Vandervoort, joined Krause's men to stop any potential German counter-attacks.

GERMAN COUNTER-ATTACKS (JUNE 6-9, 1944)

"In the morning [of June 6], Saint-Mère had been deserted by the occupier. M. Renaud came back to see me, accompanied by an American captain and a sergeant paratrooper. The latter wanted to see the German headquarters at La Haule. "Come with me!" said the mayor. So it was me who busted in the door; I had to go in first. I had a rifle in the back! We went upstairs. I knew the German leader was gone."[43] Jacques Pignot, like many Norman civilians during the battle, was more than a little surprised at the first contact with the liberators. For the American, the fear of an ambush was such that, in case of doubt, the principle of "safety first" was paramount. In other words, following a civilian, when on reconnaissance, was the safest solution. Early that morning, already, Lt. Col. Krause had equipped a civilian, slightly drunk, with a land mine, a means of eliminating the risk that this man lead the group of paratroopers into the arms of the enemy. The man was ordered to guide the American soldiers, with several rifles in his back and a mine in his hands, a great way to sober up![44]

Around Sainte-Mère-Église, the defense of the village intensified by 9:20 a.m. when three hundred soldiers of the 2nd battalion – *505th PIR*, commanded by Lt. Col. Benjamin Vandervoort, arrived in support of the 3rd battalion on the different exits of the village. Vandervoort, 29, had had an epic night, breaking his left ankle upon landing. Requisitioning two sergeants of the *101st Airborne* to transport him on a German ammunition wagon, Vandervoort, even though he had enough men by 4:10 a.m., had to wait in reserve for several more long hours. Between 6:14 and 8:17, the orders that arrived were actually counter-orders. The commander of the *505th PIR*, William Ekman, couldn't contact Krause's

3rd battalion. The decision was made to send Vandervoort's 2nd battalion toward Sainte-Mère-Église to contact the men of Lt. Col. Krause and to consolidate the town. The arrival of the paratroopers of the 2nd battalion coincided with the first German counter-attack on Sainte-Mère-Église.

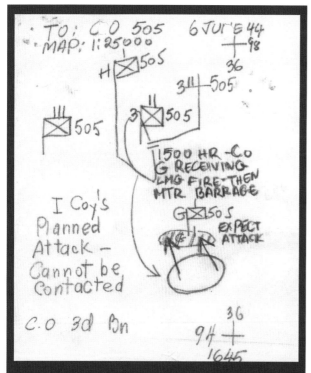

NARA.

THE GERMANS ATTACK THE SOUTHERN FLANK

Lt. Col. Krause's overlay, June 6 toward 4:45 p.m. It was addressed to Col. Ekman, commander of the 505th PIR, and was supposed to be superimposed on the General Staff's map of the sector of Sainte-Mère-Église. This document indicates particularly the different defensive positions of the 3rd battalion of the *505th PIR*, the patrol led to the south by I Company but also the German counter-attack of 3:00 p.m., coming from the south: "1500 hr, G Company receiving LMG fire then MTR barrage."

At 9:30 a.m., coming from the south, two companies of grenadiers, supported by three tanks and self-propelled guns, set off a deluge of fire on the roadblocks held by paratroopers of G and H Companies. Coordinating their efforts, the 2nd battalion (to the north) and the 3rd battalion (to the south) finished by fighting off the Germans at 11:30 a.m. "Early in the skirmishing the Germans herded cattle from the fields onto the main road and tried to drive them on so as to explode the mine field at the roadblock" according to Col. Ekman. "Private Dominique Detullio moved out well in front of the block, turned the cattle into another field and then grenaded the Germans who were driving them, killing one man, wounding a second and dispersing the rest. Detullio was killed the next day after volunteering to get water for the wounded at the aid station. He was killed by a high velocity shell."[45]

The counter-attack beaten back, Krause, who had been hit in the left thigh by mortar shrapnel, sent a group of five officers and twenty-four men of I Company toward Fauville and hill 20 to find the mortars which were continuously harassing the southern part of Sainte-Mère-Église. But the Americans got lost in the maze of hedges, and found themselves face to face with the Germans. Capt. Harold W. Swingler and seven of his men were killed on the spot, and the rest of them doubled back to Sainte-Mère-Église. Meanwhile, Edward Krause had been shot for the third consecutive time on June 6. A bullet had gone through his left thigh – the same one hit by mortar fire a few hours earlier. At this difficult time Krause would say: "The Germans are going to take back the town tonight" when he talked about it with Lt. Col. Vandervoort and Major William Hagan. Hagan would take over the command of the 3rd battalion in the following hours in order to leave Krause a little rest.

As soon as he arrived in the village in the company of his men, Lt. Col. Vandervoort was

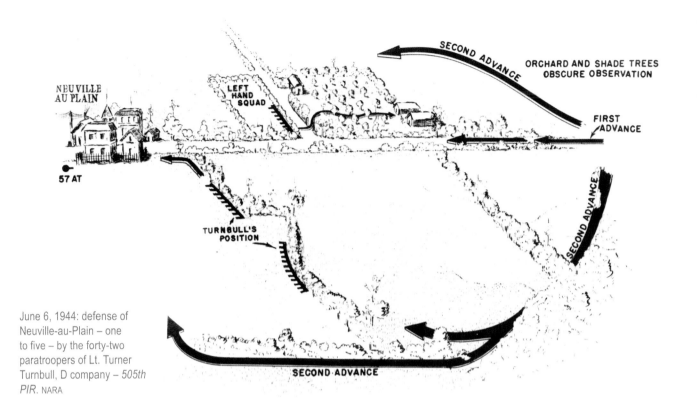

NEUVILLE AU PLAIN

57 AT

LEFT HAND SQUAD

TURNBULL'S POSITION

SECOND ADVANCE

ORCHARD AND SHADE TREES OBSCURE OBSERVATION

FIRST ADVANCE

SECOND ADVANCE

SECOND ADVANCE

June 6, 1944: defense of Neuville-au-Plain – one to five – by the forty-two paratroopers of Lt. Turner Turnbull, D company – *505th PIR*. NARA

witness to a disheartening scene as he advanced toward the square and the church. He immediately called Capt. George Wood, the protestant chaplain of the *505th PIR*. He recalls "Lt. Colonel Vandervoort asked me to do something about the men [paratroopers from the *505th* and *506th*

George "Chappie" Wood, protestant chaplain of the *505th PIR* photographed here near the aid station in the hospice of Sainte-Mère-Église.
© D-Day Paratroopers Historical Center

PIR] hanging dead in the trees down in the village square. There were six of them and it was affecting the morale of the men to see their buddies' lifeless bodies hanging there. I had no burial detail, so I got a detail of six men with an officer from the front line. There was much anger among the men over the killing of their buddies in the trees, but I explained that this was what we could expect in our kind of outfit."[46]

Before he began his advance toward Sainte-Mère-Église, Benjamin Vandervoort made the decision to send a detachment to Neuville-au-Plain, the original destination of the 2nd battalion – *505th PIR*. The forty-two paratroopers of the 3rd platoon of D company, placed under the orders of Lt. Turner B. Turnbull, took over the village a little before 10:00 a.m. without seeing a single German. They set up to the east of the chateau, along the hedges facing the National 13 road.

Only thirty minutes after their arrival, Turnbull's men could see a company of the *1058th Grenadier*

The bridge at La Fière, west of Sainte-Mère-Église and the road crossing the marshes which were flooded in 1944. Picture by the author

Regiment of the *91st Luftland Infantry Division* advancing on Neuville-au-Plain. At the head of the column totaling a hundred and ninety soldiers, the men were waving orange flags as a sign of surrender. A technique as old as time that appeared especially strange given that the Germans, in two columns along the road, were all equipped with rifles, a curious thing for troops on the point of surrender. Turnbull's men fired first, dispersing the German columns. For over eight hours, and with heavy losses, the soldiers of D Company beat back every attempt by the enemy to surround them. E Company was sent to Neuville-au-Plain to support the initial effort. At 6:30 p.m. there were only 16 survivors of the *3rd platoon* who could head back to Sainte-Mère-Église. The counter-attack from the north was stopped on the outskirts of Neuville-au-Plain, which had gone back into enemy hands.

Renault R35 tanks, felled on the road to La Fière. NARA film

The road to La Fière today. Photo by the author

LA FIÈRE CAUSEWAY

This drawing, entitled La *Fière Causeway*, was drawn a year after the terrible combats that took place from 6 to 9 June, 1944, around the manor house, the bridge (of which we can guess the outline) and the road to La Fière. Working in the framework of a detailed study of the battle by the historical service of the American Army, the artist, Olin Dows, captured this ravaged countryside on paper. Across the flooded marshes, we can see the hamlet of Cauquigny and its ruined chapel.

Drawing dated 1945 representing part of the outbuildings of the manor of La Fière, the bridge over the Merderet River and the road across the marsh area. NARA

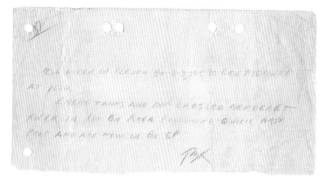

Message informing Gen. Ridgway of the German counter-attack at 4:00 p.m., June 6th, on the road to La Fière: "Enemy tanks and infantry have crossed the Merderet River in 1st battalion's sector." NARA

The exploit of Lt. Turnbull's[47] men, protecting the northern flank of Sainte-Mère-Église for several hours – at five to one! – was a real shot in the arm; first, for the men of the 3rd battalion who defended "Brooklyn, but also for the rest of the men who fought on the whole sector of Utah Beach on June 6, 1944.

To the west of Sainte-Mère-Église, bordered by marshes, is the site of La Fière. On D-Day, it was company A – *505th PIR* under the command of Lt. John C. Dolan who were given the delicate mission of capturing the bridge over the river Merderet, a strategic point that should have stopped any counter-attacking enemies from taking Sainte-Mère-Église. After a jump of an unparalleled precision, the one hundred and forty-seven paratroopers of A Company regrouped at the crossroads of the road to La Fière and the railroad to Cherbourg. The first three hundred meters heading toward La Fière were marked by German snipers which gave the reconnaissance missions a tragic character.

These isolated shots took the lives of three officers of the 1st battalion – *505th PIR*: Lt. Donald Coxon (A Co.), Robert McLaughlin (A Co.) and James McGinity (1/505). Toward 10:00 a.m., close to five hundred paratroopers, coming out of scattered groups, converged near La Fière, bringing decisive support to the capture of the bridge and its surroundings. The site was taken around 11:30 a.m. after the last Germans had surrendered. The results of this first battle were heavy for a company: twelve paratroopers killed and forty others wounded. It was the beginning of a long day, and the survivors of A Company, preparing the defense of the site, dug in their foxholes. A German truck, just captured, was placed across the bridge. Four mines were placed in front of the bridge, in the middle of the road. At first harassed by mortar fire from the other side, the 1st battalion of the *505th PIR* faced off a first German counter-attack in the afternoon of June 6. At 4:00 p.m., the defenders of the bridge, deep in their foxholes, saw three Renault R35 tanks coming at them, followed closely by two hundred German soldiers belonging to the *1057th Grenadier Regiment* (*91st Infantry Division*) and to the Panzer Abteilung 100. The intense combat finished in favor of the paratroopers of the *82nd Airborne*, particularly due to the precision of two teams of bazookas positioned on either side of the bridge. John B. Bolderson and Gordon C. Pryne

A Company's positions along the Merderet, June 6, 1944.
Photo by the author

on the right, and Leonard Peterson and Marcus Heim on the left, had accomplished the feat of routing the tanks, which forced the few soldiers of German infantry to fall back on Cauquigny. In spite of the German retreat, the American positions around the bridge were pounded by shellfire until late in the evening. William Kellam, commander of the 1st battalion of the *505th PIR* was fatally wounded by shell fire during the bombardment. Although the German counter-attack had been repelled, the nerves of the men were raw. Morale dropped as their fatigue grew and the shelling intensified. They had to hold.

By the late afternoon, the advance units of "Force C"[48], having landed on Utah Beach, were to establish the junction with the paratroopers who held the south end of Sainte-Mère-Église. From Les Forges crossroads, two kilometers to the south, the advance of Col. Edison D. Raff had been blocked by a persistent pocket of German resistance between Fauville and Turqueville. The second objective of Col. Raff's men was to take the landing zone coded "W" intended for the gliders of the 82nd Airborne Division. A first landing was to take place at 9:04 p.m. For more than two hours, the mission "Elmira" was planned to convoy thirty-six Waco gliders and one hundred forty Horsa gliders onto Landing Zone "W". The gliders fell under enemy fire as they arrived. Despite several attempts, the tanks of Col. Raff never managed to rout out the Germans installed on hill 20 in Fauville. By the evening of D-Day, in spite of a first contact between the paratroopers of the 2nd battalion – *505th PIR* and the soldiers of the *12th Infantry Regiment (4th Infantry Division)*, the village of Sainte-Mère-Église was isolated. The liberation of the little village was vulnerable and uncertain considering the bombardments that occasionally threatened the roadblocks held by the men of the *82nd Airborne*. Losses among these were heavy and the consequences for the troops' morale, disastrous.

The village looked like Fort Alamo[49] on the morning of June 7, 1944. The *505th PIR*'s combat reports tell us that between 4:00 a.m. and 9:00 a.m., officers and men experienced particularly frightening hours due to their isolation. The paratroopers held their position around Sainte-Mère-Église but there was no news of the *VIIth US Corps*. At 9:29 a.m., finally, a message from the Allied High Command in England arrived: "No info on your situation. All the general staff deeply concerned." Not exactly reassuring news, and on top of that, ironic insofar as the general staff of the *82nd Airborne Division* had not been informed of the evolution of operations and the advance of the *4th Infantry Division* from Utah Beach.

Picture taken by a soldier of the 307th Airborne Engineer Bn on June 7th, 1944. Taken from the north of the village, along the National 13, and direction south, it shows the rear of a Sturmgechütz 40 tank, taken out at 11:30 a.m. by the soldier Atchley of H Company – 505th PIR. NARA

JOE FITT, FORGOTTEN HERO OF THE BATTLE OF LA FIÉRE

Joseph Cyril Fitt, compagnie C – *505th PIR*.
© Gil Bourdeaux

Joseph C. Fitt, a young man of 22, came from Salt Lake City, Utah. He had participated in every preceding campaign as a member of the *505th PIR*. On June 6, "Joe" was dropped at about 2:00 a.m. onto Neuville-au-Plain, just like a large part of his company. After regrouping, seventy soldiers of C Company, under the command of Capt. Anthony Stefanich, went toward their initial objective, the bridge of La Fière, further west. Reaching the site toward 7:00 a.m., the "Stefanich" group participated in the capture of the manor house, alongside different elements of the 1st battalion of the 505th PIR and the paratroopers of the *507th PIR*. Once it had been taken and secured around midday, C Company took their quarters in the outbuildings of the manor of La Fière and began to set up the defenses of the site.

Around 4:00 p.m., the first German counter-attack on the Merderet River could be heard far away. The men, nestled in their foxholes, would soon do battle. Sergeant Elmo E. Bell recalls: "The attack was led by three light French-made tanks. In front of the tanks we could see 12 or 15 American paratroopers who had been dropped on the other side of the marshes and taken prisoner before they even got out of their parachutes. The German commander in the first tank was standing, ordering the prisoners to pick up the mines placed on the road by us a few hours before. They were supposed to throw them in the marshes later. They were coming ever closer, and I was wondering when they'd say to open fire. I knew full well they would say sooner or later to open fire and everyone hesitated because of those 12 or 15 paratroopers who were walking in front of the tanks..."

The machine gun of Oscar L. Queen fired the first salvo in the direction of the head tank, aiming for the German officer. He was killed outright. In the same movement, the two bazooka teams, positioned on either side of the road near the bridge, directed their fire toward the Renault R35 tanks, followed by two hundred German soldiers. On the rise where the manor was situated, in the extension of the road, a 57 mm canon took its turn and shot toward the tank up front. Elmo Bell continues: *"Once the head tank got close to the bridge, the 57mm canon shot and hit it in the track, stopping it in the middle of the road. But it still shot, reaching the area around the 57mm and killing seven of our men. Suddenly, Joe Fitt left his place. He ran across the bridge, climbed up the head tank, and threw a grenade inside killing the whole crew. The Germans then started to retreat."*

Sergeant
Simon Hannig

Oval of the 505th PIR
and paratrooper wings,
belonging to Joe Fitt.
Private Collection

M42 jump jacket worn by Joseph C. Fitt during the battle of La Fière. Some of Fitt's personal effects – including his combat vest – were sent to his mother after the Normandy campaign by Sgt Simon Hannig. "Sam" Hannig also belonged to C Company, and on June 6, 1944, he had been one of the pathfinders for the 1st battalion of the 505th PIR. In a letter addressed to his family on July 15, 1944, he wrote: *"Every time I write, I think of the fellows and good friends that I left back in France. [...] In Ste Mère Eglise, in the 82nd cemetery, I buried one of my best friends there [Joseph Fitt]. It was one of the most sorrowful moments of my life."* Collection D-Day Paratroopers Historical Center

Joseph Fitt was posthumously awarded the *Silver Star Medal* for this act of bravery facing the enemy. For, on June 13, 1944, as C Company was leaving the area around the train station of Montebourg heading for a new bivouac station near Picauville, Joe Fitt was taken in the sights of an isolated sniper. That morning, it was raining for the first time since the operations began in Normandy. Joe Fitt was buried in the divisional cemetery in Carquebut.

MISSION ACCOMPLISHED

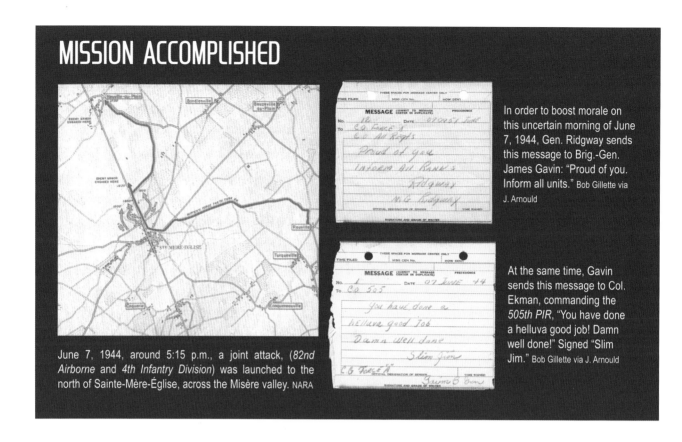

June 7, 1944, around 5:15 p.m., a joint attack, (*82nd Airborne* and *4th Infantry Division*) was launched to the north of Sainte-Mère-Église, across the Misère valley. NARA

In order to boost morale on this uncertain morning of June 7, 1944, Gen. Ridgway sends this message to Brig.-Gen. James Gavin: "Proud of you. Inform all units." Bob Gillette via J. Arnould

At the same time, Gavin sends this message to Col. Ekman, commanding the *505th PIR*, "You have done a helluva good job! Damn well done!" Signed "Slim Jim." Bob Gillette via J. Arnould

The junction between the airborne troops and the infantry that had landed on the beach did not happen on the morning of June 7, 1944. The men of the *505th PIR* had to hold up face to face against a powerful counter-attack at the north entrance to Sainte-Mère-Église. By 9:00 a.m., enemy artillery was pounding the American positions before progressing to the National 13 road out of Neuville-au-Plain. Three German tanks were destroyed during this bitter battle. The counter-attack was contained at the edge of the village toward noon. The beginning of the afternoon was spent trying to make contact with the *8th Infantry Regiment* (*4th Infantry Division*), a link finally established toward 3:00 p.m. The feeling of a job well done and the relief of the paratroopers of

June 7, 1944, in the Misère valley, a paratrooper of the 502nd PIR – *101st Airborne Division* and a soldier of the *82nd Airborne Division* care for a wounded German soldier. Picture taken by Lt. James J. Coyle, E Company - 505th PIR. Collection H.-J. Renaud

James Coyle then photographed th[e] site where about 160 Germans ha[d] been searched. A wounded German so[l]dier lies in the middle of the pieces [of] equipment. Collection H.-J. Renaud

the *505th PIR* who had held the front line up till then only lasted a short time.

By 5:15 p.m., an American offensive toward Neuville-au-Plain had started, with the intention of cleaning up around the National 13. On the western flank, the 2nd battalion of the *8th Infantry Regiment*, supported by E company – *505th PIR* of Lt. James J. Coyle, progressed along the Misère valley forcing the last German defenders to retreat or give up. Over three hundred German soldiers had been killed in the battle of the Misère valley, and one hundred and sixty were taken prisoner. Hundreds of corpses lined the ditches along the country roads.

Earlier, the tanks of the *746th Tank Bn* had reached Neuville-au-Plain, bypassing to the east the most advanced elements of the German counter-attack on the National 13. A significant advance but short-lived for lack of support, the tanks returned to Sainte-Mère-Église toward 9:00 p.m.

What was the situation at the end of the afternoon of June 7, 1944? Bill Tucker, of I Company – *505th PIR*, in position in the gardens south of the school road, draws a picture far from the smooth image of a euphoric liberation: "Toward the end of the afternoon of June 7, the artillery fire really intensified, and I said to myself: Where the hell are those other guys in town?"

June 7, 1944, in a field between Sainte-Mère-Église and Beuzeville-au-Plain, a paratrooper of the *502nd PIR* (*101st Airborne*) and a few soldiers of the *12th Infantry Regiment* (*4th Infantry Division*) are shown the position of a German field battery. NARA

The Misère Valley, where, in his photo-report published in Voir *Magazine n°4* of August 1944, Weston Haynes, war correspondent, photographed the site where the Germans were searched. Other pictures taken at the same time show dozens of German corpses lining the surrounding ditches. Keystone – Winston Haynes

All we could get was rumors or gossip according to which the 2nd battalion was busy containing the Germans, including the tanks coming from the north. About that time, Major Hagan who had replaced the commander of the battalion, Krause, who had been wounded, came to each foxhole to warn the guys that we would probably be confronting some tanks shortly. The orders were we had to stay in our foxholes and hold."[50]

Finally, a barrage of artillery came crashing down on the positions of the *3rd battalion* killing several men of I Company. These were the final victims of combat in the town, as the elements of the *82nd Airborne Division* left their positions around 7:00 p.m. on this June 7, moving toward the northwest. After 40 hours of combat, the retreat of the German troops marked the definitive liberation of Sainte-Mère-Église. Nothing more came to retake the village whose capture had been so hard. "Brooklyn" was free, but to the west, on the river Merderet, the fighting to control the bridge and the road to La Fière was heavier than ever. On June 7, toward 10:00 a.m., a new German counter-attack put American control of the bridge in danger. The situation was so serious that the paratroopers began leaving their positions given the intensity of the German bombardment. John Dolan's orders were clear: "We stay. There is no better place to die." The *505th PIR* once again stopped the German offensive on the road to La Fière.

A Company, for its part, was relieved the next day. It had lost sixty-six soldiers out of the one hundred forty-seven engaged in the previous 48 hours of the battle.

On June 9, Gen. James Gavin decided to force the passage on the road. At 10:30 a.m., the American artillery focused its fire on the enemy positions partly installed in Cauquigny. Fifteen minutes later, the 3rd battalion of the *325th Glider Infantry*

MUCH MORE THAN A PLAQUE

This bronze plate, installed in 1969, Rue Cayenne, on the wall of buildings of the farm belonging at the time to Léon Feuardent, marks the place where four paratroopers of G Company – 505th PIR were killed in a German counter-attack, June 6, 1944.

In a letter addressed to Henri-Jean Renaud in 1993, the American veteran Ronald C. Snyder, who had ordered this bronze plate, recalls for us the circumstances of this episode, tragic and poorly known: "In the afternoon

Collection H.-J. Renaud.

of D-Day in Normandy, June 6, 1944, the first platoon of G Company, 505 Parachute Infantry was digging in an irregular semi-circle pattern on the south side of Ste. Mere Eglise, stretching from Highway 13 to the road to Gambosville. Enemy artillery and small arms fire had been continuous and accurate since about 11:00 a.m. and no movement could be made without drawing enemy action. About 5:00 p.m. an attempt was made to resupply the besieged paratroopers in Ste. Mere and the sight of C-47s releasing gliders diverted the enemy's attention and a curtain of fire rose to meet the gliders and tow planes.
At the same time, a messenger arrived with orders directing that the mortar squad be detached and relocated to the second platoon area on the east side of Highway 13, so the mortars could be fired in battery.
The platoon sergeant relayed the instructions to the mortar squad leader, sergeant Stanley Smith, and when he complained about his new assignment the platoon sergeant laughingly told him "not to worry, if anything happens to you I promise to place pretty flowers on your grave." [...]
This movement was not un-noticed by the enemy and shortly an artillery shell landed nearby. This prompted the squad leader to move out immediately without waiting for the other two men and the platoon sergeant assured him that he would send them along in the right direction. But it was too late. The next shell was an aerial burst. Concussion and steel splinters smacked down on rooftops and the roadway, one fragment tore through Pvt. Robert Herrin's leg pocket and detonated a gammon grenade (two pounds of plastic T.N.T). Two of the mortar squad, Herrin and Smith, died instantly.....The other two, Walter and Holtzmann, died a short time later in the aide station. The platoon sergeant was hurled over the wall and landed in a civilian's yard, but escaped with only a mild concussion and minor abrasions.
Twenty five years later, in June, 1969, the former platoon sergeant returned to Ste. Mere Eglise on a tour sponsored by a veterans group and revisited the site where his men had died. [...]
I, Ronald C. Snyder was the platoon sergeant on that climactic day and as I departed Mr. Leon Feuardent's home a wide smile crossed my face despite the tear in my eye and I whispered softly "Smitty! I'll do more than place a few flowers on your grave, I'll enshrine your name in bronze and you will be forever acclaimed a hero long after the rest of us are dead and gone."

Regiment received the suicidal mission to run down the road and, in the process, to occupy the enemy positions.

Because of an ineffective artificial smokescreen, the soldiers of G, E and F Companies were plainly visible during their advance. Men fell one after the other. The few tanks who had followed the infantry skidded and blocked the road covered with lifeless bodies. James Gavin gave the order to the ninety paratroopers of Capt. Robert D. Rae (*507th PIR*) to support the efforts of the men of the *325th GIR*. In a scene of total confusion, Rae and a few of his men managed to get to the west side of the Merderet, pushing a hundred yards toward Le Motey. The breakthrough by the men of the *507th PIR* served to inspire and encourage the rest of the units positioned around the bridge of La Fière.

Message dated June 9, 1944, and sent to the VIIth US Corps. At 12:50 p.m. the message indicated: "Merderet crossed and bridgehead established to the north of bridge." Sainte-Mère-Église was finally secured and the paratroopers of the *82nd Airborne* continued their progress north and to the west. NARA

Cap-de-Laine Street, June 10, 1944, the soldiers of the *4th Infantry Division*, who had landed four days before on Utah Beach, head toward their new objective: Montebourg. NARA

The men consolidated the newly acquired ground as quickly as possible while waiting to be replaced that evening by the *90th Infantry Division* who had landed on the 6 and 7 of June at Utah Beach. The battle of Sainte-Mère-Église was coming to an end. A painful success that had stained the surrounding landscape with the sight of American and German corpses piled along the roads. The macabre remains of these four days of combat profoundly traumatized those who had seen and lived the battle. For the paratroopers of the *82nd Airborne Division*, Sainte-Mère-Église was only the starting point. It was, however, here, on the bridge of La Fière, in the fields around Neuville-au-Plain, or on the village square of Sainte-Mère-Église, that the bloodiest pages of the division were written.

Above and below, June 10, 1944: scattered elements of the *82nd Airborne Division* (505th and 507th PIR) moving up Carentan Street (today, rue du Général-de-Gaulle) on horseback. NARA

IF I SURVIVE....

Sergeant Fred B. Morgan Jr, photographed in Normandy in June 1944. Medic to the 1st battalion – 505th PIR, he participated in the battle of La Fière, taking charge of the numerous American casualties. Collection F. Morgan

From the town of his birth, Edgartown, situated on Martha's Vineyards Island, Massachusetts, Fred B. Morgan Jr. recalls with emotion the thirty-three days he spent in Normandy: "I was 20 when I joined the army, one month after the Japanese attack on Pearl Harbor [December 7, 1941]. In the spring of 1942, I learned that they were looking for volunteers for a new group in the army. And that's how I joined the paratroopers. Because I had started out in a military hospital in the south of Boston, I was attached to the HQ/1 – *505th PIR* as a medic, which suited me fine as I'd never been very comfortable with firearms.

Our regiment had landed in North Africa, in French Morocco, in November 1942, before we prepared our first operational jump. Sicily was our baptism of fire in July 1943. Then, we jumped in Italy to secure the city of Naples. In the autumn of 1943, a ship took us to Ireland, where the invasion was in preparation. We did more and more the night exercises up till the big day arrived. I remember the speech of Brig.-Gen. Gavin, June 5, 1944, at the airfield of Cottesmore, in England: "Look around you! Two men out of three will be taken out of action in this battle." But we didn't even think about it. We had a blind confidence in this man.

Our plane flew over the Channel without incident, and the red light came on. We got up and verified the equipment and our parachutes. We were in a hurry to get out of the plane when the green light finally went on. The jump was very short, and I landed in a tree on the edge of a marsh that was flooded. I could hear my companions all around and I yelled the password "Thunder, thunder!", hoping to get their attention. But, I had to go it alone with a pocket knife that I ended up dropping on account of the excitement. I grabbed my dagger, placed at the ankle to finally cut the straps of my harness. I saw guys landing in the marshes. I can still see them disappearing into the waters. They got themselves caught in their parachutes. Some were trapped...

In the morning of June 6, the battalion was supposed to capture the manor and the bridge at La Fière. All our officers had been killed one after the other. We had no time for rest. The Germans just kept hammering our positions. A shell exploded near me. It was a huge whiplash that threw me in a ditch along a path. I was covered by an avalanche of soil. I found myself buried alive, swallowing the dust. My head was ringing! But I managed to dig a path to the air to breathe. I stayed there several minutes, the time to get my consciousness back. My buddies thought I was dead that day!

Dying for Sainte-Mère-Église

"KILLED IN ACTION" OR "GEFALLEN"

The veteran Morgan, photographed in May 2013, at home on the island of Martha's Vineyard in Massachusetts.
Photo by the author.

It was high time to take care of the wounded, despite lacking material and medicine. A lot of the men were just in shock. They had an empty look, scared. I tried to reassure them, while their comrades died one after another. The battle lasted thirty-three days. We were miserable, dirty and tired. We fulfilled our mission, but a large number of guys I knew never left Normandy. I said to myself, if I survive this campaign, nothing else can get me. And I would marry my girl, left back in the country, as soon as I went back.[51] For several years after the war, I would sometimes wake up in the night with a jump, yelling my head off, and frightening my poor wife. I cannot forget. In fact, I still think about it, every day…"[52]

Bullets kill. The observation may seem naive but is worth examining so as not to hide once again the brutality of the battlefield. To talk about the combatant's behavior on the ground is to go well beyond the latter day sanitization of a battle that our era has made acceptable through the rituals of commemorations. The battle of Sainte-Mère-Église was bitter, cruel, and profoundly deadly, in terms of both military and civilian losses. In the aftermath of the fighting, the scenes which confronted the inhabitants contrast with the story smoothed over by the years and by memories, ever more tenuous and selective.

Raymond Paris remembers two soldiers – one American, one German – lying next to each other near the washing place at Vaulaville, their bayonets thrust into each other's entrails. Cécile Flamand recalls with fright the combats that took place around her parents' stud farm: "The night of the jumps, the stable caught fire. One of our horses was still inside, we could hear it squealing […] A few days after June 6, the shells were still falling and the paratroopers made us leave our house. We put Grandmother in a wheelbarrow with a few pillows behind her head and we headed off down the valley of the Misère. We could hear the machine guns. It was frightening. We stayed in a ditch for several hours, and then we were thirsty. My father went off to milk a cow under fire (they all had full udders). The fighting got worse at La Fière, so we left our trench. We had to pick a path over

Evening of June 7, 1944, the landscape of the Misère valley, northwest of Sainte-Mère-Église. German corpses could be counted in the hundreds in the surrounding ditches. Collection H.-J. Renaud

the bodies. The Americans were wrapped in their parachutes. I remember crossing over a German with a gaping hole in his chest."[54]

In his book, A Bridge in Normandy, Gilles Bré paints a surreal picture of the battle for the bridge and the road of La Fière. On June 9, 1944, while the 325th GIR and the 507th PIR tried to cross the road overlooking the marshes around, he wrote: "Everywhere, in every possible position, lay the dead and dying on the road and its banks. Men dragged themselves, trying to escape the bullets and shrapnel of the mortars. Many were in a pitiful state. Their bloody members were hidden by bandages done up in haste. Cries of pain could be heard on every side amid the noise of explosions. Desperate cries called out for the medics ..." All that was dead had to remain indifferent; to soften was a visible sign of weakness. Death on the battlefield – without a priest or a sepulcher – became run-of-the-mill, and had to be accepted as such. Full awareness of the horrors of death came later for the majority of the soldiers. Death was, in this context, an idea that applied to civilians, very far away.

In addition, there was death caused by friendly fire, a fact of war as common as kept secret. The blunder, as Paul Fussel reminds us, "is the trademark of great operations".[56] Of course, fear is at the origin of the errors committed by these eternal and vulnerable adolescents. Soldiers applied the principle of safety when they were risking their lives. One could say the shots were often fired out of extreme nervousness in this long night of June 6, 1944.

After having jumped over Neuville-au-Plain, the soldier Gerald Colombi, of C Company – 505th PIR, found himself alone when he arrived on the ground.

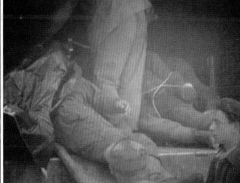

The road at La Fière after the combats: civilians volunteered to pick up the bodies of American and German soldiers who were still lying in the ditches of the road. NARA Film

He had missed *Drop Zone "O"* and had to join the other members of his unit at all costs. This was an absolutely terrifying situation in that knowing where you were in the middle of the night, in the middle of the Norman "Bocage", was not an easy task. Noises could be heard on the other side of the hedge from Colombi. Not having a cricket, our man used the password agreed to for the first twenty-four hours of the invasion "Flash!?". A reply rang out "Thunder!". Colombi answered finally "Welcome!". From across the hedge, came a comrade belonging to the same company, Nicholas Polachek. After barely the time to greet each other, Colombi accidentally fired his gun in the direction of Polachek who took it in the stomach. Colombi took his comrade-in-arms to a small farm in Fresville, to Mr. Levasseur, where the soldier Polachek died of his wounds. Overwhelmed, Colombi buried Polachek in the garden before rejoining his unit in the drop zone and fighting on the bridge of La Fière. Later, the body of the American soldier accidentally killed was taken up by the graves services and buried temporarily in cemetery n° 2 of Sainte-Mère-Église.

If, as states the poet Melville, "all wars are boyish, and are fought by boys", it is for two reasons that are obvious: these young men are physically strong and they ignore the fact that they are mortal. It is after the first battle that they are beaten down, cynical, exhausted and hopeless. On this subject, William Tucker, of I Company – *505th PIR* recalls the battle of June 7,

Nicholas Polachek, C Company - *505th PIR*, killed accidentally on June 6, 1944, north of Baudienville. Collection Sarah Miles

Gerald Colombi (left) veteran of C Company – *505th PIR*, returning to Normandy in 2004 with his friend Jean-Baptiste Feuillye, former guardian and interpreter of the temporary military cemetery n° 1 of Sainte-Mère-Église. Collection J.-B. Feuillye

MONUMENTS CAN BE WRONG

A memorial plate, erected in memory of the soldiers Jack Leonard and Bill Laws of I Company - *505th PIR*, situated in the Rue de L'Ecole. The monument indicates that on June 7, the two paratroopers were the victims of artillery fire coming from the top of the church tower. An erroneous theory, in that no German soldiers were present at that time at the top of the steeple of Sainte-Mère-Église. Moreover, no mortars and no machine guns were positioned on top of the building. The two soldiers were victims of the bombardment that had preceded the German counter-attack in the afternoon of June 7, 1944.

Photo by the author

in Sainte-Mère-Église: "Later on, there was a massive barrage of artillery for 20 minutes that hit the 3rd battalion and we had a lot of dead and wounded. Jack Leonard and Bill Laws had set their sights on a big deep trench shaped like an L that the French had dug in the garden as a sort of shelter against the bombs. That I wasn't in that hole with them was due to the foresight of Capt. Melvin who told me two men in the same hole was enough [...]. I heard a few screams and yells for medics and I got out of my hole to go see in back. I saw Jack Leonard with his face buried in the wall of his hole holding what was left of his chest. He was gone, dead. When I turned right, I saw he had pulled Bill Laws from the hole. He had been badly shot up, and lasted only a couple minutes. We talked about whether it was a shell that had blown up in the air or in the trees that had done that. All I knew at the time was that here were a couple of guys that I had really come to appreciate in I Company, through the mud, the hail, the parties, the goofing around, and, my friends, it was a great loss for us all. I began to think that I'd better get used to it."[57]

The official history of the *505th PIR*, written after the campaign of Normandy, furnishes several

precious pieces of information on the conditions up front on D-Day but also the principal causes of death: "After the first phase of Operation Neptune, one of the principal handicaps of the *82nd Airborne* – affecting this division more seriously than any other engaged in it – was that the men fit for combat had also to take care of their wounded. In every other division – *101st Airborne* included – evacuation toward the LSTs [transport vessels] via the beach, was possible by the morning of D-Day, or, in the worst of cases, in the afternoon. Three days went by before the first help came from Utah Beach. [...] Several soldiers died when they could have been saved in other circumstances. [...] Krause realized that his men knew that help wasn't following them, which multiplied the cases of behavioral disorders. The first aid post of Sainte-Mère-Église [situated in the hospice] took charge only of those hurt in the defense of the village; there was another post in the jump zone [at the farm of La Couture] that handled soldiers hurt during the jump. On the evening of D-Day, there were a hundred and thirty soldiers hospitalized in Sainte-Mère-Église. Most of them suffered from shrapnel of all kinds – artillery shells, mortars, grenades, etc. No more than six or seven soldiers had been hit by bullets. Krause had been hit by a bullet in the left thigh at about 5 p.m. – his third hit of the day. The medics sent him to the aid station."

Thirty-five days of fighting followed in Normandy. After the painful days of the battle of hedgerows near La-Haye-du-Puits, the men of the *82nd Airborne* went back to England on July 13, 1944. When it came time for accounting, the first observation was that in spite of the short duration of this campaign, the total number of losses (5,436 soldiers killed, disappeared, or wounded) for this airborne division had never been so high since the beginning of the conflict. 46% of the men had been taken out of combat, including 9.7% killed during the operations in Normandy. For this single American division, an average of thirty-three killed per day were counted, whereas the figure was five killed per day in Sicily (July 1943) and nine for the campaign of Holland (September 1944). A deadly density that is striking, to which we must add 6% of soldiers "in shock", a figure that is a testimony to the bitterness and the violence of the battle. Death is not only physical. When it destroys a being, it becomes psychic but also social when the individual is forced into psychiatric care.

CHARLES N. DEGLOPPER

In the night of the 8 to 9 June, the soldier Charles N. DeGlopper and C Company - 325th GIR received the mission to cross the marsh zone in order to establish a link with the paratroopers of the *507th PIR*. Coming from the east and using a road covered with water, known as "le gué secret" (the secret ford), C Company was to veer off to attack the chateau d'Amfreville in order to put the Germans under pressure. The military operations deteriorated when a German attack forced the men of the 1st battalion – *325th GIR* to fall back in total disarray. As the sun rose, toward 5:30 a.m., Charles DeGlopper set himself in the middle of the road, not far from the chapel of Cauquigny, to facilitate the retreat of his companions toward the bridge at La Fière. In spite of the heavy losses inflicted on the enemy thanks to his BAR rifle, the force of nature (1.96 meters) that was DeGlopper was fatally shot. Later, in 1946, this exploit won him the Congressional Medal of Honor, awarded posthumously. Until 2014, he was the only soldier of the *82nd Airborne Division* to receive this distinction for the Normandy campaign.

In March, 1944, PFC Charles N. DeGlopper, poses, pipe in mouth, along with his comrade, Kirby McDonald. Collection DeGlopper family, via the Roger family.

Left, a letter sent to the father of Charles N. DeGlopper confirming the death of his son: "It is with regret that I am writing to confirm the recent telegram informing you of the death of your son, Private First Class Charles N. DeGlopper [...] who was killed in action on 9 June 1944 in France." Charles DeGlopper was buried in the temporary cemetery in Blosville. Collection DeGlopper family, via Roger family

STEVE L. RZASA

On June 20, to the west of Vindefontaine, Private First Class Steve L. Rzasa of HQ/3 – *508th PIR* was killed in action. This young soldier from Chicago was wounded twice during the battle of Normandy. It is easy to understand the anguish of a mother who receives two consecutive telegrams, each saying that her son was out of combat, on 6 and 16 of June. However, the third telegram brought even sadder news. On June 24, Mary Rzasa was officially informed by the Department of War of the death of her son: "The Secretary of War desires me to express his deep regret that your son, Private First Class Steve L. Rzasa was killed in action on 20 June in France." In the weeks that followed, Col. Lindquist, commander of the *508th PIR*, Gen. James Gavin, commander in second of the 82nd Airborne Division as well as the governor of Illinois expressed their condolences to Mrs. Rzasa. Her son was buried in the temporary military cemetery of Blosville.

Steve L. Rzasa, photographed at Camp Mackall (North Carolina) in November 1943.

The Morning Report, dated 26 June 1944 signaling the death in combat of Steve Rzasa.

Collection Rzasa family

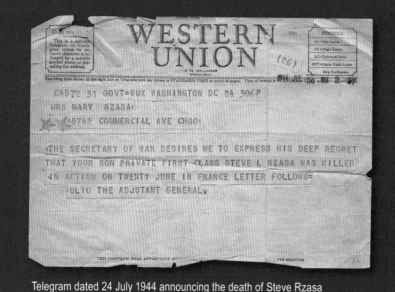

Telegram dated 24 July 1944 announcing the death of Steve Rzasa

For the three parachute regiments of the *82nd Airborne Division* engaged in the fighting around Sainte-Mère-Église, the *505th*, the *507th* and the *508th PIR*, 12% of the men were killed in action in the course of the Normandy campaign. Of the seven hundred fifty-two victims, it is worth noting that two hundred fifty-five were killed on D-Day. 34% of the paratroopers killed in action in Normandy were killed in the first twenty-four hours of the operation – a rate of fatality without precedent and which demonstrates clearly the dangerousness of this enormous operation.

Ihr Lieben all' gedenket mein,
Doch ohne Herzensschwere;
Ich brauche keinen Leichenstein,
Mich deckt das Feld der Ehre.

Soldat
Johann Pommer
gef. am 6. 6. 1944

Two death cards printed at the request of the families of two German soldiers killed in action in Sainte-Mère-Église: that of Johann Pommer, killed on June 6, 1944 near Saint-Côme-du-Mont and that of Balthazar Ulletsee, killed in action on June 9, 1944 in Gourbesville.

Collection F. Le Goupil

Christliches Andenken
an meinen einzigen, unvergeßlichen Sohn,
unseren lieben herzensguten Bruder und
Schwager

Johann Pommer
Soldat in einem Grenadier-Regt.
Hausbesitzersohn in Wagenham

welcher am 6. Juni 1944 im Entscheidungskampf bei St. Côme du Mont im 20. Lebensjahre den Heldentod für seine Heimat starb.

Das Glöcklein verkündets im Heimatland
Ein Held ist gefallen fürs Vaterland.
So schmerzlich trifft dies Los meine Lieben
Der Sohn ist auf blutigem Schlachtfeld
geblieben.
Zu Vater und Schwestern sprach ich
noch beim Geh'n:
Lebt wohl, lebt wohl, auf Wiederseh'n!
Ihr hofftet stets auf meine Wiederkehr,
Doch in die Heimat komm ich nimmermehr.
Weinet nicht meine Lieben, ich war doch bran

In Gottes heiligem Frieden
ruht fern von seinen Lieben
mein herzensguter unvergeßlicher Mann, mein
guter lieber Vater, Sohn und Bruder

Baltasar Alletsee
Obergefr. in einem Infanterie-Regt.
Inh. des Kriegsverdienstkreuzes 2. Kl. m Schw.
geboren am 25. Juni 1907
gefallen am 9. Juni 1944, beerdigt
im Friedhof Curbesville (Frankreich).

HCoM   Druck Fischer Weilheim   612

THE "NORMANDY" SYNDROME OF A GERMAN PARATROOPER

Joachim Dahms was 20 in June, 1944 when his regiment of German paratroopers, the *Fallschirmjäger* Regiment 6, was engaged in violent fighting on D-Day. In 2009, he looked back on this visibly painful past. This rich and poignant testimony gives us several keys to understanding the actions under fire of a young German soldier.

"In the spring of 1944, nature was awakening while the *Fallschirmjäger* Regiment 6 trained in Köln-Wahn. Under the command of Lt.-Col. E. von der Heydte, this new combat troop was well trained, particularly in parachuting. I was a member of this troop at its creation. I immediately understood that this would not be a walk in the park. I was a part of the 3rd battalion commanded by Horst Trebes. In May came the goodbyes. The whole regiment took the train for France where we were stationed in Saint-Georges-de-Bohon, near Carentan. As we awaited the allied landing, my comrades and myself were on constant alert right up to the night of June 5 and 6, 1944. The *Fj Reg* 6 found itself suddenly put to the test of fire with a region of about 15 by 20 kilometers to defend. I remember very well my first contact with the enemy (exchange of fire between Saint-Georges and Rougeville) as well as my first encounter with isolated American paratroopers, early in the morning of June 6, near Saint-Côme-du-Mont. The fighting, intense and relentless, first moved toward Sainte-Marie-du-Mont but my company had to defend itself equally from the forces advancing toward us from Sainte-Mère-Église.

We understood immediately that our opponents had an enormous quantity of arms and material and so we grasped what was waiting for us. We were constantly involved in combat; artillery shellfire hit us non-stop on our poorly installed positions. I saw a very young paratrooper from my unit just lose it after four hours of uninterrupted shooting. It was clear that he had didn't know what he was doing because he jumped up, threw away his helmet and his gun and fell immediately under a cloud of shells. This crazy war was far from reaching its peak because, from the sea, the gunmen on the ships could get at every one of our positions, and before sending in troops they would cover everything [...] Our losses increased substantially as we approached Angoville[-au-Plain]. In Vierville, where there is a marvelous manor house, a German aid station found itself in the line of fire of the naval artillery which caused panic among the wounded. But fear was not the only thing keeping us company. Water and cider were offered by the local population on this hot summer day. We were surprised at this friendly gesture of the locals because our faces were covered with cow manure as camouflage and offered a rather dreadful image.

The beautiful landscapes of the Norman countryside with its fields for the horses, and its "Bocage" turned quickly into something very good for fighting man to man. "Him or me", struggling for his own survival that is what guided every soldier at the front. But the desire to stay human was still stronger. At one moment, I heard some cries coming from the thickets. "Mama, mama!", cried out a very young man [an American soldier] barely older than me. At that instant, I realized the enemy had a mother too, and that, in the worst moments of distress, he called out to her with the same affection as a German. These desperate cries and this fear of death made me conscious for the first time of my life as a soldier.

I was raised in the Christian faith, and I tried to ease my conscience by prayer. But one single truth imposed itself: the shells destroyed everything, houses, trees, greenery, they dug deep craters into the earth and killed young men, in their finest age, who should have had their life before them. This terrible reality contained warnings that we had not yet learned learn to appreciate: the retreat of the enemy generally signified that we would be getting piled on by their artillery. The air and the earth trembled under the power of the strikes and everyone who stood in the trenches was invaded with a sensation of total helplessness. We could do nothing against it except to use our strength and our superiority in close combat, which intensified.

[...] I had the feeling that it would soon "be my turn" and that my survival depended on luck. That made solidarity with my comrades more necessary than ever. In a field, a dead cow offered protection from the enemy fire. What was happening to me? Was I becoming a brute? What was I capable of? Was this what my parents had raised me for: for me to die here, for the fatherland, in a fatal, senseless irreversible mesh? Nothing more? [...] In a matter of a few seconds, everything that had seemed important appeared paltry, and I felt myself once again imbued with all the beauty and all the joy of this world. An insect that moved laboriously across my hand, passing from finger to finger, monopolized all my attention. With my head in my arms to protect me from the artillery. I observed this insect who seemed to show me affection. This memory is very much alive in my head, and it gives me the strength today to carry on when I need it.

[...] The counter-attack toward Saint-Côme-du-Mont stopped and we were unable to retake the town. We hid in the furrows of a field and prepared to die there. Nothing unusual. The Americans' torrent of fire surprised us this time as they used phosphorus shells and so the fog prevented us from seeing their preparations for the attack. We couldn't see their snipers in the trees either, and our men fell one after the other, victims of a bullet in the head that seemed to come out of nowhere.

[...] The battle had started even more fiercely at Carentan. My strength and that of my comrades was exhausted after the hardships of the preceding days and it was high time that someone come to relieve us. The continuous engagement left little time to eat and there was no question of sleeping. The commander von der Heydte then did the only thing he could and ordered a retreat of the rest of the regiment (one spoke of ninety-seven men).

[...] I know that after the war, my psychic and physical existence were brought into question, and it seemed miraculous to have gotten out of a situation that had no exit. Myself, like all my generation, I must admit that I was unaware that in 1944 the national-socialist state had already decided and started to put in place the end of our existence. [...] The basis for this trust, on which the groups of German soldiers could still lean, was founded on the unique strength of an ideology and its fundamental principle: to die for the fatherland – an ideology by which an entire generation of young people were seduced, abused and deceived.

By my testimony, I hope to contribute to the demystification of this nationalist ideology and perhaps looking back at these key events will enable me to reconcile myself with my past and the "Normandy" syndrome." [58]

"Jo" Dahms and his MG42 in Normandy. Film ECPAD

IN CONTRAST WITH THE JOYFUL POPULATION: THE CIVILIAN VICTIMS

Bullets kill without distinction, and the civilians of Sainte-Mère-Église were not spared. Forty-six inhabitants lost their lives, principally by artillery fire. The battle for the liberation of the town was not an easy task, far from the skewed picture of a lightening liberation, clean and festive. It was not. First concerned by this disillusion were the twenty-eight civilians killed by the German bombardments of June 6 and 7, 1944. On the day of June 6 alone, twenty-five people of Sainte-Mère-Église perished in the German counter-attacks that had started by 9:30 a.m. on D-Day.

Among the victims of D-Day, Jules Leménicier, a shopkeeper, was hit by the shrapnel of a shell that exploded in front of his store as he was conversing with René Jamard. The two were fatally hit. Raymond Paris lived in the next house and came immediately to his neighbor's shop after hearing the explosion. As he entered the main room, the body of Jules Leménicier was stretched out on the ground, his skull opened, a horrific sight.

Name and first name of civilian victims	Date of death	Cause of death
BRISSET Juliette	6 June	Artillery fire
CUEFF Lucien	6 June	Killed by German soldier
DA GRACA Manuel	6 June	Aerial bombardment
DOREY Christiane	6 June	Artillery fire
FEUILLIE Esther	6 June	Artillery fire
HAMEL Amélie	6 June	Artillery fire
Inconnu	6 June	?
JAMARD René	6 June	Artillery fire
JOSEPH Raymond	6 June	Aerial bombardment
JOUAN Eugène	6 June	Artillery fire
LE BRUMAN André	6 June	Artillery fire
LE BRUMAN Raymond	6 June	Artillery fire
LEBOUCHER Marius	6 June	Artillery fire
LECHEVALIER Marie-Thérèse	6 June	Artillery fire
LECOEUR Marie-Olive	6 June	Artillery fire
LELAISANT René	6 June	Artillery fire
LEMAITRE Jeannine	6 June	Artillery fire
LEMENICIER Jules	6 June	Artillery fire
LEPELLETIER Germaine	6 June	Artillery fire
LIOULT Marie-Louise	6 June	Artillery fire
MASSIS Augustine	6 June	Aerial bombardment
REFFRAY Augustine	6 June	Artillery fire
VIEL Alphonse	6 June	Artillery fire
VIEL Berthe	6 June	Artillery fire
VIEL Simone	6 June	Artillery fire
CROUZET Auguste	7 June	?
REFFRAY Jean-Marie	7 June	Artillery fire of 6 June
POTIGNY Désiré	7 June	?

This reconstruction takes place in front of the hardware store of Jules Leménicier. Note multiple impacts coming from the shells that hit the front of the store, those that killed the shopkeeper. NARA

With a heavy heart, Raymond Paris cleaned up the place to spare the family of the victim this gruesome spectacle.

Later in the week, Saturday June 10, Raymond went off towards the Impasse des Ribets, at the south end of Sainte-Mère-Église. He wanted to find the shelter where a handful of civilians had taken refuge during the combats of D-Day. This little outbuilding served to stock a few barrels of cider. For the comfort of the occupants, mattresses had been laid in the interior. Until an artillery shell hit the building. Raymond recalls, with emotion: "At the impasse, I found the shed that had been visibly damaged by a shell. As I entered the room, I saw corpses in a mixture of cider and feathers. It was hard to look at. With some friends, we took the remains of the victims to the village cemetery".

Lucien Cueff was an 18 year old high school student in Valognes. He was requisitioned in the night of June 5 to 6, for his very first time, to guard the railroad between Fresville and La Fière. He had a front row view of the paratroopers landing of the railroad. The show over, he fell in with a group of lost American soldiers who wanted to go to the farm of La Couture. Lucien Cueff served as guide to the Americans until the morning of D-Day. As the A Company – *505th PIR* began its advance toward the manor of La Fière, the young man was forced to walk at the front of the group. Arriving near the gate of the fortified farm, he was the target of German snipers. He took a bullet to the head before falling to the road. He was taken to the cemetery of Sainte-Mère-Église as "Inconnu" (unknown), his papers having been taken after his death. It was a full month later that his parents came to recognize their son, chosen by History as the first victim of the combats of La Fière.

Impasse des Ribets, in Sainte-Mère-Église, at the end of which Raymond Paris discovered several civilian victims following the German shelling. Photo by the author

A monument, facing the city hall, dedicated to the 46 civilian victims, on which are engraved these words: "In honor of the French of Sainte-Mère-Église who gave their lives to buy back our liberty." Photo by the author

The small building situated at the entrance of the village cemetery of Sainte-Mère-Église where civilian victims of June 6 were placed before burial. Picture by the author

June. A shell had exploded very close and I can still see the branches falling all around us. The presence of this dead woman was frightening for all the occupants of the trench. So people began to change areas. On the 7th, everyone left in different directions. Marius Leboucher, the hairdresser, went off toward the calf market where there was a completely dry trough. In his turn, he too was killed by shrapnel from a shell."[60]

Entire families were decimated by the bombardments of the German artillery, like the Viel family. They lived near the Haule park. Jacques Pignot recalls: "The daughter, Simone, was my age. A week after June 6, I was with with Mr Deloeuvre, head of the sector for the electricity company of Valognes, and his nephew, when we discovered the bodies in the cellar, behind the house. It was a 105mm shell (according to Charles Deloeuvre) that had mutilated them horribly. I remember the gory discovery. We took them all the way to the cemetery on stretchers."[61]

The young Henri-Jean Renaud, 10, has a clear memory of the two first days of the invasion. Far from the flags and other symbols of a festive and joyous liberation, his testimony highlights the omnipresence of the risk of death during the battle for the liberation: "June 6, we took refuge near the fountain of Saint-Méen in a trench. We spent two nights in this makeshift trench with a parachute that carpeted the ground. We were several families in the place, and a few meters from me was Mrs Lecoeur. She was beautiful, very neat, with beautiful hair. She was the mother of one of my friends. She was killed in the same trench, the night of 6 to 7 of

Facing this inhabitual number of lifeless bodies, it was decided, during the first 48 hours of the invasion, to store civilian victims temporarily in the small building to the left of the main entrance of the village cemetery. Mr Reffray, assistant to the pharmacist Alexandre Renaud and his wife were also killed during the battles of the 6 and 7 June. They were added to the pile of bodies heaped for better or worse in the little building of the cemetery. It was only on Friday, June 9, that the first civilian burials could take place. "Friday afternoon, we buried our dead [in a mass grave]. No official delegation, we were alone with them.

In the ruins of Pont-l'Abbé, west of Sainte-Mère-Église, a paratrooper of the 82nd Airborne has just pulled the body of a little girl from the wreckage. NARA

Saint-Marcouf, to the east of Sainte-Mère-Église, was heavily bombed by American aviation in the evening of June 5. Thirty-six of the 175 inhabitants were killed by allied bombs. The caption of this picture claims, however, that the husband of this woman in tears was killed by German guns. An erroneous description that expresses a certain malaise about the shelling by American aviation. NARA

The liberated sector of the Cotentin at this stage extended to only a part of the county of Sainte-Mère-Église, and this part of France was still a battlefield. Many men had come to dig graves. Others went, with a small handcart, to look for those who remained under the ruins of their houses. As there were no shrouds, we tore parachutes out of the trees; those who were dear to us left for their final home draped in grand veils of the whitest silk. [...] Yet, Christ blessed our dead in the person of our priest, who recited the ritual prayers; I lowered the flag of France over them and their poor bodies returned to the Norman soil which recalled them to it."[62]

In the days after the battles, with the front moved on elsewhere, other civilians met their death through other acts of war. Seventeen of them – the eighteenth had been killed in Fauville May 28, a week before the Invasion – were killed by mines and other unlucky accidents resulting from handling munitions.

"Friendly" fire caused the death of an inhabitant of Sainte-Mère-Église: Pierre Lebarbier. Fire and the omnipresence of death bring about attitudes and behaviors inherent to the context of war. Facing the risk of death, some allied soldiers were overcome by terror. This fear of dying was the root of their mistrust of civilians. As with any armed conflict, excesses and abuses took place during the combats of June 6, 1944. The expression "collateral damage" is anachronistic to the events of the summer of 1944 in Normandy. The term would be used officially by the American army for the Vietnam war to camouflage the recurrent abuses of the civilian population.

One spoke of "friendly" fire. Entering war is, in reality, penetrating into another universe where human conduct is transformed. Thus, when the terror of being killed gained the upper hand, it caused, according to the anthropologist Edgar Morin, "an animal and destructive euphoria" which does not differ between civilians and military.

Name of civilian	Date of death	Cause
BOSVY Lucien	?	?
CHAPEY Amélie	28 May	Killed by a German soldier
CZECHOWSKY Josef	?	?
DUBOSCQ Claude	?	?
ENDELIN Auguste	24 June	?
GAUTHIER André	7 July	?
JUSTE Désiré	17 June	?
LAURENCE Fernand	15 June	?
LEBARBIER Pierre	3 July	Killed by an American soldier
LEGAILLARD Albert	18 June	Bombardment
LEMIERE Marcel	?	?
LEVEZIEL Louis	9 August	Mine
POISSON Simone	18 June	?
ROBIOLLE Léonie	11 June	?
SIBRANT Gustave	26 June	Mine
SUZANNE Alphonse	?	?
THEZARD Maria	20 June	?
YONNET Roger	?	?

RELATIONS WITH ENEMY DEAD

If war takes on its true significance the first time you come across a body of someone you know, encountering an enemy corpse has the particularity of generating three types of behavior: respect, fury and/or annihilation.

Respect seems to be the easiest to understand, even if, generally speaking, it is the rarest. If the German commander of the place had the right to be buried temporarily in the village cemetery of Sainte-Mère-Église, the majority of German foot soldiers killed in action were buried in the ditches along the roads or around the villages. This behavior comes from the way one saw the enemy. One considered him a figure radically different from oneself, an "other" who was totally antithetical. If the Japanese soldiers were stereotyped as animals of a dwarf species, although particularly pestilential, the Germans were recognized as human beings. Except that the latter were perverted, according to historian Paul Fussell in his reference work, *Wartime*. He adds: "If we could defame the Japanese so far as to treat them as animals, the Germans were merely "sick", the incarnation of "disease".[63] A persistent rumor circulated in the American army whereby German corpses turned green as they decomposed, proof of their abnormal physiology.

Fury, on encountering an enemy body, appeared to be the rule during the combats of D-Day and the following days – especially given the intensity of the battle. This fury was not exclusively physical, quite the opposite. In fact, touching enemy bodies seemed to carry such risks – real or symbolic – that American soldiers would do everything they could to avoid handling German bodies. This task was thus often left to the civilians or to prisoners of war. However, the instrumentalization of

The body of a German soldier lies in a ditch near Sainte-Mère-Église. Simple photograph, or war trophy? NARA

the enemy corpse by means of photography, for example, would be the principal method of debasing these adversaries. To photograph enemy corpses is to cross the line of obscenity, according to Stéphane Audouin-Rouzeau, "obscenity of the anatomical frontier, obscenity in the postures of the cadavers, obscenity of their nudity, finally, whether it be accidental, an effect of modern explosives, or intentional, the outcome of a final gesture of dehumanization on the enemy's part, on the part of his executioner."[64] The enemy body was a propaganda weapon as a result of realist photographs of human remains, cadavers expressing the suffering and the solitude of the final moments: photos showing enemy deaths that mobilized the troops to the rear and brought a certain comfort at the sight of the pain endured by the other camp.

Combatants, who live for long periods with dead bodies, adopt their own practices on the battlefield. Symbolic ritual mutilations of bodies mark the desire of the victor to bring back a trophy, a sign of his courage, to take the strength of the beaten and to prolong his suffering in the hereafter. These photographs became the modern form of the trophy of war.[65] Numerous soldiers fix the images of enemy cadavers on paper, as a means is of preserving the representation of inflicted death. The photographic image, however, served less to express the horrors of war, than to affirm victory and prove one's virility.

Whether it is a question of simple vandalism or whether it has a deeper significance, these practices of corporal mutilation are often concentrated in the sensitive zones, symbolic of the body, its extensions, its orifices. Plundering the corpses, resulting in mutilations and removal of body parts to make trophies remained current practice throughout the battle of Normandy and the combats of Sainte-Mère-Église. Private First Class Joseph J. Krzyzak belonged to A Company – *12th Infantry Regiment*. He landed on Utah Beach on June 6, 1944, with the *4th Infantry Division*. His service in the Cotentin was cut short when, on June 7, he was seriously wounded near the battery of Azeville, a few kilometers north of Sainte-Mère-Église. Two days later he arrived back in England to be cared for. His convalescence lasted until the end of the war so his stay in Normandy was relatively short.

Nonetheless, Krzyzak had enough time to acquire the gold denture of a dead German during the day of the 6th. A macabre souvenir, a trophy which he kept until the day of his death. In January, 2011, a few personal effects of the veteran Krzyzak were placed for sale on a well-known auction website on the internet. Among the medals and other honorable decorations was the gold denture taken in Normandy off the body of a dead German soldier. These spoils of war were undoubtedly the veteran's most precious trophy. To humiliate and mutilate the dead enemy are common wartime practices that extend well beyond our sphere of understanding..

Sexual mutilations, such as emasculation, point to rituals of affirmation of victory of the warrior, denying the vanquished his virile humanity. They are, at the same time, a determined humiliation of the corpse, a negation of his person, and a brutal

Message written June 23, 1944 by Sgt. Bob Gillette, S2 (Intelligence) – *505th PIR*, and sent to all commanders of each battalion of the *82nd Airborne*. Collection Bob Gillette

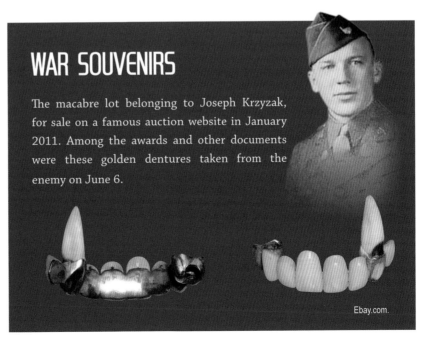

WAR SOUVENIRS

The macabre lot belonging to Joseph Krzyzak, for sale on a famous auction website in January 2011. Among the awards and other documents were these golden dentures taken from the enemy on June 6.

Ebay.com.

means of appropriating his power. Committed on both sides, these bloody practices were found in several places in the county of Sainte-Mère-Église. In the hamlet of Holdy, in the county of Saint-Marie-du-Mont, was a field battery served by about forty German soldiers. On D-Day, several American paratroopers belonging to the 1st battalion of the *506th PIR* were dropped into the center of the field battery. Rapidly taken prisoner or still stuck in the trees bordering the area, these men were horribly mutilated in the genital areas. The death report of George Bailey, who was one of the unlucky ones, registered June 7, 1944, by the men of the *426th Quartermaster Co (101st Airborne)* carries the following mention: "Genital parts missing. Body has suffered major abuse."[66]

After the capture of the German battery, early in the afternoon of June 6, the reprisals against the forty-seven Germans were equivalent to the atrocities they had committed, as forty of them were shot, then tortured with the seven remaining prisoners looking on. To put pressure on the living by mistreating their dead is an ancestral practice which is an integral part of psychological warfare. Auguste Dugouchet, who lived on a farm nearby, recalls the battle at Le Holdy: "At the crossroads, I saw a German who was trying to come out of a field. He was running away. An American officer who limped started shooting at the running man with his machine gun. It was unreal! I saw his head literally explode. The body was dragged to the middle of the crossroads and left there for ten days or so. When I moved it, it was flat as a cigarette paper. The vehicles didn't stop running here."[67] An enemy body had no more value than a poor animal abandoned on the road. This was the ultimate degree of denial of the other and the dehumanization of the lifeless body of the vanquished. In June 1944, Private Murray

PHOTOGRAPHING ENEMY CORPSES

An everyday image of combat: the body of a German soldier, outstretched on the side of the road, is photographed by an American in the vicinity of Sainte-Mère-Église. Although the GIs, before landing in Normandy, were told not to bring any cameras with them, it is clear that an enormous number of pictures were taken by the troops. This picture was taken back to the States and shown with pride alongside other trophies of war.

Collection P. Dawson.

NARA.

This picture, taken during the battles of the Cotentin by an American war correspondent, shows the lifeless body of an American medic. The image is as upsetting as it is uncommon. Indeed, allied self-censoring was imposed on war photographers to not take pictures of "friendly bodies" so as not to shock American public opinion. Except, in this case, it is a picture of an American medic, a service which was not required to bear arms as stipulated by the Geneva Convention of 1929. The object here was to demonstrate the barbarity of the enemy, attacking even soldiers without arms. By precaution, the face of the soldier was censored (scraping of the negative), to avoid any unfortunate recognition.

Moonhatch, of D Company – *506th PIR*, jumped in error near the bridge at La Fière, well away from Sainte-Marie-du-Mont. For three days, he participated in the battle for the bridge at La Fière alongside soldiers of the *82nd Airborne Division*. "Andrew Sfrisi and I landed in the marshes of the Merderet. I knew right away this was the wrong place. We waited until dawn to head for our regrouping zone. Later, we came across a group of the *505th PIR*. The officer ordered us to join his group which had to take the bridge [of La Fière] situated about 500 yards from where we were. [...] The guys of the *82nd Airborne* lost a lot of men during the three days of combat. The German artillery hammered us without stopping. The men had their nerves on edge. [...] Then, on June 9, Sfrisi and I started off to find our company. From Sainte-Mère-Église, we went south toward our CP [at Angoville-au-Plain]. The ditches along the roads were filled with German bodies. They had been searched, very often. Their tags, watches, insignia, their rings, personal papers, etc. had been taken as souvenirs."[68]

The taking of dog tags in combat had a very special significance. It was the main thing that allowed the identification of a soldier killed in action. It was a prized souvenir in wartime for two reasons: first, it was compact, and further, it gave the victorious soldier the identity of the vanquished. It was a double death inflicted on the soldier in question, as identification was rendered virtually impossible, plunging the family into an eternal uncertainty. To take the identity plates was to vanquish the enemy symbolically on the battlefield, but also to shatter the hearts of those left behind.

« WAR IS HELL »

An American M1 helmet liner. This model, made by Hawley, belonged to an unknown first lieutenant. It was found in 1991 on a farm at Amfreville, west of Sainte-Mère-Église. In spite of a fairly poor state of conservation, a detail inscribed on the interior caught the attention of its finder. The mention "War is hell" lets us imagine the intensity of combat in this corner of Normandy. Even if this observation may seem naive, it remains no less pertinent. It makes each of us consider the suffering bred by any armed conflict. War, such as tortures the body, such as bruises the soul, is then not a game. Here, we are far from the traditional gatherings and other historical reconstitutions that delight some of our contemporaries.

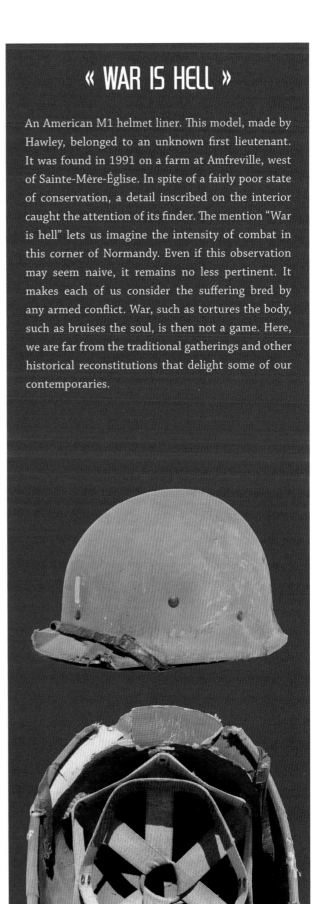

14 July 1944: Taps resounds at the funeral of Brig.-Gen. Theodore Roosevelt Jr. at temporary cemetery n° 2, Sainte-Mère-Église. NARA

TEMPORARY CEMETERIES

WM A LOUDERMILK
34198753

STENCIL USED ON WHITE WOODEN CROSSES
TO IDENTIFY WAR DEAD U.S.A.
IN TEMPORARY CEMETERIES ETO 1944-45

POUR IDENTIFIER LES SOLDATS U.S.
INHUMES ICI DE 1944-1948

The military cemeteries of Sainte-Mère-Église's county

BURYING THE DEAD: THE FIRST CEMETERIES

The frontline was not very far away, yet already the first bodies had been buried in gardens, on the side of the road, along the hedges and sometimes in village cemeteries. This month of June 1944, the county of Sainte-Mère-Église was covered with a coat of white crosses, marking inevitably the surrounding landscape. Here and there, an isolated mound of earth marked the place of a military tomb, often dug in haste, often bereft of anything else to mark it. In Sainte-Mère-Église, the first allied victims of D-Day – notably those paratroopers who were killed on the town square – were buried in the town's cemetery, next to the villagers. Jacques Pignot remembers, "In the days following June 6, someone brought the body of the German commander, who I knew well, being his neighbor. He must have been killed at

Fauville. He was buried in our cemetery." Three nations were thus temporarily reunited in the cemetery of this town. What a powerful symbol, while the battle raged on only a few kilometers away. Among the Americans buried here was the soldier Alfred J. Van Holsbeck of F Company – *505th PIR*. He was the unlucky paratrooper who landed in the middle of the flames of Pommier's house on the evening of June 5, 1944. The report of his death presented below says: "Previously buried in isolated grave located at French Civilian Cemetery, Ste Mere Eglise." His body was exhumed on July 19, 1944, and transferred to the temporary military cemetery n° 1 in Sainte-Mère-Église.

Other American paratroopers were shot down elsewhere, behind enemy lines. This was the case for Private James R. Hattrick of I Company – *508th PIR*. During the airdrops of the 6 June, 1944, a handful of men landed around the village

The report of burial of Private First Class Alfred Van Holsbeck, *505th PIR*, killed in action on the 6th of June after landing in the flames of the Pommier's house. Before being buried in the temporary cemetery n° 1 in Sainte-Mère-Église, the paratrooper was initially buried in the village cemetery. NARA

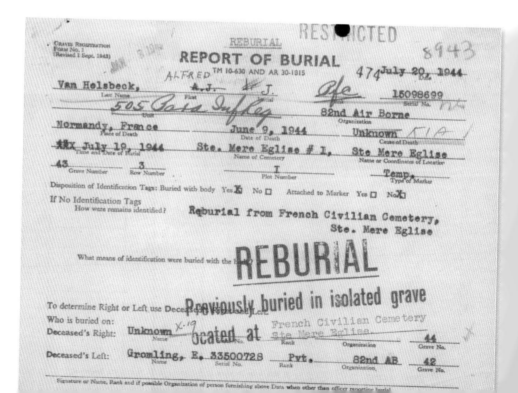

of Gourbesville, situated seven kilometers from Sainte-Mère-Église.

James Hattrick landed close to the chateau, then the property of Michel Delaune. In the same house was installed the headquarters of a German medical company and an aid post. A report of the American army, dated July 7, 1944, mentions the presence of "100 armed medics". Camouflaged in the leaves of the park, Hattrick killed nine German soldiers on D-Day before being taken in the German sights. Seriously wounded in the head, he was taken to the aid station and was treated by the German doctor who was already treating several other American prisoners. Toward 6:00 p.m. he died of his wounds. Members of the German medical unit buried him in the village cemetery next to fourteen German soldiers. Three weeks later, June 28, 1944, the men of the graves services exhumed the body of the paratrooper to transfer him to the temporary military cemetery n° 1 at Sainte-Mère-Église.

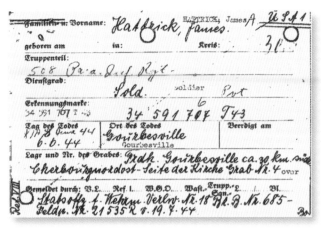

The report of losses established June 6, 1944, by the German doctor of the aid station of Gourbesville showing the death of the paratrooper James Hattrick, *508th PIR.* NARA via J.-B.Feuillye

The people of Gourbesville, who had brought flowers daily to the tomb of the soldier who lay in their cemetery, put up a monument, or more exactly a plate, dedicated to the young local hero. Today, the discreet plate can be seen at the foot of the monument to the dead of World War I, 1914-1918.

Lt. Lloyd Brown, observing the temporary German graves dug in haste in the sector of Saint-Côme-du-Mont, July 15, 1944. NARA

On the German side, taking charge of the dead was even more difficult, given the fact that the Wehrmacht was retreating from day to day, making the task particularly complicated. The frontline got bogged down, often for a few hours, as was the case for La Fière, where, on the afternoon of June 7, 1944, a cease-fire was requested by the Germans in order to gather the many victims who lay on either side of the road. It was an apocalyptic spectacle of desolation. An American observer estimated the number of Germans killed on the road that crossed the marshes to be in the vicinity of two hundred. The cease-fire of thirty minutes was lengthened and the Germans spent close to two hours evacuating their dead and wounded. What became of the German dead? They were probably conveyed to Saint-Sauveur-le-Vicomte, or even Bricquebec, to be buried in a divisional cemetery. Earlier, the officer in charge of graves, the *Gräberoffizier*, would have taken half of the ID plate in order to identify the dead. Later that half-plate would be sent to Berlin, to the seat of the WASt (the German administration charged with those killed in action) to inform the family of the victim.

In several parts of the American sector known as *Utah Beach*, little cemeteries could be found. Around the beach of La Madeleine, in Sainte-Marie-du-Mont, the men of the 1st *Engineer Special Brigade* undertook the construction of a cemetery that would hold the bodies of all those killed on or near the beach.

The "interim" cemetery of the hamlet of La Madeleine, near Utah Beach, received 365 soldiers, American and German, between 6 and 25 June. Collection Utah Beach Museum

The organization of the recent bridgehead on June 6, 1944, included the creation of a cemetery a few meters south of the chapel of La Madeleine. On D-Day+1, the cemetery was opened and 365 tombs were dug, up until a divisional cemetery was finally opened, June 9, for the *4th Infantry Division*, to the north of Saint-Martin-de-Varreville. The transfer of bodies to the temporary cemetery n° 2 of Sainte-Mère-Église began on June 25, 1944.

Inland, on the territory of the village of Hiesville, was another "interim" cemetery. On June 6, 1944, the doctors, surgeons and medics of the *326th Medical Co.* belonging to the *101st Airborne Division*, installed a divisional hospital in the compound of the chateau of La Colombière, a beautiful building dating from the late XVIth century.

The temporary graves of Gen. Wilhelm Falley (commander of the *91.Luftland Division*) and his aide-de-camp, Maj. Bartuzat, both killed on D-Day in an ambush near the chateau of Bernaville. Collection Airborne Museum

At 9:00 p.m., under the orders of Maj. Albert J. Crandall, and with the help of the Cotelle family, the owners of the place, an improvised operating room was installed in the milk room of the farm and five tables were operational by the evening of D-Day. Up to three hundred stretchers were laid out in the courtyard of the chateau as well as in the centuries-old buildings. In the afternoon of June 9, the wounded, just operated on, began to be transferred to the aid station on *Utah Beach* before being sent back to England.

BURYING THE ENEMY

Burial report of the German paratrooper, Karl ***, *Fallschirmjäger-Regiment* 6, killed in action June 8, south of Sainte-Marie-du-Mont and temporarily buried in the German square of the Hiesville cemetery until July 4, 1944, before being transferred to the German cemetery in Orglandes.

Nota bene: The author has been requested to keep the personal information (name, birth date and serial number) presented here to the right confidential.

WASt, Berlin.

The bodies of the first victims of the Landing are stored in the cemetery of La Madeleine, officially called "607 Macon".
Collection Michel De Trez

HIESVILLE'S AID STATION

The Field Hospital of the chateau La Colombière, at Hiesville, where the doctors and surgeons of the *326th Airborne Medical Co. - 101st Airborne Division* – took charge of 998 patients, American and German, from 6 to 9 June, 1944. Pictures NARA

That same day, late in the evening, about 11:45 p.m. a light German bomber dropped three bombs on the chateau in spite of the huge red cross on a canvas spread on the ground. The chateau was severely damaged, and some of the wounded soldiers who were waiting to be transferred to England found themselves in a desperate situation. Close to sixty wounded soldiers, American and German, as well as medical personnel died that night of June 9, 1944. Each major aid station had its cemetery. It was the same for the aid station at Hiesville. Fifty meters from the chateau, in a big parcel that had served as a landing field for the American gliders in the morning and evening of June 6, the *426th Airborne Quartermaster Company (101st Airborne)* undertook the construction of a divisional cemetery. The men of Col. Rich landed at *Utah Beach* during the day of June 7 and went straight to the divisional command post. The historical records for this stewardship unit, available from the National Archives, shows us a few details concerning the creation of this military cemetery of the *101st Airborne Division*:

« D plus 2	8 June 1944	Location of Company CP's near Hiesville. Capt. Linker, M/Sgt Bradley, T/5 Barksdale and Cpl Long, Pfcs Mraz and Vanlaningham formed the Division Graves Registration Services platoon and started the Division cemetery.
D plus 4	10 June 1944	21.00- Company attended services for Pfc Vanlaningham. Services are held each night at 21.00 for those buried during the day.
D plus 28	4 July 1944	Normal-General Taylor paid a second visit. Division Cemetery at Hiesville moved to Les Forges Cemetery in vicinity of Blosville. It was VIIIth Corps Cemetery.[69] »

Report of burial of the soldier James Campas (*506th PIR*), killed June 6, 1944, after having landed in the middle of the German field battery at Le Holdy. He was buried on June 8 in the American square at the Hiesville cemetery. NARA

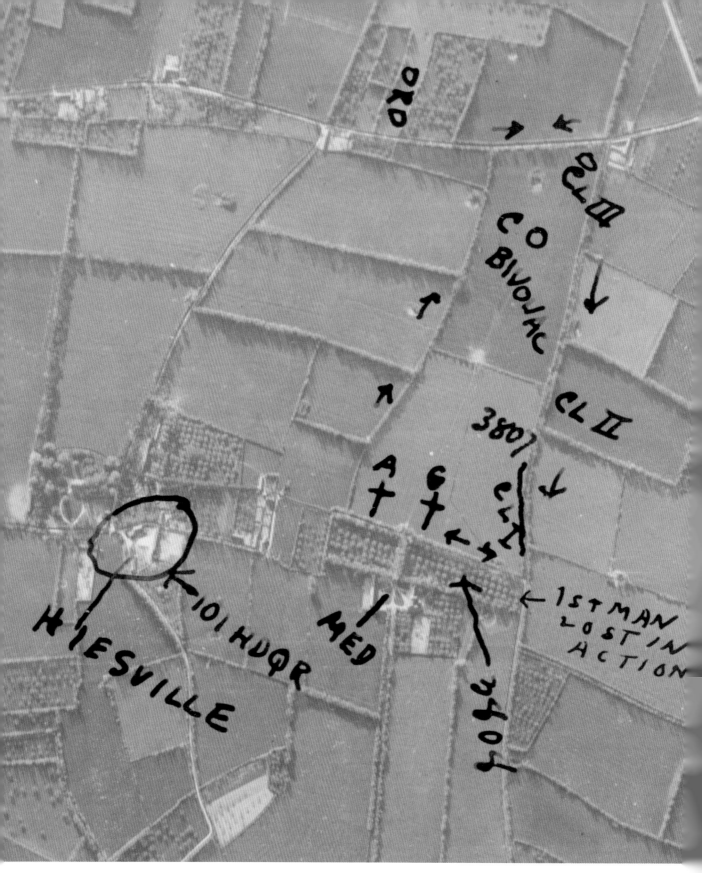

Aerial photograph of the village of Hiesville. Document marked up in June 1944, by the soldiers of the *426th Quartermaster Company –
101st Airborne Division* – showing the place of the command post of the *101st Airborne* "101 HDQR", the hospital of the chateau La Colombière
"MED", and further to the north, the sites of two temporary cemeteries, "A," American, and "G", German. NARA

Construction of the temporary cemetery of Hiesville by German prisoners under the gaze of a paratrooper of the *101st Airborne*. NARA

THE CEMETERY OF THE *101ST AIRBORNE DIVISION*

"Saturday morning I went to place where de division cemetery had been established. None of the bodies had been buried yet, but there were several hundred lying side by side waiting to be buried, some already wrapped in a parachute. I was shocked to find so many of my faithful boys among the dead. [...] All were in God's merciful hands now. German prisoners were digging the graves for both the American and the German dead. I read the burial ritual for all and remained most of the afternoon for the actual burial."

Recollection of Francis L. Sampson

Cemetery of Hiesville, June 10, 1944: the Catholic chaplain of the *501st PIR-101st Airborne Division*, Father Francis Sampson, blesses the bodies of American paratroopers wrapped in their parachutes. NARA

Images captured from the documentary *Sainte-Marie-du-Mont: kilometer 00*, released in 1964. Germain Cotelle presents the vestiges of the cemetery of Hiesville and the clumps of nettles indicating the position of graves (empty) of 256 American paratroopers. © INA

In a story written in 1964 by a local writer, Gilles Perrault, called *Sainte-Marie-du-Mont, kilometer 00*, another testimony, every bit as precious, adds to our knowledge about the cemetery of Hiesville. In a filmed interview, Germain Cotelle looks back on the history of this site which, 20 years later, still carried the scars of this month of June, 1944:

"Sir, you have here the locations of 256 graves of American soldiers who were buried here in the first days of the Invasion. When they were exhumed six weeks later, [four, in reality], in order to refill the holes, they used the soil from the bottom last. As this soil was less rich, it grew back with nettles. Between graves, there are no nettles. We cut them twice a year...".[70]

Everywhere else, it was the men of the *603rd Quartermaster Graves Registration Company* (*603rd QM GR Co.*) who had to select temporary sites and to bury the men fallen in combat. This unit, nicknamed the "Fighting 603", was put into action on January 24, 1943, in Camp Lee, Virginia. Its men came from the four corners of America to join the ranks of this company charged with the registration of graves.

But many didn't know what the principal mission of this unit was. For example, Jack Watt arrived at Camp Sutton (North Carolina) in February 1943 and Sergeant Peel asked him:

Extract of the "Weekly report of burials" for the cemeteries of Normandy. The document reports the burials of soldiers of the *4th Infantry Division*, in the cemetery of "Saint-Martin" up until 14 June, 1944. NARA

QMC Form No.2-GRS
QM 314.6 Q-GRS (Trans).

RESTRICTED

SUBJECT: QMC Form No.2 GRS
Weekly Report of Burials. No. 96

AUG 18 1944

NAME	SOLDIERS NO.	RANK	ORGANIZATION	DATE OF BURIAL OR DEATH	CEMETARY
1741 HILL, Donald G.	35023669	Pfc	23rd Inf.Rgt.	15Jun44	St. Laurent Cem.
1742 KENT, Lonnie J.	18007824	Pvt	23rd Inf.Rgt.	16Jul44	"
1743 LAPORTA, Frank J.	36626695	Pfc	23rd Inf.Rgt.	16 " "	"
1744 SMITHEY, Ira	18013567	Pfc	23rd Inf.Rgt. 2nd Inf.Div.	22Jun44	"
1745 SKURMANN, Paul	32791513	Pfc	38th Inf.Rgt. 2nd Inf.Div.	16Jul44	"
1746 WOODHEAD, Joseph J.	39274085	Pfc	23rd Inf.Rgt.	16 " "	"
1747 SOWERS, Vincent J.	32835254	Pvt	23rd Inf.Regt 2nd Inf.Div.	15 " "	"
1748 WALKER, Gordon F.	32140999	Sgt	17 Armd.Engr. Bn.	20Jun44	"
1749 WARD, William S.	36437087	Pvt.	149 Engr. C Bn	9 " "	"
1750 WARE, Robert B.	O-367982	Capt	116th Inf.Rgt.	9 " "	"
1751 WHITE, Donald R.	33137293	Pfc	18th Inf.Regt.	13 " "	"
1752 WILSON, Robert J.	11132701	Pvt	16th Inf.Rgt.	9 " "	"
1753 WILSON, Wallace	35728829	Pvt	18th Inf.Rgt.	15 " "	"
1754 SANFORD, Norman C.	32334784	Pfc	12th Inf.Regt. 4th Div.	9 " "	St. Martin Cem.
1755 SCHWARTZ, Howard F.	36162730	Pfc	12th Inf.Rgt. 4th Div.	14 " "	"
1756 SHERIDAN, John P.	32088551	Pfc	20 FA 4th Div	14 " "	"
1757 SIGNORILE, Joseph W.	32008166	Pvt	8th Inf.Regt. 4th Div.	14 " "	"
1758 SMITH, Eugene W.	34434997	Pvt	8th Inf.Regt. 4th Div.	14 " "	"
1759 SMYTHE, James A.	32044896	Pfc	12th Inf.Regt 4th Div.	14 " "	"
1760 STRUM, Edward	36013415	S/Sgt	12th Inf.Regt 4th Div.	10 " "	"

"Have you got the slightest idea what this unit where you've landed does?" To which Jack replied, "No. None at all." Disappointed, Sgt. Peel added: "Well, buddy, you're a gravedigger starting today. I've got 48 shovels in the shed, and one of them has your name on it."[71] Accompanied by their faithful mascot, a little dog named Tombstone, the soldiers of the *603rd QM GR Co* followed specialized training in many camps in the US. In his memoirs, Sgt. Charles Butte recalls this period: "We were going to do something different. We were all novices except for two men who had experience in civilian life in funeral operations. We learned how to lay out cemeteries, process personal effects, drive different types of vehicles, complete Emergency Medical Tags (EMT's), apply first aid, and complete burial forms. We did not learn how to handle the deceased, armament, ammunition, or to familiarize ourselves with any language which would help us gather information relative to deceased soldiers from either civilians or prisoners of war.

Laying out a cemetery was no great problem. You look at a diagram, get a tape measure, a few tent pegs, and a hammer. Picking the proper terrain and area could have been a problem, however, this was solved by assigning two men to the unit who had a background in civil engineering. […] First aid training was given to a selected few in the unit. In this specialized unit the Medics were a group of enlisted men selected to bear the burden of completing EMT's for deceased military, both friendly and enemy, brought into the cemetery. No demand was buried without a completed EMT. As strange as it may sound, the Medics first had to ensure the individual was indeed deceased, then determine the type of wound that killed him. We were told, this was important for history in determining the tactics, type of weapons, and armament which were most lethal in battle."[72]

Then came the transfer to the European Theater of Operations (ETO). On February 25, 1944, the "gravediggers"[73] landed in England and, sooner than expected, this unit went into action in April 1944, following the disaster known as "Tiger". The 750 victims of this botched rehearsal of the D-Day landing on Slapton Sands were supported by the *603rd QM GR Co*, with the bodies being later being buried in the British Military Cemetery in Brookwood.

While a handful of men arrived in Normandy on a glider during the day of June 6, the rest of the *603rd QM GR Co* landed at *Utah Beach* between the 6 and 13 June. In accordance with allied plans, the twenty-two soldiers of the 1st Platoon were to create a temporary cemetery dedicated to the victims of the 4th Infantry Division. Situated in Saint-Martin-de-Varreville, precisely at the intersection of La Croix-Saint-Martin, this divisional cemetery had a history as short as it was stormy as Ronald A. Milton explains in detail: "Our platoon was supposed to hit the beach at H plus 12 hours and contact Lt. Raker's platoon of the 607 Graves Registration. There were a lot of rumors about what was going on on shore. None of them made us feel any better. […] We all assembled on the beach and found that Allshouse was missing. […] Lt. Dubrov took part of the platoon and started out to pick up bodies. There were some bodies on the road that the Infantry was using. One of the bodies was marked booby trapped. Tied a rope to it and stopped the infantry while we pulled the body. The rope broke but we got the body loaded into the truck. Our first body had been a sailor. […] We cleaned out some crashed gliders. It was a mess. Back to the bivouac area where we stacked the bodies in the next field. Asked Lt. Dubrov if we might see the maps and find out where we were. He said lay the blanket on the ground and he would get the maps. He was just about to unroll the maps as some planes went over and he said not now they might see us looking.

These three photos show the construction of the German square in the cemetery of Saint-Martin-de-Varreville, in mid-June, 1944. German prisoners are charged with digging the graves while those responsible for the registration of graves, take charge of the bodies at the collection point. Collection F. Le Goupil

It became apparent that it was no use to try and contact Lt. Raker, so we set out to look for a cemetery site. We found a place right out of St. Martin but it was decided not to start the cemetery until the next morning as things were still hot in that area. We returned to the beach to pick up some ammunition. [...] The next morning, 8th June, we moved to St. Martin to open the cemetery. Thought that we were further from the front than we were even though there were fresh killed Heinies in the field. Lt. Dubrov put up signs pointing to the cemetery and Jennings started laying out the cemetery. Had no sooner arrived than bodies started coming in. The division QM had notified the units where we were to set up. June 9th we were able to get Frenchmen and some men from the *90th Division* who had lost their equipment to dig graves. Bodies were piling up and somebody got the idea that a bulldozer was just the thing. Got one and started to dig a plot with it. It did not work. Had to cover it up and start digging the separate holes again. [...] We had just finished working when the German planes came over. Everyone edged towards their

holes in the hedgerows. The ack-ack opened up on them. They hit one plane. He circled and it looked like he was going to crash right where we were but he crashed in the next field. I had just gotten into my hole when I heard the other plane come diving in. I could hear it screaming. It hit in the middle of the cemetery. Dirt and shrapnel was thrown all over the place."[74]

Among the civilians who participated in the construction of the St. Martin site, the young fellow from Sainte-Mère-Église, Jacques Pignot, 17, began his incredible and atypical experience in the American army: "I spoke a little English; so the mayor [of Sainte-Mère-Église] sent me off right and left to help out the Americans... In June, the first cemetery was at Saint-Martin-de-Varreville, near the farm De La Dune. It was, by the way, the only time I dug a grave. I was with M. Bonhomme. But, it seems, the location didn't suit the Americans."[75]

In the light of these problems, it seemed clear that the future of the cemetery would be challenged. This fear was confirmed on June 11 when the *3rd platoon* of the *603rd QM GR Co.* opened a cemetery at Sainte-Mère-Église. This one would now receive the dead of the *VIIth US Corps.* The order was given to close the temporary cemetery of St. Martin as soon as possible. Two days were needed to transfer the remains of two-hundred-sixty Americans (to the cemetery n° 2 of Sainte-Mère-Église) and three British soldiers (to the Bayeux military cemetery). One-hundred-eighty-nine German bodies remained there. Until 1947, the year when they were transferred to Orglandes, the little cemetery, although placed in the care of the Americans, would barely be maintained. In this context, on July 11, 1947, the mayor of the village addressed the following letter to the Prefect of La Manche[76] :

"Mayor's office, Saint-Martin-de-Varreville

The mayor of Saint-Martin-de-Varreville has the honor of indicating to Monsieur Le Prefect that at the time of the Landings, one-hundred-eighty-nine German soldiers were buried at Saint-Martin-de-Varreville, in the hamlet of La-Croix-Saint-Martin. These bodies were never exhumed, and the graves have remained without maintenance.

Might they be transferred to one of the large German cemeteries of the region? If not, who should we ask such that the graves do not remain abandoned?"

The Mayor

Departmental archives of La Manche

"BLOSVILLE", THE AMERICAN CEMETERY OF CARQUEBUT

From June 7, 1944, until November 23, 1947, 5,804 American soldiers were temporarily buried in a big cemetery, incorrectly called "Blosville" by the American Army. Situated in fact in the commune of Carquebut, three kilometers south of Sainte-Mère-Église, this site originally witnessed the landings of the gliders of 6 and 7 June, 1944. In the days that followed, the 4th platoon of the *603rd Quartermaster Graves Registration Company* was responsible for the creation of the largest allied temporary cemetery in Normandy.

The National 13 road that runs from Caen to Cherbourg, separated the village of Carquebut from Blosville and Sébeville. This triangle, formed by the three villages, was chosen by the allies as a Landing Zone for the gliders of 6 and 7 June. This *Landing Zone* (LZ) coded "W" had to await the evening to see the first Waco GC-4 gliders and the other Horsa gliders arrive. Located in the heart of this LZ "W", the farm Vigilant, in Carquebut, housed the De La Rüe family in 1944. Yves De La Rüe was sixteen. He remembers the arrival of the first allied soldiers on D-Day: "In the afternoon of June 6, the first tanks came from the beach and took position as a battery right beside us, aiming their canons toward Fauville. Later in the evening, there were gliders behind the farm, and in the whole sector."[77]

On LZ "W", the first glider mission, known as "Elmira", would see 36 Waco gliders and 140 Horsa gliders land between 9:00 p.m. and 11:05 p.m. on D-Day. 1st-Lt. James Fraim (*407th Airborne Quartermaster Co. - 82nd Airborne*) and Sgt. Elbert Legg (*603rd QM GR Co.*) were in the second wave. They landed in a field near Sébeville near 9:15 p.m. on board the n° 32 Horsa glider in the company of nine soldiers and a jeep. Elbert Legg says: "After take-off, it was a two hour trip to Normandy. Flying over the Channel, there were thousands of ships, smoke, a choppy sea and a mess of equipment on the beach was clearly visible. [...] You could see gliders in free flight in every direction. Landing was hard but everybody was ok."[78]

Before nightfall, Lt. Fraim and Sgt. Legg reached the crossing of Les Forges at the frontier between Blosville and Carquebut. There were already several victims in the area: "Lt. Fraim told me there were several bodies in the area, and we had to pick a site for a cemetery. I reminded him that our mission was to establish collection points for the victims, but nobody had said anything about

Morning of June 7: gliders prepared to land at LZ "W" at the crossroads des Forges between Carquebut and Blosville. This view enables us to perceive clearly the parcel that will welcome the future temporary cemetery of Carquebut. NARA

June 8, 1944: a truck "captured" by Private William Fike, is discharged of its German bodies by three civilians. From left to right: Yves De La Rüe, René Legendre and Paul Dupont. NARA

"Bert" Legg lands at Sébeville at 9:15 p.m. during his airlifted mission "Elmira". Collection Legg via Yves De La Rüe

burials before we got there", added Elbert Legg. On the evening of June 6, fifty dead soldiers had been gathered in a parcel near the crossroads of Les Forges, where they awaited burial. Lt. Fraim had found thirty-five Frenchmen to begin burying the dead the next morning. The question arose of paying these Norman volunteers: "I asked him how he was going to pay these men. He showed me a sack overflowing with invasion bills, francs destined to this effect", adds Elbert Legg.

On the morning of June 7, a field was finally selected by the two men. The situation next to a main road, and the quality of the soil were two decisive elements at the moment of the choice. Indeed, the parcel in question which belonged to Raymond De La Rüe did not contain the slightest rock. His son, Yves, says: "An American officer [James Fraim] came to see my father about dealing with the first of the dead. Thereafter, for two or three weeks, he was the intermediary between the American troops and the civilians. My father was occupied with bringing volunteers who were mostly pretty old. There were mostly World War One veterans. The first days, they behaved rather badly with the German bodies. They threw them directly in their graves, rather than lowering them with ropes. It was an American officer who made them understand

that they had to be respectful of the enemy dead, despite the antagonisms."

The civilians arrived with their tools. With the help of a few soldiers, the first fifty graves were dug in rows of twenty in a corner of the field, near the wrecks of five gliders. A simple parachute served as a shroud before the victim was buried with one of his two dog tags. The other was nailed to a wooden post.

On June 8, military and civilians continued to bury their victims. The volume of work would intensify under the watch of Lt. Col. George L. Riddle, chaplain of the *82nd Airborne Division*. First Lt. Fraim and

In a field of Carquebut, the bodies of American and German victims lie in their parachute silk, temporary shrouds awaiting the covers specified in the technical manual. NARA

Sgt. Legg were assisted by three soldiers. Private First Class John A. Gardner and Private Rufus H. Honeycutt were charged with identifying the bodies and collecting personal effects, while Private William L. Fike drove a German truck that served to collect bodies and bring them back to Carquebut. On the French side, Yves De La Rüe presented himself with his shovel, but an American officer invited him to accomplish a more challenging task: "For two weeks, I was charged with searching the dead. First, I had to remove any ammunition and grenades. Then, I had to take the personal effects that I grouped in a little canvas sack.

To begin with, the grave markers were simple wooden pickets with dog tags nailed to them. Collection Legg via Yves de la Rüe

The first days, the money and cigarettes were collected in a sack, and then in the evening these were shared among the workers." Yves De La Rüe continued his distressing task the first Saturday following the Landing when he lifted a cover and recognized with horror two young GIs with whom he had shared a glass of cider on June 6. "They were burnt badly. A truck had picked them up between Les Forges and Fauville. This, for me, was the most difficult moment."

On June 9, while waiting for the rest of the men of the *603rd QM GR Co* to arrive from Utah Beach and go to Carquebut, seventy Frenchmen worked, without rest, before they saw one-hundred-fifty German prisoners of war arrive, requisitioned by 1st Lt. Fraim at the end of the day. It was inconceivable for the civilians to loan their tools to the Germans. They had to go back to their camp, near the beach.

Until June 13, with the help of one-hundred-fifty German prisoners, three-hundred-fifty GIs and one-hundred German soldiers were buried

The cemetery of Carquebut photographed toward the end of June, 1944. A few Waco gliders, serving as offices for the different units charged with grave registration were regrouped in the north-west corner of the site. We note the grave markers in the form of Christian crosses replace the simple pickets planted initially. Collection F. Le Goupil

at Carquebut. Finally, the same day, the 4th platoon (*603rd QM GR Co*) landed on *Utah Beach* one day late. An anonymous soldier, belonging to this unit charged with grave registration, tells of setting up Carquebut: "Once we got off the beach, the platoon went to Blosville, our zone of action. On the road, we passed the infantry who were moving to the front. We arrived at the cemetery before dark. There was nobody in the cemetery.

German prisoners take advantage of a moment of rest around the signs indicating the divisional cemetery of the 82nd Airborne Division in Carquebut.

© D-Day Paratroopers Historical Center

It was a big field with four or five gliders in it. We examined it. It was sad. An officer told us Legg would be there in the morning. It was so calm that we slept out under the stars. We started early the next morning. We installed our HQ in one of the gliders and Legg arrived around 9 o'clock. He only had a few forms in poor shape, and the working material was just absent. We went to work. No row and no grave was aligned. The French dug the graves. They only drank wine or cider. No water for them, they didn't believe in it…

We started the first day looking for bodies in the area. An MP had noted the presence of a parachutist a few fields lower. He was laid out in a trench. His dog tags were still on him, but someone had undressed him. We were worried about moving him at first, having heard stories about bodies being booby-trapped. So we attached a rope to him and started to pull. The rope came through. That made me sick, it was really sickening. I would have preferred to be in the infantry at that moment. That whiskey

(labeled "Medical materials") that we had brought from England helped."[79]

On June 16, there were five-hundred-thirty graves. Four days later, on June 20, Sgt. Legg, who was one of the main organizers of the temporary cemetery at Carquebut, was transferred along with his platoon to Orglandes where a German cemetery would be seen shortly. "The rumor was that we were going to Orglandes to build an enemy cemetery. Before we left, the military staff of the *82nd Airborne Division* came by to pay a final tribute to the paratroopers buried at Blosville. Gen. Ridgway told Lt. Miller to bring his platoon because he wanted to thank them for the work done. He addressed the platoon and said he was happy to see us wearing the insignia of the *82nd Airborne*, and he hoped to see us wearing it again soon."[80]

Starting on June 24, 1944, the site at Carquebut was chosen to become the cemetery for the *VIIIth US Corps*. It was the turn of the *3041st*

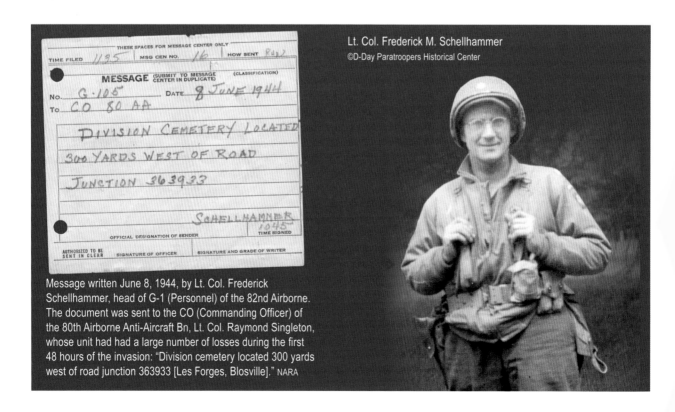

Lt. Col. Frederick M. Schellhammer
©D-Day Paratroopers Historical Center

Message written June 8, 1944, by Lt. Col. Frederick Schellhammer, head of G-1 (Personnel) of the 82nd Airborne. The document was sent to the CO (Commanding Officer) of the 80th Airborne Anti-Aircraft Bn, Lt. Col. Raymond Singleton, whose unit had had a large number of losses during the first 48 hours of the invasion: "Division cemetery located 300 yards west of road junction 363933 [Les Forges, Blosville]." NARA

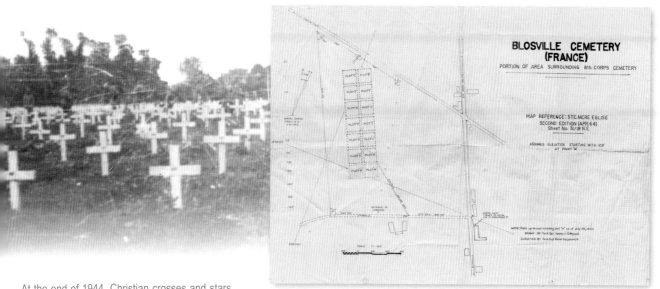

At the end of 1944, Christian crosses and stars of David have replaced the stakes.
Collection Y. De La Rüe

Plan dated July 29, 1944, showing the degree of advancement of the work on the cemetery at Carquebut. Collection Utah Beach Museum

Quartermaster Graves Registration Company to take charge of the enlargement and the maintenance of the site. On July 4, the bodies of those who were buried initially at Blosville were exhumed and moved a few dozen meters further, to the other extremity of the parcel. In the same manner, the two-hundred-fifty-six paratroopers of the *101st Airborne* who had been buried near the chateau of La Colombière, at Hiesville, were transferred to the site. Grave markers in the form of Christian crosses and Jewish stars of David were substituted for the primitive stakes. The names and serial numbers of the soldiers were stenciled on, and a dog tag was nailed to the back.

On the evening of December 24, it was action stations for everyone at Carquebut: victims were brought there by the dozen from Cherbourg. On that evening, the *U-486 submarine* had torpedoed and sunk the *USS Leopoldville*, a boat which was carrying two regiments of the *66th Infantry Division* and some medical personnel. It sank with its crew in icy waters. The seven-hundred-eighty-two victims who were pulled from the sea were sent to the temporary cemetery of Carquebut, the only site where the space could be enlarged enough.

Yves De La Rüe, this evening of Christmas 1944, was particularly bitter: "As we left the midnight mass, trucks came by with new bodies.

The *3041st QM GR Co* at work in the month of July, 1944.
©D-Day Paratroopers Historical Center

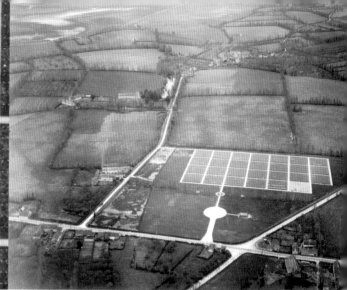

Details of an aerial picture dated June 29, showing the creation of the last two squares of the cemetery of Blosville. NARA

The temporary cemetery of Blosville, seen from the sky in February 1946. In the foreground, the crossroads of Les Forges. To the left of the cemetery, the farm of Le Vigilant. NARA

Large canvases were once again strung up around the squares of graves to avoid people seeing the various stages of handing the corpses."

Starting on July 1, 1945, the cemetery was placed under the authority of the *American Graves Registration Command* (AGRC), the independent military organization charged at the same time with seeking out military personnel lost in the battlefield, identifying unknown soldiers and maintaining and assuring the management of the temporary cemeteries. The superintendent named to Carquebut was Sgt. Lionel Blais, 35, from Franklin, New Hampshire. He had landed on *Omaha Beach* on June 8, 1944, with his unit, the *734th Field Artillery Bn*. As a recompense for his loyal services, the American army placed this francophile at the head of the largest temporary cemetery in Normandy. At his side, and to watch over the security of the site, the soldiers W. A. Campbell and Michael Sandy, two honor guards of the American army, were assigned to this temporary cemetery.

The farm of Le Vigilant, today. Photo by the author

Dated June 28, 1944, the photo shows members of the *3041st QM GR Co*. In the background, we see the farm Le Vigilant, property of Raymond De La Rüe. Collection Legg via Yves De La Rüe

Until its closure to the public in November, 1947, the cemetery at Blosville did not stop receiving new victims as opposed to the two other large American temporary cemeteries situated at Sainte-Mère-Église.

The last burial was registered on November 6, a little more than two weeks before the final closing of the site. In June 1945, the number of graves was 5,333. A year later, this figure rose to 5,476 and finally to 5,804 graves – exclusively American – at the beginning of November, 1947. Evocative numbers which demonstrate the titanic work led by the teams charged with investigating and identifying the isolated graves in the field during 1946 and 1947.

THE AMERICAN MILITARY CEMETERY AT BLOSVILLE [81]

Infantry	Navy	Merchant Navy	American Civilians	Unknown	TOTAL
5 698	26	1	3	76	5 804

The temporary cemetery of Blosville in June, 1946. On this date, two new squares (top, right) were under construction. Also, two buildings were constructed at the entrance of the cemetery to receive guests. NARA

SAINTE-MÈRE-ÉGLISE N° 1

If the allied plans had not formally preselected the village of Sainte-Mère-Église to hold two great temporary military cemeteries, it nevertheless prevailed in the eyes of the *603rd Quartermaster Graves Registration Company* as an inevitable site. This busy crossroads was the point of convergence of roads coming from *Utah Beach* and it served the main towns of the department of La Manche as well. One might say that all roads led to Sainte-Mère-Église. Its proximity to several country hospitals as well as being the collection point for the bodies of men killed in action made this village the first choice for the construction of a first temporary cemetery which opened June 11, 1944, east of the town. The creation of this new military cemetery was carried out by the 3rd platoon of the *603rd QM GR Co.* The story of this little unit – conserved by the NARA – retraces the major steps taken:

"Half of the platoon went down to St. Martin to help the 1st platoon, and the rest of the men started out for Ste. Mere Eglise, to find a site for a cemetery. Had to wait for Ste. Mere Eglise to be taken. There were just a few paratroopers an[d] some civilians in Ste. Mere Eglise. [...]

We picked a site just back of the civilian cemeter[y]. It would be large enough for the division cemeter[y,] the officer said. Bodies were lying every plac[e.] The body of one GI who had been killed by on[e] of his own guards while camouflaging his vehicl[e] was brought in. Picked up some Heinies lyin[g] in the road that the traffic had mashed beyon[d] recognition. [...] The crew came back from the firs[t] platoon and told us that Supel and Ketcko wer[e] happy. They had been stripping Heinie bodies a[ll] day to identify them.

On 10 June 1944, we moved up to Ste. Mere Eglis[e] to open the cemetery. Bodies started coming i[n] fast. The first night a bomb hit in the next fiel[d] killing two cows. [...]

That night Tamborini and Cragle were on guar[d.] Standing near the end of the cemetery aroun[d] 24.00. One came whistling in. Cragle fell off th[e] ledge he was on and managed to squeeze himsel[f] into a very small hole. Tamborini took off, trippin[g] over the tent rope and slid into his foxhole[.]

June 16, 1944: at the collecting point of Sainte-Mère-Église n°1, Sgt. Peter F. Slusarcyzk, from Ohio, inventories the personal effects of soldiers killed in action. The bodies are placed in the "cover, protective, individual", this brown, water-proof sack would be used, if necessary, by the soldiers to fight against a gas attack.
NARA

A JUNE DAY IN CEMETERY N°1

Filmed at cemetery n° 1 in Sainte-Mère-Église, these previously unpublished images were taken from two reports made on 13 and 15 June, 1944, by cameramen of the American army. They show the intensity, the labor and the range of thankless tasks that fell to the members of the American graves services. After discharging and aligning the bodies, friend and foe, the American soldiers had to complete the identification and the collection of personal effects. During this time, a large number of German prisoners were occupied with digging graves to an average depth of 1.5 meters. Black troops of the American army were charged with this same task, when they weren't delegated to surveying the prisoners. We note in these pictures a marked difference in the treatment of enemy corpses, simply thrown from a stretcher into the grave. American soldiers, on the other hand, were given a shroud and were placed carefully, using straps, in the grave. At the end of the day, the column of prisoners was escorted to the different prison camps of the Utah Beach sector.

Pictures taken from NARA film. Pictures NARA

The sign indicating the entrance to cemetery n° 1, and a captain belonging to the 35th Infantry Division. Collection musée Airborne.

A zinc plate (8.5 x 3 cm) fixed to the back of the grave marker. Substituted for the ID plate (dog tags) when these were missing. Joseph G. Bachulak belonged to A Company – 502nd PIR and was killed in action on 6 June, at the age of 24. He was buried at cemetery n° 1, as indicates mention "SM1". Collection Airborne Museum

Things quieted down until in the early morning hours. Were walking in the cemetery when the first 88 came over. Took to the open graves. Cragle landed in one with a permanent occupant but he did not mind. The whistling was what worried him."

The 3rd platoon opened the cemetery at Saint-Mère-Église on D-Day +5 [June 11]. Plot B was under construction and eight germans dug the graves. There were parachutes in the trees and bodies aligned in endless rows. The first days were very intense. We lived and worked in the cemetery. We didn't wash for two weeks. A part from that, the only way to go was to put some water in your helmet for a brief toilet.

PFC's Paul Mann and Edwin Knowlton registered the funerals. The bureau was situated near a hedge. Then a company of negroes[82] came to give us a hand.

The *9th Infantry Division's* HQ wanted us to build a plot for it [a square of 200 graves] and that gave us plenty to worry about. It was almost impossible to group the bodies from the same division. We did our best."

The construction of cemetery n° 1 at Sainte-Mère-Église was not an easy task. Among the men of the 3rd platoon who worked tirelessly in response to the unending inflow of bodies was Sgt. Charles Butte of Ohio. His story tells us a bit more about the intensity of these first days of June:

"The first deceased we came in contact with after landing in Normandy was a soldier who had been dead for sometime and was twice his original size with his clothing the only thing keeping him from bloating even larger. We learned from experience, to relieve the body of the gas, roll him over on his stomach, put a knee in the middle of his back, and apply pressure. One develops a strong stomach quickly: the gas escaping is the worst you will ever encounter. [...]

The 3rd Platoon moved to Ste. Mere Eglise on 9 June and established a cemetery for the *90th Division.* On or about 12 June it was decided to make St. Mere Eglise cemetery the *VII Corps* Cemetery. Over the next four weeks, with the exception of the 4th Platoon which opened and operated the cemetery at Orglandes for German deceased, the remainder of the company joined the 3rd Platoon at Ste. Mere Eglise.

We operated the cemetery with local civilians digging the graves during the first few days, however, we were unable to open sufficient graves to bury the number of deceased arriving at the

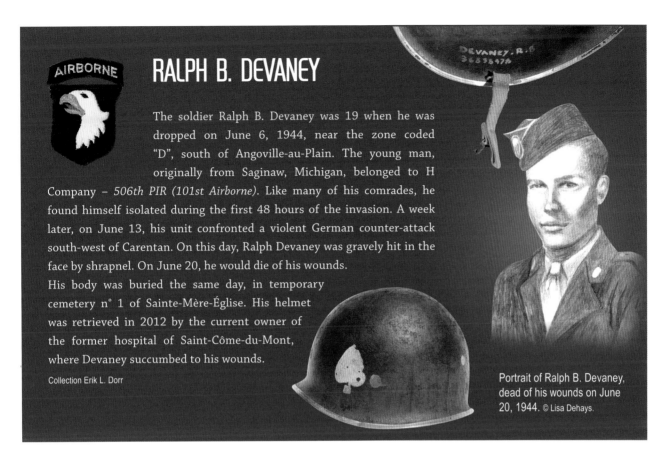

RALPH B. DEVANEY

The soldier Ralph B. Devaney was 19 when he was dropped on June 6, 1944, near the zone coded "D", south of Angoville-au-Plain. The young man, originally from Saginaw, Michigan, belonged to H Company – *506th PIR (101st Airborne)*. Like many of his comrades, he found himself isolated during the first 48 hours of the invasion. A week later, on June 13, his unit confronted a violent German counter-attack south-west of Carentan. On this day, Ralph Devaney was gravely hit in the face by shrapnel. On June 20, he would die of his wounds.

His body was buried the same day, in temporary cemetery n° 1 of Sainte-Mère-Église. His helmet was retrieved in 2012 by the current owner of the former hospital of Saint-Côme-du-Mont, where Devaney succumbed to his wounds.

Collection Erik L. Dorr

Portrait of Ralph B. Devaney, dead of his wounds on June 20, 1944. © Lisa Dehays.

cemetery. Prisoners of war and a Quartermaster Service Company operating as a Guard Company were attached in order to open the number of graves needed to handle the remains arriving daily. General Collins visited the cemetery often as did all Division Commanders. During each visit General Collins made it quite clear that all remains at the cemetery would be buried each day. This made for long and very hard days for Graves Registration Personnel, guards, and prisoners alike."[83]

On June 10, Brig.-Gen. James Gavin, commander of the *82nd Airborne Division* came to visit the brand new cemetery.

These three African-Americans worked for the graves services and had been attached to the cemetery n°1 of Sainte-Mère-Église. As they were allowed to serve in normal infantry, they were often employed to dig graves. These thankless tasks and the rest of the responsibilities in the domain of logistics that were reserved for them, testify to the racial segregation encountered during World War II. Collection S. Lamache

IN SEARCH OF ISOLATED GRAVES WITH "JACK" PIGNOT

Jacques Pignot was 17 when he lived the first hours of the Invasion on the square of Sainte-Mère-Église. To this extraordinary experience was added another, every bit as uncommon. In the weeks that followed, this young man found himself enrolled in a unit registering American graves, in search of isolated graves across the countryside of Normandy.

Collection J. Pignot.

"Toward the end of September, 1944, I met Mr Rouxel, the foreman of cemetery n° 1. He hired me because I spoke English. It was the labor bureau in Cherbourg who paid us every two weeks. I stayed at the reception of cemetery n° 1 for a while. There was always something to be done. I stayed there several weeks, but when the terrain was cleared, we had to go get the soldiers who had remained on the battlefield. It was our job to rake the countryside, there were posters everywhere in the villages, to find the last isolated graves.

I remember a German soldier, near the beginning. It was on the route to Beuzeville, near an armored car, the body was burned down to the belt.
It had to be done. We left in a jeep and a trailer, or a GMC. As we went along, we sometimes saw German bodies, but they didn't interest us. The only Germans taken up by the Americans were those killed around the temporary cemeteries or in the prison camp of Foucarville. Bodies were brought to cemetery n° 1 at first, then after that to Orglandes. I went all the way to Brittany and to Calvados. I remember well the accidental explosion at Longueville that made one hell of a crater near the mayor's office. A woman was completely disfigured and killed that day. At Mortain, there had been a hell of a battle. I had to get into a tank in order to recover the ashes of a soldier. We found a ring and his dog tags.

Around Périers and Saint-Lô, there were still minefields. So, when there was a body to get out from the middle of a minefield, the Americans let us take care of that kind of thing. We looked for dog tags first. The remains of the soldier were placed in a shroud and later the Americans themselves studied the body. In case of non-identification, we looked for a number on the collar, in the clothes. The bodies were placed on stretchers.

Later, we put them in shrouds (big white sacks) like that; that way no one touched the bodies. Until spring 1945, the research teams were very limited, understand that. They got structured later. At this time, Capt. Crisson was responsible for Sainte-Mère, Marigny, Saint-Laurent, Saint-James and the one at Mayenne from mid-1945 until 1946. On June 30, 1947, after having worked some time at the camp "John B. Franks" in Carentan, in the graves services, I left the AGRC to do my military service."

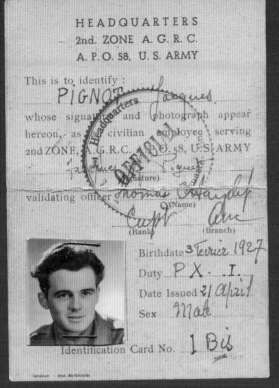

Various identity cards, proving his attachment to the American grave services. Collection J. Pignot

On board his Dodge, WC52, he roamed the Norman (and Breton) countryside, looking for isolated graves.

From September 1944 to June 1947, Jacques Pignot, from Sainte-Mère-Église, worked for the American graves registration service. We see him here, in 1946, beside a Puerto-Rican soldier in the vicinity of L'Isle-Marie near Picauville.

As anyone could see, these bodies needed burying – the priority being given to the victims of the *90th Infantry Division* – the general, usually calm, cried out, *"Don't go looking for their baptism certificates! Bury them now!"* The order was to bury them as they came in. Thus, June 12, cemetery n° 1 became the cemetery of the *VIIth US Corps*. The dead, belonging to six American divisions engaged in the battle of the Cotentin peninsula had to converge on Sainte-Mère-Église. The main consequence of the massive inflow of bodies was the closure of the site in under two weeks. As the interment capacity had rapidly been reached, no more bodies could be buried in n° 1. In total, 2,195 American soldiers had been buried alongside 1,000 German soldiers assembled in five of the most distant squares. On June 25, the second cemetery of the *VIIth US* Corps was opened west of Sainte-Mère-Église, on the road to Chef-du-Pont.

The people of Sainte-Mère-Église were the privileged witnesses of the establishment of these military cemeteries. Placed at the forefront, they could judge, once again, the human costs engendered by the liberation of France. The relations between the inhabitants of this Cotentin village and the victims of the fighting could only be strengthened as they saw, displayed before their eyes, an idea still considered the most noble: "the spirit of

A young girl of Sainte-Mère-Église places flowers on the first graves of cemetery n° 1. Collection Airborne Museum

sacrifice". These people were shaken, shocked, and inevitably found themselves changed.

A handful of locals volunteered to the American authorities in order to participate in the establishment and also the management of these cemeteries. Léon Mignot, apprentice carpenter, was 16 in June, 1944; he recalls his hours working for the American graves services: "At the end of June, [1944], I had been evacuated to a farm in Vaulaville [to the west of Sainte-Mère-Église]. I had no news of my employer and the Americans needed volunteers to dig the graves.

The original caption with this photo shows that the civilians of Sainte-Mère-Église dug the initial graves while the children brought flowers. NARA

The work had to be clean. We were paid, and we got some rations, too. We brought our own tools. So I worked for several days at cemetery n° 1. Trucks arrived one after the other, and the soldier's bodies lined up. We saw bodies burnt, horribly mutilated. Lots of paratroopers rolled up in their parachutes. Soldiers were charged with identifying them, they wore gloves. We put Americans to one side and Germans to the other. We were several Frenchmen digging the graves. But the burials, only the Americans took care of that. German prisoners carried the stretchers. One day, my boss came looking for me saying the work at the shop was starting back up."[85] The 3,195 military graves of cemetery n° 1 of Sainte-Mère-Église which had been placed under the responsibility of superintendent Eitland and under the protection of the inhabitants of the village, were nonetheless closed to the public starting July 16, 1948, before the bodies were transported to the permanent cemetery of Colleville-sur-Mer for 40% of them, and to the United States for the rest. The remains of German soldiers were transferred to the German military cemetery of Orglandes. "One Sunday in spring, there was a ceremony of adieu to all these dead who left our soil"[87], wrote Maurice Lecœur.

Another aerial view of cemetery n° 1 dated June, 1946. Note the addition of several brand new buildings added at this date (a reception and an additional workshop.) NARA

The temporary cemetery n° 1 of Sainte-Mère-Église photographed in February 1946. The site held 3,195 graves of which 1,000 were German. Five squares of 200 graves (plots G,H,K,L, and M) were conceded to the German dead. Three of these squares were situated apart in a section called for the occasion "the enemy sector". Note in the distance, near the top at right, a part of cemetery n°2. A photograph highlighting the proximity of the cemeteries with the little town and its people. NARA

JEAN-BAPTISTE FEUILLYE, RECEPTIONIST OF CEMETERY N°1

Jean-Baptiste Feuillye, at 13, would become the mascot of a laundry unit stationed near Fresville.

"I was 13 at the time of the Landings. I lived in the little town of Fresville. I found myself on board with the Americans right from June 1944. I became the mascot of a laundry company at Emondeville. I was known as "Bobby". I served with the *681st Laundry Co* for close to a year, all the way to Laon in Champagne.

When I came back, in May 1945, my parents' neighbor came to see us because the sergeant who was responsible for the cemetery n° 1 of Sainte-Mère-Église was looking for someone who mastered English preferably, in order to receive visitors and take care of putting up the flag in the morning and taking it down in the evening. The next day I met Sgt. Espinoza [superintendent of the temporary cemetery]. He found my English was very basic, but he took me on anyway. I started the next day as the receptionist. So I was hired June 1, 1945 at the temporary cemetery n° 1 of Sainte-Mère-Église. I received visitors and accompanied them among the graves. In the large trees of the cemetery there were still parachute harnesses hanging and very visible. I showed them to the visitors.

There were French personnel that worked at the cemetery to cut the grass (these were still the days of the sickle and scythe). Messrs. Joseph Baril, Leroux and Cauvin were the gardeners of the site. About M. Cauvin, he took his scythe home with him every night and sharpened it. At cemetery n° 1, M. Rouxel, of Chef-du-Pont, the horticulturist, passed through the rows every morning. If he noticed paint was missing, M. Crestey, the painter, removed the cross with M. Touroude. It was repainted and they applied a rigid stencil. To avoid smearing, he used a shaving brush. In his shed, Crestey had all the stencils arranged alphabetically. It was often the same ones we had to change, mostly those under the trees. As for the German squares, they weren't so well maintained. Sgt. Eitland (successor to Sgt. Espinoza) was the new superintendent of cemeteries n°1 and n°2 of Sainte-Mère-Église. He lived near n° 2 in Vaulaville. He came every day to make sure I left on the hour and that I didn't drop the flag. He was very demanding on that

For a year, the young man followed the 681st Laundry Co. across France. Here he is with Dave Levosky and his brother, in camp "Chicago"; at Sisonne in L'Aisne. June 1, 1945, he was hired by the cemetery n° 1. Collection J.-B.Feuillye

point. He arrived every day at 5 p.m. in his Dodge. M. Rouxel gave me a hand to bring down the flag. That same year, the Honor Guards arrived. They were American military, two per cemetery, they lived on site. Among them, Julius Steinke was chosen for having fought heroically in the Pacific, at Bataan. During his time at Sainte-Mère-Église, he met a young girl from Chef-du-Pont, Fernande Ozouf. They were married in a military barracks near Verdun, and she went to the States with him. These Honor Guards were the most deserving. We also had Jim Vomhof, "Bent" Straight and Ted Liska [*12th Infantry Regiment – 4th Infantry Division*] for several months. The latter had landed on Utah Beach on June 6, 1944.

In 1947, at plot P, the most northerly one, there were seven graves which were a bit strange that four officers coming from Germany came to see. They asked me to find four people to dig two graves. They wanted security around the graves. They had a tarpaulin two meters high. They enclosed the seven graves, but only dug two. "We want to be alone", they told me... We had no idea what they were doing. Later, I learned they were the seven guys of Hémevez[86] . A big guy, in a raincoat, took pictures for the inquest of the massacre of Hémevez."

Pay slip from the labor department of La Manche, dated September, 1946.

View of cemetery n° 1 in Sainte-Mère-Église in the direction of the church, visible in the background. In certain places, the harnesses of parachutes were still visible in the big trees according to Jean-Baptiste Feuillye. Collection J. Pignot

SAINTE-MÈRE-ÉGLISE N° 2

On June 25, 1944, the 3rd platoon of the *603rd QM GR Co* was forced – in the absence of space available in n° 1 – to open a second temporary military cemetery near Sainte-Mère-Église. Dedicated to the victims of the *VIIth US Corps* killed in the combats for Cherbourg, Sainte-Mère-Église n° 2 received 4,798 graves of American soldiers up until July 16, 1948, date of its closure to the public. No German graves were dug in this cemetery, the bodies went directly to the German military cemetery of Orglandes from June 25, 1944. Once again, it is worthwhile to look at the story of the *603rd QM GR Co* and the passage presented below, concerning the establishment of cemetery n° 2:

"Ste Mere Eglise was nearing its capacity and Corps decided to open another one just out of Ste. Mere Eglise on the road towards Chef Du Pont.

Sgt. Alcayde, Hurst and Carelyne went over to lay it out. The Heinies lobbed in a few shells and they took to the ditch. Sgt. Alcayde say a cow smelling of the transit and, shells or no shells, out he went for the transit. Got the cemetery laid out and started digging there but continued burying at Ste Mere Eglise n° 1. The company left part of the 3rd platoon to finish up n° 1, and moved to n° 2.

Colonel King was one of the first funerals that was held. Cragle was mad because his body was wrapped in two mattress covers. Showing special privileges. Not much was said when General Roosevelt was buried with full military honors. Even the body was taken on a practice run for the funeral. There was a lot of stars there to attend the funeral. The cemetery was cleared of the GR personnel and the funeral held. The town mayor's wife won out on who would adopt and take care of the General's grave. [...] Our next destination was Marigny."

On July 2, 1944, cemetery n° 2, Cpl. Robert O. Reisterer, Michigan, writes details using a brush on the shroud which will carry the body of PFC Frederick R. Smith. NARA

July 20, 1944: funeral of Lt.-Col. Harry A. Flint, commander of the *39th Infantry Regiment* (*9th Infantry Division*). Three days earlier, "Paddy" Flint had been the target of a German sniper and died of his wounds the next day. Like many other soldiers buried in "n° 2", Flint was not buried in a coffin. Here he is disposed between two stretchers, a starry flag covering his body. NARA

The very first interments concerned the 365 bodies earlier buried in the short-lived cemetery of the hamlet La Madeleine, near *Utah Beach*. Subsequently, burials took place at a frenetic pace up until the month of October 1944, by which time no more bodies could be buried at n° 2.

The extract above indicates that exceptional funeral practices were held for several American officers, which provoked – with regard to this last testimony – a certain bitterness among the personnel charged with graves registration. A simple white shroud was generally used to accommodate the body of each soldier.

Report of burial of the soldier James A. Hattrick, company I, 508th PIR, killed in action at Gourbesville, June 6, 1944. First buried by Germans in the village cemetery of Gourbesville, Hattrick's body was not identified as his dog tags were kept by the German doctor. Thanks to multiple markings "H-1767" inscribed in particular on the inside of his combat vest, the unknown X-16 was finally identified as James A. Hattrick. He was buried on June 28, 1944, at cemetery n° 2 in Sainte-Mère-Église. NARA via J.-B. Feuillye

At the head of the procession, Lt. Marcus Stevenson, aide-de-camp to the general (at right) and Capt. Quentin Roosevelt II, fourth and last child of Gen. Roosevelt. Quentin landed at Omaha Beach on June 6, 1944. Doctor of Natural History, the young man developed an interest early on for the eastern world and China. In January 1940, the magazine Life published his works about the Buddhist religion. He died in December, 1948, at the age of 29 in a plane accident near Hong Kong. NARA

On July 14th, as known as Bastille Day, a major event in the construction of the friendly link between the village of Sainte-Mère-Église and all of America took place in cemetery n° 2. Men, women, children and old folks gathered around the grave of a General unknown to the local population but whose name rang out in all ears. Brig.-Gen. Theodore Roosevelt Jr., son of the 26th president of the United States of America, and by the same token, cousin of Franklin D. Roosevelt, the president of the United States at the time, had landed June 6, 1944, on *Utah Beach* with the first wave of assault. His volume of poetry in his pocket, he led the *4th Infantry Division* to the capture of Cherbourg. Yet, this man with his fragile health, succumbed to a heart attack July 12, 1944, near his command post in Méautis.

An extraordinary funeral was organized two days later attended by the likes of Generals George Patton, Omar Bradley, not to mention Joseph Lawton Collins. Behind these great strategists of the American army, a son: Quentin Roosevelt Jr. He, too, had landed in Normandy (at *Omaha Beach*) on D-Day with the men of the *1st Infantry Division*. The cortège was led by the military band followed by the General's coffin on a half-track. As the people of Sainte-Mère-Église watched, the Protestant chaplain of the *4th Infantry Division*, Rev. George W. Knapp, officiated. Once closed, the Protestant and Catholic chaplains of each of the six divisions engaged in the battle of Cherbourg, blessed the grave in cemetery n° 2.

ROUGH RIDER

Photograph of Brig. Gen. Roosevelt sent by his widow, Eleanor, to Mme. Renaud, wife of the Mayor of Sainte-Mère-Église. In a letter dated August 26, 1945, Eleanor B. Roosevelt wrote: "I am sending you a photograph of the General that I hope you will like to have. It was taken on the morning of the very day he died, July 12th, 1944. [...] My husband is standing up in his Jeep, and if you look closely you can see a bullet hole in the windshield. The General had written me about this hole sometime before I think this photograph is the best ever made of him." Collection H-J. Renaud

Like cemetery n° 1, several French civilians worked in the management and maintenance of cemetery n° 2 of Sainte-Mère-Église. Placed under the orders of Sgt. Eitland, superintendent of the sites, a dozen locals worked there every day. There was Mr De La Mare, the overseer charged with inspecting the general state of the cemetery; the reception of visitors was given to Fernand Leger, nicknamed "Shorty". Several local women were also hired for cemetery n° 2, such as Madeleine Valognes. Originally from Montebourg, she fled the town at the beginning of the Landings, taking refuge at Emondeville. She recalls: "One evening, an American officer came to tell us we had to leave immediately. We left and walked in single file to another farm further south [Ecausseville]. And the Americans then took us in a truck to Sainte-Mère-Église. We slept in the church... At cemetery n° 1, I remember seeing trucks arrive with dismembered bodies, feet hanging down."

The people of Sainte-Mère-Église pay homage to the General.
Collection Utah Beach Museum

14 July, 1944: outdoor mass at cemetery n° 2. Twenty-some priests and pastors bless the square where Gen. Roosevelt was buried. L'Abbe Rouland, priest of Sainte-Mère-Église, appears in the center. NARA

A COFFIN FOR THE GENERAL

Léon Mignot, the apprentice carpenter of Sainte-Mère-Église, worked in June 1944 for the American graves services. As the carpenter's shop, situated on the Carentan road, had started back up, the young man went back to work for his boss. One day in July, a very special order arrived.

Léon Mignot, photographed in 2011 at his home in Chef-du-Pont. ©Julien Paquin

"July and August [1944], we only made coffins, because during the Landings, civilians were buried urgently, straight in the ground. A mass grave was dug in the churchyard. Later, the families wanted to give them a decent burial. As a result, my boss and I made coffins every day. One day, an American officer came to see the boss to order a coffin. I found that strange as I knew the Americans were buried with a shroud and nothing more. I came to understand quite quickly that the coffin was for General Roosevelt."

A few days later, there was a grand ceremony at the military cemetery. I recognized the coffin we had made as the half-track passed in front of me. We made some special shapes. It wasn't just ordinary wood. I was struck by the band, all the military music (funeral march). I had never seen that before. The shots. It was the evening, the end of the afternoon. Lots of the inhabitants of Sainte-Mère-Église came to the ceremony. When the Americans buried their dead, they put them in their grave, and the priests of every confession recited their prayers. We could hear the cannonade in the distance. In the end, the body was covered."

Images of the funeral of General Roosevelt, July 14, 1944. NARA

14 July, 1944: funeral of Gen. Roosevelt at cemetery n° 2. Contrary to the rest of the soldiers, buried in the temporary cemeteries, the General had the benefit of a coffin in wood, partly made by Léon Mignot. NARA

Jean-Baptiste Feuillye, receptionist, interpreter and guide of cemetery n° 1, adds: "When they exhumed Roosevelt, I was with Fortier. The General had a solid coffin, a strong case. The guy who wanted to lift the coffin with his shovel, he broke a bit of it off."

An aerial view of cemetery n°2 of Sainte-Mère-Église; dated February 1946. NARA

It must have been one hell of a job to identify those unrecognizable bodies. Later, I worked at cemetery n° 2, road to Chef-du-Pont. I had learned that the Americans were looking for laborers. They were calling for volunteers. We had really nothing to do at the time. You had to do that just to live properly. My main job was to paint the crosses white. We took care of stenciling the names, ranks and serial numbers of the soldiers. There were three or four women who did that. Another woman, Marie-Madeleine Alexandre, from Montebourg, started work with me but then married an American. She followed him to America. We wore combat boots, a pair of pants and top from the American army.

In a way, we felt good about this because it gave us something to eat. I gained a lot of weight at the time. I also sorted used military clothes for the Americans. There was a little of everything. There was a sorting center over by Audouville. There were a lot of us doing this work. In cemetery n° 2, there was a big tent situated up at the top. That's where the Americans identified the dead. Once in a while we would find a body on a stretcher in a special sack. When they identified a German, they took him to Orglandes. Several German bodies were buried with the animals in the fields. There wasn't always respect for the enemy corpses. There were still some German prisoners who painted crosses.

The following summer, 1947, new buildings were built including the chapel. Collection J. Pignot

They worked separately from us in another tent, near the "morgue". You know, I worked there every day... On December 25 [1944], when the *Léopoldville* sank off Cherbourg, as I went to work, tarpaulins were strung up. There were maybe three hundred soldiers lined up, and they were all in strange positions, they must have tried to hold on before they drowned. You got used to seeing things like that."[88]

The chapel of cemetery n° 2.
Collection A. Levesque

Henry D. Delock, horticulturist and chief landscaper of the temporary cemeteries of Normandy.

Collection J. Pignot

The three photos presented on this page date from 1946. War photographer D. Tobey was making a story of the celebrations of D-Day at Sainte-Mère-Église. In the photo below, we see the procession heading toward the center of town. The inhabitants are situated on either side of the road to Chef-du-Pont while the detachment of paratroopers of the *508th PIR* (from Frankfurt, Germany) enter the village followed by a few firemen. In the foreground, note the dog tags fixed to each of the crosses. NARA

America watches over its dead

TOWARD THE CREATION OF THE AMERICAN GRAVES REGISTRATION COMMAND[89]

In the days following a fratricidal war that had divided America in two, from 1861 to 1865, the plains of Antietam or of Gettysburg offered a macabre spectacle, without precedent. The remains of thousands of soldiers, their bones scattered over the battlefield, profoundly shocked American public opinion. Happy were those who had been able to benefit from a grave – communal for the majority – often dug in haste and only rarely indicating who was buried there. In order to remedy this enormous disgrace, and to finally pay individual homage to the soldiers fallen for the fatherland, Congress put forward the Act of February 22, 1867, attributing responsibility to the American Army for the graves, maintenance thereof, and the management of national cemeteries. In order to put in place this commitment to individualizing the death of soldiers, each grave should have a stone, or a plate, presenting a number of the grave referring to a register that would indicate the identity of the dead.

Forty-odd years later an American Quartermasters Corps was officially created in 1912. It was necessary to wait a few months after the entry of the United States into the war (April 1917), under the impetus of Gen. Pershing, for the creation on August 7, 1917, of the Graves Registration Service (GRS). In total, four companies who had received specific training were sent to Europe to take charge of those fallen, mostly in Belgium and France. After contributing to the building of eight permanent American cemeteries in Europe following WWI, after having buried 30,902 American citizens, the GRS was placed on standby in peace time, up until the entry of the US into the Second World War in December, 1941.

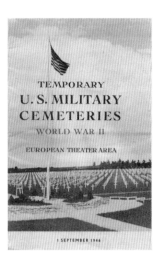

Plan dated 1946 on behalf of the AGRC. Each temporary cemetery appears on a map of France and is accompanied by a historical comment.
Private collection

On February 18, 1942, one month after sending the first men to Europe, the GRS was re-activated. On that date, a supplementary mission was given to this corps, more than ever belonging to the Quartermasters: the collection of personal effects.

At the end of 1943, the Graves Registration Service was renamed the *American Graves Registration Service*[90] (AGRS) within the framework of preparations for the invasion of Europe planned for Spring 1944. Beginning with a principal unit (199 men plus 6 officers and 12 army doctors), different groups belonging to the AGRS were already at work by May 1944. As the allied plans projected large losses during the "first shock", in other words during the first twenty-four hours of the assault, "emergency" cemeteries had been set up along the southern coast of England. Three principal cemeteries situated at Weymouth, Portsmouth and Plymouth were prepared to accept the first victims of the landing in Normandy. In addition, sixteen civilian cemeteries were planned near the embarkation zones. The plan was to leave two companies charged with graves registration in order to receive the first victims of D-Day.

Hotel Trianon, headquarters of the AGRC. Collection J. Pignot

AGRC Headquarters installed a command post in the hospice of Sainte-Mère-Église, road to Montebourg. NARA

the development and maintenance of these fourteen sites (between Paris and Brittany) in August, 1944. Graves registration was by far the principal task of the Quartermaster's services, sometimes making use of ancillary services (washing or transportation). In December 1944, reviewing the gigantic project, Maj.-Gen. Littlejohn, commander of the *Quartermaster's Corps* estimated at four to five additional years the time it would take to build the military cemeteries of the theater of operations in Europe.

The size of the job led to the creation of an independent organization, distinct from the rest of the American *Quartermaster's* Corps, an organization whose responsibility consisted of taking charge of the national cemeteries of Europe. On September 22, Maj.-Gen. Littlejohn obtained the creation of the *American Graves Registration Command* (AGRC) as a definitive replacement for the AGRS. This brand new organization took its quarters in Versailles, at the Hotel Trianon. It was to continue to maintain the American military cemeteries in Europe, accelerate the searches for the last of the isolated graves – in Normandy for example – and, equally, to set up a logistical infrastructure in connection with the return of the bodies to the United States or toward one or several permanent national cemeteries that were yet to be defined in 1945.

In Normandy, the AGRC installed its quarters in the fields of Saint-Hilaire-Petitville, a town situated at the entrance of Carentan, where one of the most important allied military camps between 1944 and 1949 was erected. This camp, called "John B. Franks"[92], served as headquarters to the *Second Zone*. This geographic entity grouped the military cemeteries of the north-west of France. In charge of the *Second Zone*, the following men served from 1945 to 1949:

However, it was not to be. The plan to send the dead back to England was never applied, to the extent that on D-Day + 1 (June 7) each American sector had a temporary military cemetery. To the soldiers wounded in Normandy and who died being transported to England, were added the number of those killed in accidents there. These last were buried in the cemeteries of Brookwood and Cambridge.

In Normandy, the rapid advance of the front and the number of victims rapidly obliged the AGRS to establish a plan of permanent support of these cemeteries – American only – including

George C. Traver (from February 1946 to June 1947), Samuel N. Lowry (June to December 1947) and Richard T. Mitchell (December 1947 to March 1949). For the *Second Zone*, from February 6, 1947, there were forty-four officers, one hundred forty-five soldiers, one hundred American civilians and eight hundred and ten French civilians (or "natives" in the text).

Jacques Pignot, the man from Sainte-Mère-Église who had since June 1944 been engaged in the service charged with American graves registration recalls of the camp "John B. Franks": "It was in the old military hospital of Carentan. Early 1946, there I was. At the entry, there were the administrative buildings and the lodgings of the camp commandant, Capt. Lowry. We weren't very many at first. Just a little company. I was alone for a long time. In 1946, we were to scour the whole countryside. There were posters in every

Dating from 1947, this aerial photo shows the camp "John B. Franks" at Saint-Hilaire-Petitville. Note the straight road (RN 13) going toward Carentan to the west. © IGN

village in order to find the last isolated graves. Capt. Crisson, who had landed at Utah Beach on June 6, 1944, was responsible for the cemeteries of Sainte-Mère, Marigny, Saint-Laurent, Saint-James and the one in Mayenne from September 1945 up until 1946."[93]

The 14 temporary military cemeteries of North West France placed under the responsibility of the AGRC, September 22nd 1945[91]

Sites	American graves	German graves	Openings	Closings
« Blosville » (Carquebut)	5 804	0	7 June 1944	23 novembre 1947
Saint-Martin-de-Varreville	0	189	8 June 1944	End 1947
Sainte-Mère-Église n° 1	2 195	1 000	9 June 1944	16 Jul 1948
La Cambe	4 534	3 070	10 June 1944	29 Sep 1947
Saint-Laurent-sur-Mer	3 797	1 293	10 June 1944	28 Jul 1947
Orglandes	0	7 358	19 June 1944	1956
Sainte-Mère-Église n° 2	4 798	0	25 June 1944	16 Jul 1948
Marigny	3 070	4 238	31 Jul 1944	25 Jul 1948
Saint-James	4 367	2 077	5 Aug 1944	12 Oct 1947
Le Chêne-Guérin	1 202	1 205	7 Aug 1944	18 Jul 1948
Gorron	752	1 100	15 Aug 1944	2 Aug 1948
Saint-Corneille	521	280	16 Aug 1944	16 Aug 1948
Saint-André-de-l'Eure	2 066	1 098	24 Aug 1944	23 Aug 1948
Villeneuve-sur-Auvers	303	0	25 Aug 1944	6 Sep 1948
TOTAL	**33 409**	**22 929**		

PFC John J. Yazum, left, equips a French civilian charged with administrative tasks at camp "John B. Franks". NARA

Normandy, in particular those of Naqueville, La Glacerie, Tourlaville and Foucarville. Their dismantling, in mid-1947, obliged the AGRC to recruit twice as many French civilians at the end of that year. Their mission: participate in the closing of the temporary cemeteries of the Second Zone and contribute to the administrative tasks relating to the follow-up of the bodies.

In the tents and other buildings provided at Saint-Hilaire-Petitville, the work consisted of following the process of identifying the last unknown soldiers and, equally, putting in place the program of transferring the bodies which began at the end of the summer 1947.

Note, in the tableau below, the intensive employment of German prisoners up until mid-1947. The use of this labor force can be explained by the presence of several big prison camps in

Once the temporary cemeteries of the *Second Zone* were closed, the camp was dismantled in

AGRC Personnel (Second Zone) between 1945 and 1948

Date	American officers	American soldiers	American and British civilians	French civilians	Polish personnel	Prisoners of war	Totals
Dec 1945	31	144	65	289	-	880	1 409
Dec 1946	35	145	50	350	75	600	1 255
Dec 1947	47	176	140	730	64	-	1 148
Dec 1948	23	74	32	157	51	-	337

In May, 1946, PFC Clinton Moore, veteran of the 35th Infantry Division, stands guard at the entrance of the camp "John B. Franks", seat of the AGRC. NARA

December 1948, after transferring the personnel of the *American Graves Registration Command* to Granville on October 13. Jean-Baptiste Feuillye was among the men sent to the other side of the Cotentin: "After participating in the closures of the cemeteries of Marigny, Le-Chêne-Guérin, Gorron, Saint-Corneille and Saint-André-de-l'Eure, I came back to Carentan. Later the Americans sent us to Granville. There, they rented the Bains hotel, the Normandie Chaumière [the Grand Hotel, an annex to the Bains hotel in Saint-Pair-sur-Mer and a garage in Jullouville]. We worked at the port, in a former school, to file all the documents we received concerning the identified graves. There were about two hundred of us. There were American civilians among us. Every morning I received the archives, I sorted them. My job was to go to Jullouville to write the "bulletin du jour" [daily notice] in shorthand. It was difficult keeping clean... That job lasted a year. After that, they were off to the *Third Zone*, near Épinal. The graves service was transferred to the Astoria hotel in Paris. As for me, I was sent to the *Cablehead Office* in *Urville-Nacqueville* [near Cherbourg] until 1952, when I left for the United States."[94]

Document dated 14 May, 1947, presenting the American staff of the Second Zone based at camp "John B. Franks". NARA

In 1946, Maj. Robert C. Crisson, member of the high command of the AGRC Second Zone, returns to Utah Beach, where he had landed with the 4th Infantry Division (company C, 8th Infantry Regiment) in the morning of June 6, 1944.
Collection J.-B. Feuillye

TO EVACUATE, IDENTIFY, COLLECT PERSONAL EFFECTS AND BURY THE SOLDIERS KILLED IN ACTION

The procedures relating to the management of mortuary care for the personnel of the American army (both military and civilian) was the responsibility of the *Quartermaster's Corps*.

The principal tasks of this organization were the registration (as much as possible) of military graves, to make available to the family of the deceased his personal effects but also to acquire land for the construction of cemeteries and, finally, to maintain and develop these sites for the respect of the dead and the solace of the living. If the circumstances required it, the treatment of civilian victims, allied and enemy, had to be carried out with the same attention to detail by the unit responsible for the registration of military graves.

The first step in this procedure was to evacuate and to transport the victim from the battlefield toward a collection point. This mission fell to the soldiers themselves to the extent that searches of the terrain by the service charged with registering graves could not be undertaken until the combats were far enough away.

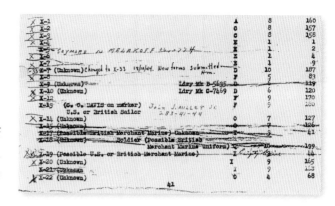

Extract of the listing of temporary cemetery n° 1 of Sainte-Mère-Église. The document presents 21 cases of unknown soldiers in the course of being identified. Note that the unknown corpses "X-9" and "X-10" have laundry marks, respectively "Ldry Mk B-5635" and "Ldry Mk C-7469". These precious indications inscribed a number of times on different clothes of military personnel would permit the identification of these men. NARA via J.-B. Feuillye

We cite, for example, the *79th Infantry Division* which, to the south of Cherbourg, called on members of the Band (the orchestra of the division) to take charge of the transportation of the dead.[95] The victims killed at the front were transferred to the rear to a collection point assembling the dead of the division. Here began the work of the Graves *Registration Service*.

When the bodies were received, they had to be handled with the greatest respect so as not to affect

On the ground, a research team exhumes the remains of an American soldier from an isolated grave. NARA

Storage room for bodies awaiting identification. Before any handling, the remains were doused with a disinfectant liquid. NARA

the morale of the troops situated at the edges of the collection point.

The corpses had to be covered rapidly and it was even required of the truck drivers to take secondary roads and paths in order to avoid the troops advancing toward the front.

The precautions concerning the handling of bodies during evacuation proved especially necessary in that several cases involving booby-trapped bodies came to complicate the work of the graves service, as explained in the extract below; from a report of the GRS dated January, 1945:

13. Special precautions in handling bodies and neutralizing booby-trapped bodies.

a. Aside from normal precautions taken to preserve identity and to handle the dead with respect, it became apparent early in the European Theater of Operations that extra precautions would have to be taken in the inspection and handling of bodies because of mines and booby-traps. It is believed the subject of booby-trapped bodies and mined areas wherein the dead lay is worthy of special consideration. That we faced an enemy who would resort to booby-trapping the dead was realized early enough to warrant inclusion of the following statement in FM 10-63, Graves Registration: "In the search for bodies great care should be taken to avoid booby-traps and anti-personnel mines which may have been placed under bodies by enemy forces." To implement such instructions, unit Graves Registration officers developed their own methods to counter set the danger involved in the handling of bodies. The following is typical of the means employed by many:

(1) At all times, bodies being picked up on the battlefield should be jerked by a rope at least 200 feet long in order to make sure they are not booby-trapped. He had definite indications of booby-trapping dead bodies with egg and rifle grenades.

(2) Take every possible precaution as the Germans have booby-trapped American dead by attaching hand grenades to the dog tag chains so a pull on the chain will fire the grenade.

b. The procedure was to delay the collection of bodies in an area believed or known to be mined until the area was cleared by personnel trained in mine-clearing operations. The fact that one Graves Registration Company in the European Theater of Operations lost 12 men who set off mines while removing bodies caused certain recommendations for changes in personnel and equipment to be made.[96]

The second step, and by no means the simplest, consisted of identifying the soldier killed in action. It appeared vital, in the eyes of the American army, to execute with rigor and accuracy this phase of the registration protocol. The challenges here were of a diverse nature. One had, above all, to ease the grief of the families who remained in the States, to give them a response when they asked questions about a son or a husband. There was also, from the administrative or legal point of view, the certainty that relatives' pensions would be forthcoming. War, being by nature an "awesome" tool facilitating technical progress, it was question for the Quartermaster's corps – untested – to test and evaluate the methods employed by the *Graves Registration Service*. This duty of excellence, relating to the identification of soldiers killed in action, was sure to influence morale at the front, but even more at the rear.

In order to handle the identification of a body and the verifications that followed, it was essential to conserve insofar as possible the dog tags of the deceased. When, by luck, the two dog tags remained around the neck, one of them was buried with the corpse, and the other was nailed to the grave marker. In a case where only one of them remained, it was buried with the body and information was indicated on the grave marker. Finally, if both were missing, every means needed to be put to work to identify the body.

HOW THE CENTRAL IDENTIFICATION OF THE AGRC WORKED

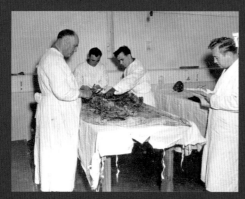

Technicians carefully inspect the clothing and other remains of the soldier to find the indications that would permit an identification. NARA

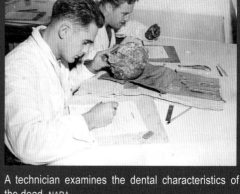

A technician examines the dental characteristics of the dead. NARA

Fingerprints. The document will then be sent to Washington and the prints will be compared with those taken at enrollment. NARA

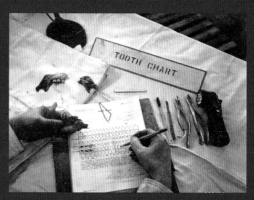

A technician completes the dental chart. NARA

The slightest element permitting the identification of the body was then placed in a flask buried next to him.

With the exception of dog tags, the principal elements permitting the identification of a soldier killed in action could be a military record, a pay slip, a bracelet, named jewelry, a letter, or other personal documents. Another method consisted of finding laundry marks among the clothes of the deceased.

Laundry marks were made obligatory such that every man and officer could quickly identify any pieces of uniform left temporarily in the hands of the Quartermasters charged with washing them.

Thus, the first letter of the last name had to be followed with the last four numbers of his matriculation. In reference to James Hattrick's (*508th PIR*) report of burial, page 111, we note that his identification was made thanks to the markings "H-1767" inscribed in his pants and his combat vest. In case of doubt, it was *de rigueur* to obtain certificates of identity from at least two soldiers having belonged to the same unit as the deceased.

In the case of an unidentifiable soldier, the title "unknown" was delivered when no formal proof was available (body burned or drowned, advanced decomposition). The individual was designated by the letter "X" followed by a number respecting the order in which he arrived.

A technician measures the humerus of a soldier, whose remains were incomplete, in order to determine the size of the individual. NARA

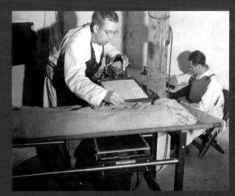

The remains of an unknown soldier are given x-rays, to know the number of missing bones. NARA

A secretary verifies and reproduces, in triplicate, the anatomical chart enumerating the parts missing from a skeleton. NARA

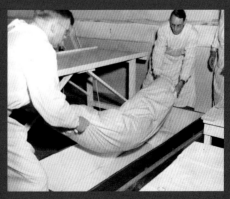

The remains of a soldier are replaced in a shroud and, occasionally, as in this case, in a coffin. NARA

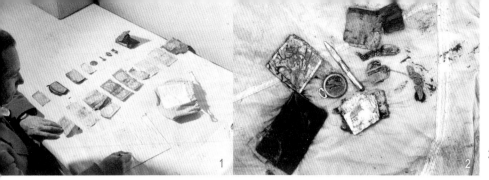

1. A French civilian inventories objects and money found on the body of a soldier killed in action. The objects would be transmitted to the family via this little bag and the money by a postal mandate. NARA

2. Objects found on the body of a downed American pilot. NARA

The collection of personal effects and their sending to the legal representatives was the third phase of the process of graves registration. The return of objects belonging to soldiers killed or lost in action, to prisoners of war and to men hospitalized had been, since 1776 and the Declaration of Independence, a fundamental principle. On September 20 of that same year, Congress adopted a text called "Original Rules and Articles of War". Article I, section 4, pronounced the foundation as follows: "When an officer, noncommissioned officer, or soldier shall happen to die, or to be killed in the service of the United States, his commanding officer would collect the dead man's personal effects and forward them to the person entitled to receive them".[97]

In Normandy, in each temporary cemetery, the officer in charge of burials had the responsibility, therefore, of assembling the objects and personal documents found on the body. The actual collection of these items was performed in certain cases by French civilians, as was the case for

Yves De La Rüe at the cemetery of Blosville. Each element was noted on the burial report and on an annex inventory sheet. The money that was found, on the other hand, was sent to the Bureau of Finances of the *US Army* where it was converted to a postal mandate and sent to the family of the deceased.

During the first days of the invasion, in the area of Sainte-Mère-Église, little sacks were made using parachute tissue. Then little bags arrived, with a waterproof form sewn on one of the two sides. These *Personal Effects Bags*, once filled, were sent to the depots of the vicinity where the content was cleaned and the bags were stored temporarily. Order was given to remove any trace of blood, and "to remove and destroy any objects which could cause embarrassment by their presence". The first of these depots was put into service on July 10, 1944. Previously, in England, a company specialized in personal effects was attached to the *64th Quartermaster Base Depot* and landed in Normandy on July 3. This site, coded

The Personal Effects Bag.
Private collection

A pair of American jump boots identified as belonging to PFC Wilburn Savage (C Company – 507th PIR) collected by a civilian of Sainte-Mère-Église during the construction of temporary cemetery n° 2. An object valued by Norman civilians wh had lacked everything during the four years of the war. Collection M. Quilez

FROM CARQUEBUT TO SALT LAKE CITY

On June 13, 1944, the soldier Joseph Fitt was killed by a German in the vicinity of the train station of Montebourg. The body of the young man was buried the same day at 5:20 pm, in the temporary cemetery of "Blosville", plot A, row 3, grave 44. A few minutes before he was placed in the ground, all the personal effects were assembled and inventoried by a member of the graves services to be sent to the family of the deceased.

On August 15, 1944, Cyril R. Fitt, father of the soldier killed in action, addressed these few lines to the bureau in charge of personal effects based in Kansas City (Missouri): "It seems as though sufficient time has elapsed for the return of my son's personal effects, such as his Kodak, pen and pencil set, clothing, etc.." However, it was only in January 1945 that the parents of the young man received a little package enclosing a ring, a wallet, a bracelet and his parachute wings.

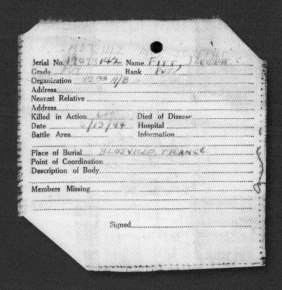

Water-proof label taken from a bag containing the personal effects of Joseph C. Fitt. Only the major information is noted (serial number, family name and first name, unit, date of death, place of burial).

Joseph E. Fant (left) and Joseph C. Fitt (right), the inseparable pair of C Company – *505th PIR*. The picture dates from the spring of 1944 in England. While the first survived the war, the second was killed in combat near Sainte-Mère-Église in the morning of June 13, 1944. "Joe" Fitt was buried in the temporary cemetery in Blosville the same day. Author's collection

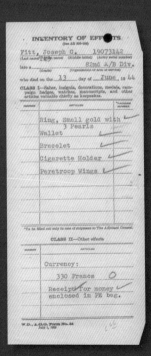

Inventory of the personal effects of the soldier Joseph C. Fitt made one week after his burial by 1st Lt. Edwin Miller, commander of the *603rd Quartermaster Graves Registration* Co. Among the objects found on the body of the young paratrooper, a ring belonging to his mother, a wallet, a bracelet and his paratrooper's wings. NARA

Parachute wings belonging to Joe Fitt. The object was returned to his family by the intermediary of the graves registration service of the American army. Private Collection

At La Cambe temporary cemetery, this film was made July 29, 1944, by the American army. Titled "Graves", it shows the different phases of the management of American military victims. An orderly comes to see the cause of death, while two members of the graves service collect and inventory the personal effects of the deceased. Finally, the personal objects are placed in a little cloth bag. A shroud (*White Cotton Mattress Cover*) is laid over the deceased. The body will be placed in the shroud a little later. Film NARA

"Q-290", rapidly received 13,000 of these little sacks awaiting treatment.[98] One month later, beginning August 6, 1944, 35,000 sacks were transferred to 41, rue du Val-de-Saire, Cherbourg. The base in Isigny-sur-Mer, set up in a cheese factory, served as an advanced collection point before being transferred to Le Mans on August 27, 1944, and then to Paris on September 25, 1944.

Sent next to the port of Liverpool, to the Quartermaster depot coded "G-4", the bags containing personal effects then crossed the Atlantic to go on to the Bureau of Personal Effects of the American army at Kansas City, Missouri. This organization, created September 11, 1942, stocked the sacks between one and six months before delivering them to a widow, a father or a mother.

The burial constituted the fourth step in the process of registering the grave. In the event that the GRS, at the time responsible for this task, was not available, it was up to the chaplain of the regiment, accompanied by a handful of men,

A view of the principal entrance of the cemetery of Blosville in June 1946. The flag at half-mast showed that burials were on-going. The legend says "June 20, 1946, eight soldiers coming from isolated graves were buried. Two of them were from the US Air Force. Permission to photograph the ceremony was denied." NARA

Identification capsules meant to contain burial form n° 1. This indicated the information relating to the deceased in case of non-identification (dental chart, distinguishing features). The capsule was to be buried with the body and placed under the left arm.
Collection of the author

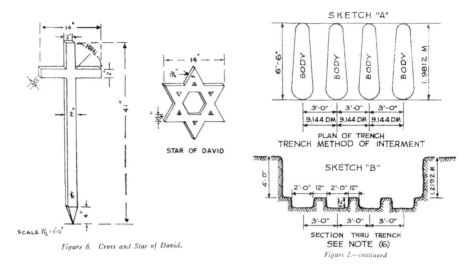

Figure 6. Cross and Star of David.

These two diagrams define the dimensions of the trenches as recommended by the Field Manual FM 10-63. The depth was close to 1 m 20 while the length could reach two meters. To the left are illustrations defining the dimensions of Latin crosses and stars of David. NARA

to take charge of the burial of the victim(s), and in the nearest cemetery. In cases where this was impossible, the grave(s) had to be dug on the site of death.

Sites containing fewer than twelve graves were forbidden. Nevertheless, isolated graves were common in Normandy. If possible, they were to have a marker of the type "Name Pegs" (wooden stakes) specifying the name of the soldier, his rank and his serial number. In other cases, a simple stake, a big stone, a rifle, a helmet or a bayonet could indicate an isolated grave. One of the two dog tags would be placed at the foot of the temporary monument.

On the subject of interments held in the temporary cemeteries, the funerals took place once a day, every day of the week. They had to be held early enough that the graves could be filled before nightfall. Each soldier had the right to a religious funeral and to a military cortège. Earlier, bodies had simply been placed in shrouds

– airborne troops, for their part, were placed in their parachutes – closed with a safety pin.

For the Norman temporary cemeteries, the staff of the *1st US Army* decided to build squares of two hundred graves in order to preserve morale for the troops through a certain rapport with the individual and in order to avoid any impression of mass deaths with plots of 300, 400 or 1200 graves as had happened in the past. American soldiers subject to the death penalty or deserters as well as allied soldiers or German soldiers had separate squares reserved for them.

For each square, white crosses or stars of David were to be placed at the head of the grave in a perfect alignment laterally, longitudinally and diagonally. Cemeteries were soon landscaped to fit in with the surrounding environment. A mast, carrying an American flag from sunrise to sunset, had to be built as quickly as possible. During interments, the flag flew at half-mast.

In an interview transcribed in a report of January, 1945, with the Graves Registration Service on the theater of operations in Europe, an anonymous officer of the GRS - *3rd US Army* – declared on the subject of the enhancement of temporary cemeteries: "Beautification of cemeteries was started the day they were opened. Not only was the morale of the Graves Registration personnel improved, but also that of soldiers visiting the graves of friends. Flag poles, prayer rostrums, fences, shrubbery, good roads, and well painted crosses were installed. The area was meticulously policed and cemetery apparatus and tools were placed out of sight as much as possible."[99]

A series of interments in a temporary Norman cemetery for which the exact location unfortunately remains unknown to this day. The cases visible in this picture are definitely not coffins which were never used in the temporary cemeteries (with rare exceptions). They are transport cases in which the remains of soldiers coming from isolated graves were placed. Collection J. Pignot

The temporary military cemetery of Marigny. On the other side of the road, we find the cemetery known as "enemy". In the foreground, the American cemetery with the "death penalty plot" in the bottom left. The bodies of 37 soldiers, condemned by court martial of the American army for rape or murder, later rejoined the 57 executed in the theater of operations in Europe at the permanent cemetery of Oise-Aisne. The bodies are today grouped, far from the public gaze, in plot E, better known as the "square of shame". NARA

LA MANCHE COUNTRYSIDE IS SEARCHED WITH A FINE-TOOTHED COMB

The "sweeping" – this was the expression used by the AGRC – of the departments of La Manche, Calvados and the Orne, in order to find all the isolated graves (American and German) began immediately after the Battle of Normandy. From September 1944 until the autumn of 1949, the American army moved heaven and earth to bring all the American soldiers, sailors and aviators, killed in action, to the national cemeteries. This great enterprise received the collaboration of the mayors of France who were informed in a document dated September 19, 1944, of their role alongside American Army. In this document, the secretary-general of the French Veterans association addressed the various prefects of France, themselves charged with distributing the document to the mayors of France, especially in Normandy. It was particularly stressed that close cooperation between the mayors of the towns and the American service of graves registration should be rapidly established in order to reunite all the American personnel killed in action – without exception – in military cemeteries. The secretary-general of veterans added: "It will not escape your attention that it is important to satisfy them because the French graves service could never assemble the means of transport or a labor force equivalent to that which is already at the disposal of the American services."[100]

After the victory of the allies and the unconditional surrender of the German army, on May 8, 1945, the German graves service was refused access to French soil to take care of their dead. The bodies of German soldiers buried in isolation were now the responsibility of the French service of graves registration.

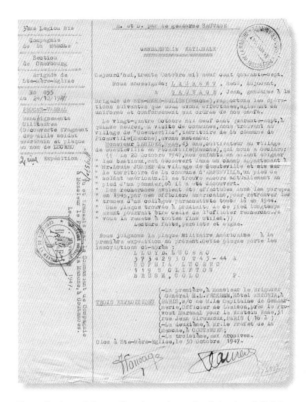

The minutes of the national gendarmerie (brigade of Sainte-Mère-Église) dated October 24, 1947. The document speaks of the discovery by a farmer of the grave of an American paratrooper in the commune of Amfreville. A copy was sent to the American service of graves registration. Departmental Archives of La Manche

It was the responsibility of the mayors to establish precise registers indicating the placement of graves on maps.

After the activation of the *American Graves Registration Command* in the fall of 1945, the research on the ground intensified visibly during 1946 with the creation of teams with a variety of missions. The first type of team was charged with talking with the mayors and other personalities of the villages; a second type of team performed research and other investigations; finally, a third type exhumed and transferred the bodies to the temporary cemeteries. On September 18, 1946, the Prefect of La Manche addressed the following letter to the mayors of the department:

"Subject: Searching for isolated graves of American or allied soldiers

I have the honor of making it known to you that an officer of the American army (graves registration service), accompanied by an interpreter, will be visiting all the communes of the department searching for the graves of Americans or allies as well as the remains of any military personnel who might not yet have received a decent burial.

I beg you to immediately do all that is in your power to ease the task of this officer. You can already look for and take note of the situation of such graves, so as to be able to inform the American service upon its passage.

It seems opportune that you invite the population to collaborate in this research, such that a grave worthy of the name may be given to these soldiers who fell for the liberation of our nation."

The "advertising" teams, those who were charged with contacting the mayors, notables, shop keepers, local priests etc., put up posters in every village inviting the population to support their effort and the research of the American graves registration service. It was impossible to ignore this vast research campaign. On the radio, from the November 26 to December 2, 1946, one could hear the following communique:

"Here is a communique from the American military graves service.

When the harvest is over and the crop has been put in the barn, we see our fields crisscrossed by women and children going to glean the last forgotten ears. Often times, they return with a pretty sheaf of wheat, a well-earned reward.

Well, Frenchmen, our friends, such a thing may apply to the research performed in the past by the American graves registration service. Thanks to the assistance that the Radio Diffusion Française has been willing to grant us, and to your inestimable efforts, we have obtained extraordinary results. Now that our principal results have been accomplished, we come to ask you to glean around yourselves the final information. Perhaps you heard that an aviator had fallen in your region, or that during a battle, a fallen soldier had been buried in an isolated corner. Write us at the AMERICAN MILITARY GRAVES in Carentan (Manche). Every piece of information is precious.

We have already relieved a lot of pain but deep in certain hearts yet shines a light of hope. Help us! Please be assured of all our recognition, one more link in the deep friendship that will unite our two countries in the future." [101]

The research went on for months. Arriving at the camp "John B. Franks", Jean-Baptiste Feuillye, former receptionist and interpreter of cemetery n° 1 in Sainte-Mère-Église, remembers the time when it was his turn to be sent in search of the last isolated graves: "In 1948, the general staff was still in Saint-Hilaire-Petitville. Since 1946 they had put up posters in all the towns asking to help us find the graves. We were rather surprised at some of the letters: we received numerous letters of denunciation. A lot of denunciation. Mr. X had collaborated with the Germans under the Occupation, another had sold them butter... We trained teams, the Fortier-Feuillye duo had to take care of the cemeteries in the area. As soon as we arrived aboard a jeep, with an American, we contacted the mayor. In particular, I found an American pilot on the Isle of Chausey, and a German in Picauville"[102]. Among the principal sources of information used by the Americans charged with the searches are the German "burial cards" ("green cards"), reports of loss of allied aerial equipment by the Germans under the Occupation, the French military graves service, the American and International Red Cross, what was called the "project of the French Church" involving the priests of each parish where the isolated graves were being sought. The results for Normandy show that 60% of isolated graves were indicated by the French service of military graves, 30% were thanks to the American graves research and 10% were due to other sources.

No enterprise, as rigorous as it may be, can be exhaustive.[103] If the work accomplished by the AGRC between 1945 and 1949 to find the greatest number of isolated graves containing Americans can be qualified as monumental, there still remain several hundred of these graves to be found. For just the regions of Upper and Lower Normandy, the number of temporary American graves hidden somewhere in the Norman Bocage is estimated at 876.[104]

A poster made by the services of the AGRC in 1946 inviting Norman civilians to notify American authorities of the presence of any isolated military graves. Departmental Archives of La Manche

A campaign of posters undertaken by the AGRC Second Zone in 1946 to call the local population to contribute to the research for the last isolated graves. NARA

The children of Sainte-Mère-Église in the temporary cemetery n°2 in 1946. NARA

THE BIRTH OF
A SPECIAL BOND
WITH AMERICA

Honor the dead to bring peace to the hearts of the living

SIMONE RENAUD, "OUR MOTHER OF NORMANDY"

Looking back at the events of the summer of 1944 and those that were played out in Sainte-Mère-Église, one name stands out in the accounts of witnesses: Alexandre Renaud, the mayor of the town from May, 1944. But when these same witnesses remember the years after the war, it is the name of Simone Renaud, the wife of the mayor that comes to mind. This charismatic woman, with an indefatigable will and great devotion, personified the indelible link between Sainte-Mère-Église and the families of those who were buried in this corner of Normandy. This deeply passionate woman became, for the rest of her life, a substitute mother for all these young men, dead and buried far from home.

Veterans of the *82nd Airborne Division* returning to Normandy in June 1945, on the first anniversary of D-Day. They were about to rejoin the port of Le Havre before returning to the US. In the center of the picture, Alexandre and Simone Renaud pose in front of their pharmacy situated on the edge of the square of Sainte-Mère-Église.
Collection H.-J. Renaud

Simone Renaud (born Cornière) was a local girl. She was born in 1899 in Saint-Germain-de-Tournebut, a village situated fifteen kilometers north of Sainte-Mère-Église. Her fascination with the language of Shakespeare took her to England where she was an assistant for a year at a high school. After having improved her English, her love of arts and letters encouraged her to go to Paris where she studied at the Sorbonne. Placed under the protection of a well-known playwright, Edmond Rostand (author of *Cyrano de Bergerac*) the young lady was inevitably influenced by this man and also by his wife, Rosemande Rostand, who shared with Simone Cornière her passion for poetry.

It was in Paris that Simone met Alexandre Renaud, a brilliant young man, who spoke several languages and was equally passionate about the arts and letters. The marriage of Simone and Alexandre took place in 1923 in the capital. Then the couple seized the opportunity to take over a pharmacy in Sainte-Mère-Église, not far from the native village of the young woman. Enjoying a completely peaceful life before the outbreak of the Second World War, they had three sons: Paul, Henri-Jean, and Maurice.

After the battle to liberate Sainte-Mère-Église, Simone Renaud was present at the construction of the three military cemeteries around it. It was with great emotion that she watched the trucks go by with their macabre loads to reach the cemeteries which grew and grew as the days went by.

But the event that would push Simone Renaud to the front of the international stage took place on July 14, 1944, the day of the funeral of Brig.-Gen. Theodore Roosevelt. The whole village had come to pay homage to this man whose name alone made

FLAGS UNDER WHICH GENERAL ROOSEVELT SERVED ARE CARRIED INTO CHRIST CHURCH WHERE FOUR GENERATIONS OF ROOSEVELTS HAVE BEEN CHRISTENED, MARRIED, BURIED

ROOSEVELT BURIED

Services for "Young Teddy" are
held on Long Island and in France

In an ivy-covered church on Long Island and at a graveyard in Normandy, funeral services were held for Brig. General Theodore ("Young Teddy") Roosevelt, oldest son of President Theodore Roosevelt. On July 12, near the battle lines, the General died of a heart attack brought on by the strain of front-line service. To Christ Church in Oyster Bay went his widow, Mrs. Eleanor Alexander Roosevelt; his daughter, Mrs. William McMillan; and two of his three sons—Corne-

lius, a Navy lieutenant; and Teddy III, also a Navy lieutenant and wearer of the Air Medal awarded him by Admiral Nimitz for bravery in the Pacific. To the graveyard in Normandy went his third son, Quentin, a captain in the First Division and the holder of the Silver Star, Purple Heart and Croix de guerre. As the band played Chopin's Funeral March and three volleys rang out under the elm trees, Quentin watched his father's coffin being lowered into the red soil of France.

FAMILY ARRIVES: FIRST, MRS. ROOSEVELT AND SON THEODORE III; NEXT, SON CORNELIUS AND THEODORE'S WIFE; IN REAR, DAUGHTER GRACE AND HUSBAND, COMMANDER McMILLAN

Page 26 of Life magazine, covering the burial of Brig.-Gen. Roosevelt. Private collection

Page 27 of Life magazine on the funeral of Brig. Gen. Roosevelt. Private collection

him stand for America. This day of July 1944, Simone Renaud took the initiative of adopting the grave of the general, pledging herself to maintain and to flower his grave as long as necessary.

Mrs Renaud invited the people of Sainte-Mère-Église to do the same, a way of paying tribute to these men, and above all, of ensuring that they would not be forgotten.

The same day, among the army's numerous war reporters covering the event, the photographer Ralph Morse – who had come first of all to meet Gen. Patton in person – thought it would be highly symbolic to show Mrs Renaud flowering the grave of Gen. Roosevelt. What could be better, indeed, than the wife of the mayor of Sainte-Mère-Église taking under her protection the son of the 26th president of the United States? This picture was later selected, unbeknownst to the photographer himself, to illustrate the article about the General's funeral in what was, at the time, the most popular patriotic revue of America: *Life* magazine. Thus, in the issue dated August 7, 1944, the photo of Simone Renaud on her knees, on the grave of Gen. Roosevelt, overwhelmed America. At this time, while the Battle of Normandy raged on, numerous American families remained without news of a son, a husband, a brother recently killed in action. The Department of War furnished families with a bare minimum of information; one can easily imagine the anxiety that weighed on the hearts of some parents. What had become of the bodies of these young soldiers? How did the army take care of its victims? "Where is my son buried?" asked thousands of mothers. Ralph Morse's photo brought to the families an element of a response, a ray of hope.

The impact of this photo on the morale of those close to the soldiers killed in action in Normandy was surprising. It was followed by an emotional explosion which had taken the form, by the end of the summer of 1944 in Sainte-Mère-Église, of thousands of letters received by the mayor who already had to share his time between his pharmacy and the administrative burdens of his office.

This explains why he agreed to delegate to his wife the responsibility of answering the American families. Feeling herself invested with a mission, Mrs Renaud dedicated all her time to the writing of personal letters. She answered all the families

Cover of Life dated August 7, 1944. Private collection.

Lt William B. Fulmer's grave (83rd Infantry Division) at cemetery n°2. This kind of photographs were mailed to the next of kin by Mrs Renaud. Collection H.-J. Renaud

who wanted to know exactly where their son was buried. In each letter, she enclosed a photo of the grave[105], as well as a rose petal freshly gathered from it. By this symbolic gesture, she enabled the families to establish a direct link, concrete and tangible, with the site where the military victims were laid.

Not content to go to the three military cemeteries of Sainte-Mère-Église every day, Simone Renaud occasionally went to Saint-Laurent-sur-Mer, in the department of Calvados, to respond to the requests of families. In early 1945, she received a letter that illustrates this precise case. Mr. White, Kansas, had been shaken by the article and the photograph in *Life* on August 7, 1944. He addressed a request to Simone Renaud concerning his son, Harry White of the *2nd Infantry Division*.

The letters, more poignant than ever, continued to arrive and left no doubt that, for certain American families, a close link had been born with Sainte-Mère-Église embodied by Simone Renaud. On either side, there was an immense sentiment of gratitude toward the other. Then, one day in 1947, in addition to letters came

**« Mᵐᵉ Renaud,
Sainte-Mère-Église, France**

Hutchinson, Kansas, U.S.A.

In the August 7th, 1944 issue of the *Life* Magazine is a picture of you decorating the grave of Brig. Gen. Theo. Roosevelt's grave. Also a short article telling about how you are keeping it decked with flowers. To say the least, I am sure that millions of Americans like myself who loved General Roosevelt and his father before him, deeply appreciate what you are doing.

We, too, lost a son in France. Pvt Harry R. White was killed in action in Normandy, July 26th, 1944. We think he was killed somewhere near St Lô, but of this we cannot be quite sure. Just a few days ago, we received word from the Quartermaster General's Office giving us the location of the grave. The letter said that our son was buried in Saint Laurent sur Mer cemetery n°1, France, Grave number 191, Row 10, Plot U. We have searched all of the maps we can find, and we have been unable to locate this place. We even went to the local Red Cross but they do not have any maps that show it.

His mother and I wondered if it would be asking too much to ask you to write us and tell us where this place is located. We would like a map of that section of the country, if it is available, and if it would not be violating the military regulations to send it to us. It may be somewhere near your home. I found Ste Mère Eglise on a map which I have, but not St Laurent. Everything you can tell us about our son's last resting place, I assure you, will be greatly appreciated by a sorrowing family.[106] »

PARIS, le 15 Janvier 1946

MONSIEUR LE CURÉ
de Sainte-Mère-L'Eglise
(Manche)

Monsieur Le Curé,

Madame Louis Tansak, employée depuis de longues années chez mes cousins de New York, a eule malheur de perdre son fils lors du débarquement des troupes améri- caines en France.

Les renseignements que Madame Tansak a obtenus du service de l'armée américaine, montre que son fils est inhumé au cimetière militaire américain de SAINTE- MÈRE-L'EGLISE, sous le N° 155, 8e rang, division B.

Madame Tansak, peu fortunée et ne pouvant se rendre sur la tombe de son fils, me demande de vouloir bien lui obtenir une photographie de l'emplacement ou repo- se son enfant regretté. Ne pouvant me rendre moi-même à Sainte-Mère-L'Eglise, j'ai recours à votre bonté pour me dire s'il est dans vos moyens de vous charger de cette pré- cieuse mission.

Madame Tansak étant Catholique désire également qu'une prière soit dîte sur la tombe de son fils en même temps que quelques fleurs y seraient déposées, afin que la photographie lui montre une tombe fleurie et non aban- donnée.

Il est bien entendu que je vous dédom- magerai de tous ces frais et en même temps j'y joindrai une obole pour vos paroissiens qui ont été éprouvés.

Je vous remercie vivement à l'avance, de ce que vous pourrez faire pour cette pauvre Mère, et je vous prie de croire, Monsieur le Curé, à l'expression de mes respectueux sentiments.

Letter dated January 15, 1946, and addressed to the Abbé Rouland, priest of Sainte-Mère-Église. It concerns the request of a mother whose son was buried in the temporary cemetery of Carquebut. Collection J. Pignot

Abbé Rouland; July 14, 1944, in the company of an American chaplain. NARA

At cemetery n° 1 in Sainte-Mère-Église, Alexandre Renaud (right) and two of his deputies collect the earth covering an American grave. Samples would later be sent to the families of the soldiers buried there. Collection H.-J. Renaud

THE GRAND CEMETERIES UNDER THE SNOW
(American military cemeteries of Sainte-Mère-Église)

Dedicated to the American Mothers.

THE snow, this night
Has fallen softly from the clouds
To spread its marvelous mantle
On the wooden crosses.

NATURE, for once, has made herself
Merciful and maternal for the poor dead,
By gently weaving thousands of flowers
And thousands of wings (feathers)
In order their shroud might be more soft.

FEATHERS of swans, flowers from heavenly gardens,
A net as light as air
Laid on their last wound and their last gesture,
Like a breath and a kiss...

WHETHER it be the newly born,
Or the pure forehead of the Virgin
Or the silver chalice so bright on the altar,
Nothing is more pure and limpid
Than your flakes falling
From the skies, O snow!

AND who better than you
Silent and smooth
Could build a more radiant wall
Between the bitter world, sensual and wicked
And these bodies of martyrs given in sacrifice?

WHAT better than your white shroud
Could separate those who breathe only
For vulgar passion, and gold, eating and drinking,
And these proud knights who fell in sacred
devotion!

MAY the struggle cease in this holy place.
Also the passion of the living,
For more living are those who died for their dream,
The face toward the rising sun!

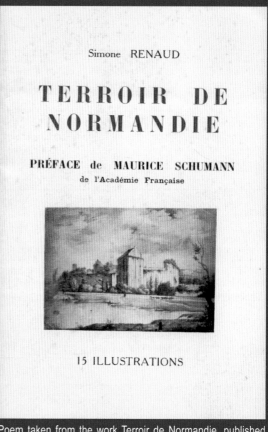

Poem taken from the work Terroir de Normandie, published in 1975. Simone Renaud gathers a large number of texts written in French and English. Private Collection

KEEP them from ugly things,
Oh beautiful, clear, pure snow.
Push aside all the mud and wickedness
From their sacred ashes.
Be for them a crystal reliquary!

PIOUSLY watch over these shadows in exile,
Rock them, rock them patiently
In your tender arms,
Like a Mother rocks a child!

Simone Renaud

packages from the United States. To the great surprise of the people of Sainte-Mère-Église, the packages contained medical materials, food, clothing, candy and playthings for the children of the village. This act of generosity was itself generated by the photos showing Simone Renaud in the pages of *Life* from August 1944. In fact, two inhabitants of Locust Valley, NY, Martha Breasted and Col. Augustin Hart, Jr. (veteran of the *82nd Airborne*) were profoundly moved by the gesture of Simone Renaud. The program of adoption and mutual assistance to the French population which was established was called "Operation Democracy". On the occasion of the celebration of Thanksgiving, 1947, the first shipment was sent to Sainte-Mère-Église. This initiative inspired nearly 200 other American cities to send supplies to French cities of their choice and this continued up until the beginning of the fifties. It is worth noting, however, that it was hardly a unique phenomenon and even less a new one.

In fact, the first deliveries of clothing destined for stricken Norman families (those of Saint-Lô, Condé-sur-Noireau, or Caen) were in operation as early as 1944. Certain cities of the Paris region, such

The Renaud couple on either side of Cap. Briand M. Beaudin, a doctor with the 508th PIR, who came back to Sainte-Mère-Église in June 1945. Collection H-J. Renaud

as Vincennes, came to the aid of the populations of La Manche or Calvados who had lost everything during the Battle of Normandy.

Panel erected at the south entrance of Sainte-Mère-Église, recalling "Operation "Democracy" of 1947 and the help brought by the American people to French civilians. Photo by the author

Simone Renaud posing in a jeep, at the entrance of the temporary cemetery n° 2. Collection H.-J. Renaud

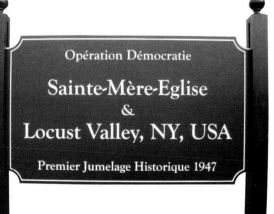

PILGRIMAGES AND FIRST VISITORS

When the three military cemeteries of Sainte-Mère-Église opened, although the graves registration personnel were at work, visitors were permitted, up to a point, to visit the still recent graves. This is nothing compared to the 1.2 million visitors today to the American cemetery in Colleville-sur-Mer. Access to these sites was monitored extremely carefully and restricted. During the first months, visits remained quite rare, up until certain soldiers came to salute the grave of a friend or a brother as described below by Father Francis Sampson. On July 11, 1944, while the *101st Airborne Division* was preparing to return to England, some news came to trouble the Catholic chaplain of the 501st PIR: "When the regiment was bivouacked near Utah Beach waiting for the boats to take us back to England, a young soldier by the name of Fritz Niland came to see me. He was very troubled in mind. The company commander of his brother, who was with the 508th Regiment [505th PIR], told Fritz that this brother had been killed and was buried in the Sainte-Mère-Eglise cemetery. We jumped in my Jeep and drove the twenty miles back to that town [Blosville]. In checking the cemetery roster I couldn't find the boy's name. "There's no William Niland [Robert] listed here, Fritz" I said encouragingly, "though there is a Roland Niland [Preston] listed". "Father... that's my brother too. He was a lieutenant in the Ninetieth Division [*4th Infantry Division*]". The unhappy boy tried to choke back the tears. After saying a few prayers at the grave we went to another cemetery just a few blocks away where we found the grave we were looking for originally. A third brother had just been killed in the Pacific [simply wounded]."[107]

Upon his return to England, Father Sampson began the procedures for bringing Frederick Niland back to the US. This was accomplished the day before Operation "Market Garden", September 17, 1944, and the airdrop over Holland. Fritz Niland finished his military service in the United States, in the military police of New York. Finally, during the summer of 1945, Edward Niland came back to his family after being held captive for a year in Burma.

Other soldiers came back during the summer of 1944, for example, Clyde Page. Clyde was posted in Cherbourg and he wanted to go to the cemetery where his friend, Joe Fitt, killed June 13, 1944, was buried. He wanted to send a photograph of the grave to the mother of this soldier, buried in Blosville. In a letter sent to his own mother, Clyde Page gives us an interesting description of the temporary cemetery of Blosville.

These photos are of a ceremony held at temporary cemetery n° 1, organized in honor of the soldiers of the *9th Infantry Division* who fell during the battle of the Cotentin. Gen. Eddy, commander of the division that contributed to the liberation of Cherbourg, is accompanied by a detachment of the *39th Infantry Regiment identifiable* by the marking "AAAO" for "*Anything, Anywhere, Anytime, bar nOthing*", present on several helmets. NARA film

Dear Mom,   Monday, Sept. 4, 1944

Well, today I got a day off, so I went to Ste Mère Eglise to see if I could find Joe [Fitt] 's grave. I had quite a time finding it. There are three cemeteries in that vicinity. I finally found the grave registration office, and they told me where he was. He's buried in the monarch cemetery about three miles south of Ste Mère Eglise, in a small town of Blosville (blow'- ville). In case Mrs Fitt wants to know, he is buried in plot A, row 3, grave 44. Well, when I got there, they told me I could not take any pictures of the cemetery.

I don't know why. I may be able later on. The place doesn't look very good now, anyway. They are just starting to level the ground and set the crosses in straight lines. When they get it all leveled off, they are going to plant lawn so I imagine it will be much nicer then. I certainly will try to get a picture, later on. I'm awfully sorry I couldn't get one today.

You should see the flowers the French people bring and put on the graves. At the cemetery where Joe is buried, there were several large wreaths, brought in by the people of many of the small towns in vicinity, and across each wreath was a wide ribbon, on which was written, "In honor of the liberators of our villages". Those think a great deal of the Americans. [...]

Well, Mom, that's about all for now. Write soon.

All my love.

Clyde[108] »

It wasn't until the spring of 1945 that the cemeteries began to take on a smoother and greener appearance. The grass had finally covered the perfectly levelled plots; the paths were done with gravel, and the white crosses were stenciled with the name and serial number of each soldier. The sites were more welcoming from a certain point of view, but nevertheless a fairly moderate number of visitors came to the cemeteries during the first twelve months. This observation is no doubt connected to the role of the various superintendents whose mission was to keep the sites as calm and peaceful as possible. One might say, simply, that they didn't really appreciate the presence of Norman civilians in too great a number.

Eleanor Roosevelt, widow of Brig. Gen. Roosevelt, visiting cemetery n°2 in 1946. Collection H.-J. Renaud

For their part, veterans of D-Day remained very special visitors, notably during the first year. In June, 1945, on the first anniversary of the Landings (organized largely thanks to Simone Renaud) some of them came back to Sainte-Mère-Église a few weeks before sailing from Le Havre to the USA. These men had the opportunity one last time, they thought, to see their companions in arms of June and July, 1944, before going back to the States.

Jean-Baptiste Feuillye, the young receptionist of the temporary cemetery n° 1 of Sainte-Mère-Église, saw these men come as well as the first American families: "At the end of 1945, we saw these veterans arrive but also the very first American families and those close to the victims, a lot of paras who had fought here and who were in Germany at that moment. Many of them came to say a last goodbye to their buddies before they went back to their homeland. These lucky ones who had escaped came from Le Havre where GIs were camped out in huge bases that had the names of cigarettes. Mrs. Harvey was one of the first American mothers to come to visit the grave of her son, Capt. James Harvey Jr. [*90th Infantry Division*]. She only had this one son and would come to the cemetery for about a half an hour, each day, for two weeks. She would come to visit in the Reception room. At first, she slept at Mrs Renaud's. I took her to the train to Paris. She sent me her father's shotgun, which I still have. The wife of the captain killed in Normandy on June 15, 1944, lived in San Antonio, Texas. So she was high priority when her husband's body was to be sent home in 1948. Mrs. Harvey tried to get the body sent to Seattle (Washington) since her daughter-in-law had remarried. [...] A lot of VIPs came, usually secretly and on a personal level. In 1946, a rainy day, it really came down, I saw a khaki car come, in the form of a mushroom. A stranger at the wheel. I went to see the driver on the parking lot.

Veterans of the *508th PIR* returning to Normandy in June 1945, to salute their comrades killed in action. This break gave them the opportunity to visit the civilians who had helped them a year earlier. The group of paratroopers took part in the ceremonies on *Utah Beach.* The veterans were taken care of by Simone Renaud, visible on the right. Collection H.-J. Renaud

MRS. HARVEY

Mrs. Harvey was the mother of James Harvey Jr., captain of the 359th Infantry Regiment (90th ID). Her son, killed June 15, 1944, was buried temporarily in the cemetery n°1 in Sainte-Mère-Église. She was among the first mothers of soldiers to come to visit the grave of a son. She is shown here in the reception building of cemetery n°1.

Collection J.-B. Feuillye

It was my job. I was always supposed to be behind him and on the left. He went down the middle. I asked him if he wanted to sign the guest book (we didn't ask everybody... The kids always wanted to put something in it). He took off his sunglasses.

It was Eisenhower! That really struck me. He was in civilian clothes. He had tears in his eyes. He felt responsible for the deaths of these guys. He went back to his car with his secretary at the wheel." [109]

Extracts from the memorial booklet offering a description of all the American temporary cemeteries taken over by the AGRC. Collection J.-B. Feuillye

Jean-Baptiste Feuillye, in charge of reception at temporary cemetery n° 1 between 1945 and 1948, gave American families the memorial booklet published by the AGRC in 1946 when they took charge. Photo by the author

THE COMMEMORATIONS OF JUNE 6

The war was barely over, with the unconditional surrender of the German army May 8, 1945, when Sainte-Mère-Église and its inhabitants started to prepare the first anniversary of the Landings. The battle that had raged in the vicinity remained very much alive in their memories and, because they knew all too well the human cost that the battle had caused, it was time to celebrate life, the living and the survivors.

Organized and set up by the mayor, Alexandre Renaud, the first anniversary of the Allied invasion of France was to take place in the presence of some veterans of the *82nd Airborne Division*. As such, a request was addressed to Gen. James Gavin in the spring of 1945 asking him to send a detachment of paratroopers to participate in this "glorious celebration".

Dear Mr. Renaud:

APO 469, US Army
10 May 1945

Your kind letter of 25 April was received today, and I hasten to convey my sincere appreciation for your most generous proposal.

Due to the victory of the Allied Forces in Europe, it is difficult to predict what the situation surrounding the 82 Airborne Division will be on the 5th of June. I assure you, however, that if circumstances permit, a representative group will be sent to Sainte-Mère-Eglise for the glorious celebration.

At the earliest possible date, I shall notify you so that you may complete your arrangements.

The troopers of the *82nd Airborne Division* often speak of your picturesque village and its noble citizens.

Thank you, again, for your very nice letter.

With warm regards,

James Gavin[110] »

Collection H.-J. Renaud.

This would be the beginning of a fascinating process of glorification of American paratroopers, these "angels come from the sky" and wreathed in victory. The infatuation with these men was already well anchored and this process of turning them into stars was exemplified by numerous gestures of affection and the first requests for autographs. This effervescence peculiar to Saint-Mère-Eglise and this cult of the paratroopers' corps are more alive today than ever. But in 1945, there was a feeling of urgency in the hearts of each one, because, of course, it wasn't known if these men would come back one day, whence the urgent and somewhat overblown character of these first commemorations. In order to describe as precisely as possible the atmosphere of these celebrations, we will use an amazing anonymous testimony. This brings out the festive, even spectacular character of the event to which the all the official departmental VIPs were invited.

GRAND CELEBRATION IN SAINTE-MÈRE-ÉGLISE ON JUNE 5, 1945 IN HONOR OF THE PARATROOPERS OF THE 82ND AIRBORNE DIVISION

In the town decorated in the greatest taste by the entire population, Monsieur the Prefect, accompanied by Mme Lebas, makes his entry. Monsieur the Under-Prefect, accompanied by Mme Moulin, follows a few minutes behind. They immediately enter the banquet hall where they are received by Monsieur the Mayor of Sainte-Mère-Église and Mme Renaud who, in the name of her village, presides over the banquet.

In an immense American hall decorated with enormous care with flowers, garlands and the allied flags, three immense parachutes, red, white and blue, installed in the ceiling, shed a soft light. Enclosed in green, a big canvas painted by a local artist of Sainte-Mère-Église, admirably decorates the back of the hall and represents in moonlight, as on June 5, 1944, the arrival of big transporter planes and the descent of American paratroopers on the town of Sainte-Mère-Église.

Immense tables, decorated with flowers, fill the hall: three hundred guests will take part in the banquet, and we notice the following personalities: M. the Prefect of La Manche and Mme Lebas, M. the Under-Prefect and Mme Moulin, the mayor and Mme Renaud, the deputy (congressman) of the region, the officers and soldiers of the 82nd Airborne Division, sent especially from the north of Berlin, practically every mayor and all the official authorities of the region, will assist in the celebration in honor of the paratroopers.

The banquet, a true Norman dinner, was spent in the greatest of gaiety. At dessert, M. the Mayor was the first to take the floor. After having thanked the departmental and county authorities for coming to this celebration, he spoke vividly of the paratroopers without whom the county would have been totally annihilated. He showed, equally, the immense role played by the splendid *82nd division* in the establishment of the first American bridgehead in France. Without these paratroopers, he cried, the Landing on the coast could have been impossible, or at least, the troops landing and the fleet would have suffered far greater losses.

Monsieur the Mayor thanked next, in English, the paratroopers for coming from so far away to participate in these festivities and he declared that from now on, they would always be children of Sainte-Mère-Église and they would always be "at home" among us.

After the banquet, there was a recording explaining the moonlight jump of the paratroopers to the sound of alarms, among the tracer bullets that rose and seemed to crash into the cabins of the planes in this fairytale night of June 6, 1944; among the deafening purr of the powerful motors, 13,000 paratroopers and gliders in formation converged on the county.

After this, the town square, admirably illuminated, was extraordinarily animated; the crowd seemed marked by the tragic and unforgettable hours. The first notes of "Liberty Jazz" were heard and soon the couples were dancing until daybreak. The night was splendid, the century-old trees covered with multicolored lights softly waved their arms and seemed, as well, to participate in the first anniversary of the Liberation. " [111]

THE COMMEMORATIONS OF JUNE 6, 1945

Collection H.-J. Renaud and the Airborne Museum

The "barrel": this American construction of corrugated steel was used for the banquet and festivities.

The north entrance to Sainte-Mère-Église and the homage to the paratroopers.

Veritable stars, these veterans sign autographs for the pleasure of the inhabitants.

A "fake" Sherman tank, in the colors of free France, was recreated for the first anniversary of D-Day. It is visible here at the crossing of the road to Ravenoville and the rue de Cap-de-Laine.

The procession from cemetery n°1 to n°2.

THE COMMEMORATIONS OF JUNE 6, 1946

Collection H.-J. Renaud and the Airborne Museum

The military parade, rue Cap-de-Laine, included fifty vetrans of the *508th PIR*.

Gen. Le Gentilhomme, military governor of Paris, places the Légion d'Honneur on 11 officers of the *508th PIR* (*82nd Airborne Division*), in the Park of La Haule, in the place of the current museum. Note those curious enough to climb the trees to watch the ceremony.

On the stand installed in cemetery n°1 of Sainte-Mère-Église, Alexandre Renaud, the mayor, listens attentively to a member of the ARGC, who was a member of the *4th Infantry Division*.

The small fellow, in the center, is Capt. Malcolm D. Brannen. On D-Day, he commanded HQ Co of the 3rd battalion (*508th PIR*). During the first few hours of the attack, he fatally wounded Gen. Falley, commander of the German 91.Luftland Division near the chateau of Bernaville.

THE COMMEMORATIONS OF JUNE 6, 1947

Ceremony in the cemetery n°2 of Sainte-Mère-Église in June 1947. A member of the AGRC places a wreath at the foot of the grave of Brig. Gen. Roosevelt, under the gaze of the inhabitants. Collection H.-J. Renaud.

Ceremony in cemetery n° 2 in honor of the unknown soldier. We note among the members of the AGRC the strong representation of African-Americans. In the photo in the extreme lower left, Abbé Lemercier, curate of Carquebut. NARA

The establishment of these commemorations fulfilled a need to bring together the civilian as well as veterans in order to remember the great hours of this village of the Cotentin. To commemorate this first anniversary of D-Day was to assert and to appropriate the memory of this event on a local scale. It was, furthermore, a means of affirming a strong sense of identity with the presence of the three military cemeteries in the county of Sainte-Mère-Église.

Everyone felt involved and people said to themselves that "we owed them at least that". The duty of memory, a notion that the historian distrusts as a general rule[112], gave way to the establishment of a ritualization of memory but, equally, to examples of astounding behavior within the military cemeteries.

SAINTE-MÈRE-ÉGLISE: KILOMETER 0 OF "LIBERTY ROAD"

The idea of the project created by Col. Guy de la Vasselais after the victory of the Allies in Europe, was to commemorate the triumphant route of Gen. Patton's 3rd Army from Normandy to Bastogne, in Belgium. Along this "sacred way", milestones made by the sculptor François Coigné would be installed every kilometer.

Installed September 16, 1947, in Sainte-Mère-Église, opposite the Hotel de Ville, the milestone of kilometer 0 of the Liberty Road led to a gentle battle of belfries with the neighboring village of Sainte-Marie-du-Mont, where the American troops had landed on June 6, 1944. This modest memorial conflict, with its touristic and economic stakes, pushed the neighboring village to put up its own monument: the milestone of kilometer 00. With a touch of humor, an anonymous member of the municipal council of Sainte-Marie-du-Mont testified to the microphone of Gilles Perrault, in 1964: "Each one wanted his piece of the cake, if you will. In Sainte-Mère, there is no water. For a landing, you had to have some water. It seemed natural to have a milestone of kilometer 00 in Sainte-Marie. There is no water in Sainte-Mère, there is just the fountain of Saint-Méen!"

Collection J. Pignot.

Collection J. Pignot.

Sacred places, new rites

A CORNER OF AMERICA IN NORMANDY, EXOTIC AND DIFFERENT

The establishment of the three American temporary military cemeteries in the county of Sainte-Mère-Église affected not only the landscape but also the behavior of the locals. The sudden presence in a limited space of 13,103 military graves obliged the inhabitants to adopt a new type of attitude toward the dead. For the village of Sainte-Mère-Église we can, in 1946, count 1,261 inhabitants[113] on a territory of 17.82 square kilometers, in other words, a density of 71 inhabitants per square kilometer. That same year in this same village, we count 7,993 military graves (of which 1000 German) located around the village. The density of these graves suddenly represented 448 military graves per square kilometer, providing a ratio of 6 to 1 "military graves per inhabitant". It became impossible to ignore the presence of these thousands of military graves and cemeteries and they became part of the local landscape that was impossible to ignore. In consequence, these places generated new activities on the part of the inhabitants, both collective and individual.

Among the collective practices engendered by these great temporary cemeteries, we have already mentioned the setting up of ceremonies by the Renaud couple. In addition to the festivities and the rejoicing of the first years after the war, there were the moments of contemplation, solemn occasions when the population was called upon to commune with the dead each June 6 or at each Memorial Day. In the image of this type of ceremony celebrated on the other side of the Atlantic, the cemeteries brought with them a new way of life à l'americaine and the rites that went with it. The people of Sainte-Mère-Église saw a continuation

June 6, 1945, in the village of Carquebut, an outdoor mass is officiated by an American chaplain.

To the right, wearing a white chasuble, Léon Poisson, the churchwarden, addresses the Abbé Lemercier, the priest of the village. To the left, Raymond De La Rüe, the proprietor of the parcel of land where the temporary cemetery was installed. NARA

of the cultural shock experienced at the Liberation and that each of them had felt. The wonder and fascination they felt when faced with the abundance of American material and the discovery of products "made in USA" left a permanent memory in these Normans who had lacked everything these last four years of Occupation. Once the war was over, the military camps and the temporary airports dismantled, there was nothing left for the witnesses but the temporary cemeteries to get a glimpse of a tiny bit of America "on Norman soil".

The temporary cemeteries, American islands in the heart of the Norman countryside, were spaces that had a meaning, following an architectural logic which was heavy with symbols. For the American designers, there was a desire to mark the cemetery as somewhere different from the exterior world (by means of barriers or dense vegetation) seeking to reinforce the idea that this was a special territory. The continuation of culture shock within the temporary cemeteries resulted in particular from the immaculate treatment of the infrastructures, and the fundamental principle of symmetry, which left visitors with a striking image of the way in which America paid tribute to her dead.

The ceremony of Memorial Day within temporary cemetery n°2, May 30, 1946. NARA

In the cemetery n°1, on Memorial Day, a firing squad fires three shots in honor of the American soldiers fallen in combat in the summer of 1944. NARA

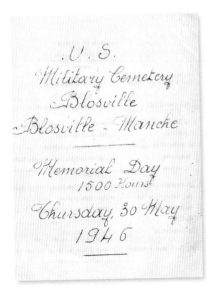

A poster announcing a ceremony for Memorial Day in the cemetery of Blosville.
Collection Airborne Museum

June 20, 1946, "the pilgrims of peace" enter Sainte-Mère-Église where they will visit the American temporary cemeteries. The members of this organized trip come from seven different countries. Among them, fifteen parents have come from the United States to visit the grave of a son fallen in France. NARA

The panels situated at the entry of these sites, the barriers, the architectural rigor mentioned above, the buildings – like the white chapel of cemetery n°2 – all these names with far-away sounds inscribed with a stencil, everything recalled the birthplace of these young men fallen in Normandy.

These places, destinations for a particular kind of outing, fascinated all those who strolled the graveled paths of the temporary cemeteries. They found exaltation of the greatness of sacrifice, an idealized image of a mythical America. To go to the military cemeteries of Sainte-Mère-Église was, all proportions retained, to be the witness of an American show, where the terrifying aspects of war and death on the battlefield seemed to be erased, denied. This staging and beautification of death considerably marked and moved the Normans who were unfamiliar with such sights. In parallel with the collective tributes, they wanted to show their recognition in a personal and private manner.

Among the individual practices that took place inside the temporary cemeteries, meditation was surely the most common. People regularly came and placed flowers on the same grave(s). By the nature of things, people came to adopt, informally, the grave of an illustrious unknown, yet become so familiar in certain respects. The phenomenon of adopting military graves began in July 1944 when Simone Renaud, during the funeral of Brig.-Gen. Roosevelt, took the initiative of adopting his grave to flower it. She later invited other mothers of the village to do the same. A few days earlier, her husband, Alexandre Renaud, had, in his turn, called upon the mothers and women of the village to take care of these military graves. On July 4, 1944, the magazine *The Stars and Stripes* recalled a part of the mayor of Sainte-Mère-Église's speech, reproduced on the next page:

The forty-some pupils of the class of 1935, the "little singers of the American cemeteries" photographed here in temporary cemetery n°1 at the commemoration of 11 November 1918. Collection Airborne Museum

"Ste-Mere-Eglise Folk Pay Tribute to U.S. Dead

By Andy Rooney
(Stars and Stripes Staff Writer)

"STE. MERE EGLISE, July 4- One thousand men and women of this battered little French village paid solemn tribute today to 2,200 American soldiers buried a quarter of a mile from town. Through their mayor, M. Alexander Renaud, they promised that the graves of those soldiers who died to free France would be cared for now and forever by the people of Ste. Mere Eglise.

The ceremony began in the church of Ste. Mere with Frenchmen who made their way here on horseback cart, and bicycle from the surrounding countryside, hearing Mass said for the fallen Americans. Following the prayer, the procession walked slowly in step with the toiling church bell to the cemetery. Two hundred small children leading the procession filed through the rows of new-painted white crosses and knelt to place bouquets of red roses on the soldiers' graves. Flowers had already been placed at the graves of many by the townspeople.

Maj. Ralph W. Yuill, of Cedar Rapids, Iowa, the Allied Officer in charge of the Civil Affairs office here, spoke briefly followed by Mayor Renaud. "These boys who have died for the freedom of France," Mayor Renaud said in English, "would all have mothers and wives at home shedding tears for them. They cannot be here but I can assure them that the mothers and wives of France will take care of these graves now and will continue to care for them when the war is over."[114]

The Levesque family, of the Sigosville stud farm, on a walk to the north of Sainte-Mère-Église. Like many of the families of the village, each Sunday, they would go see the Spitfire carcass abandoned near Pointe-Colette. Collection A. Levesque

The Levesque family and cousins in front of temporary cemetery n°2. Collection A. Levesque

The entry of cemetery n°1. Collection A. Levesque

Then, we headed toward the American cemeteries to "hide out in the USA" for a few minutes, in a way. Here, in cemetery n°1. Collection A. Levesque

Inevitably, a close link was progressively established between the families of Sainte-Mère-Église and the young men who had come from so far. Like Simone Renaud, certain women developed a maternal relationship with the American soldiers much as a mother wolf takes her little ones under her protection.

The neighbors of the cemeteries, these neighbors by circumstance, by process of maternization, became very close in certain cases. In adopting the history of a man, one could forge a link so strong that nothing could break it. This close and indelible link with certain men reinforced the idea that one could be proud of the cemeteries. Proud, because they were concrete witnesses to the suffering endured at the Liberation and which, in the following months, became transcended to a paradise, a garden on earth.

In this way, the American cemeteries of the county of Sainte-Mère-Église, which so marked the countryside, became destinations for walks. They were, at the same time, parks such as had never been seen in this area, and equally, a great source of escapism. These cemeteries, they were America! It was the birth of long Sunday walks with the family, which always ended up in an American cemetery because this was the highlight of the show. The change of scenery was guaranteed, as writes André Levesque in his "Memoires d'outre-bombes" (Memories from beyond the bombs): "After the Sunday meal, if it didn't rain, we went for a hike to the "Spitfire" at Pointe-Colette or else we went out to the American cemetery on the road to Chef-du-Pont. The Americans had buried their dead in two cemeteries on the edges of Sainte-Mère.

Geneviève Marie, 10, is photographed in the cemetery n°1, to immortalize the day of her First Communion. Collection G. Pasquette

Simply called n° 1 and n° 2, they held eight thousand soldiers killed during the first combats of D-Day. [...] Although temporary, these cemeteries equaled the majesty and perfection of the great military cemeteries offering a perspective to the millimeter of their thousands of white crosses and the broad graveled paths leading to the mast where flew the star-spangled banner. [The] trees broke the solitude of the squares of successive graves while giving a false air of a park that encouraged strolling as much as contemplation. We circulated among the alleys trying to count the stars of David, and then we stopped before the grave of Gen. Theodore Roosevelt Jr., the hero of Utah Beach who died of a heart attack a few weeks after D-Day. It was a little corner of America with its little buildings painted white and their porticoes with neo-classical triangular gables. We entered to sign the guest book in one of these little buildings where a friendly soldier received you with a smile, and then we lingered a bit in the tiny chapel with its strange steeple resembling a semaphore; instants of serenity, of respect and of peace that intimidated more than one of us."[115]

For the children of Sainte-Mère-Église, going to the cemetery was a trip to the park. For the adults, the cemetery was a place for socializing where one could meet other families from the village or around. Going further, on certain occasions, after a marriage (a strange honeymoon), or a baptism or a First Communion, people went to the American cemetery to immortalize the occasion on film with this exotic backdrop. This was the case for little Genevieve Marie and her family. July 6, 1946, just after her First Communion whose ceremony was held in the church of Sainte-Mère-Église, the family went to the temporary cemetery n° 1: "It was a meeting place and it was so pretty" recalls the young girl of 10. These surprising practices testify to the close link between the American cemeteries and the inhabitants of Sainte-Mère-Église, these sites having become part of the surroundings of the local families. These were "our" cemeteries!

27 May 1945, Sunday visit in the temporary cemetery of Blosville. One of the men bends over to read the names of soldiers inscribed on the wooden crosses, given that it was strongly discouraged to walk among the graves. NARA

THE CHILDREN OF SAINTE-MÈRE

"And then, there were the festivals! The commemorations of June 6. I spent those days in a state of complete excitement. Everything was known, and everything was unexpected: the arrival of my cousins and the arrival of a president [Vincent Auriol in June 1948]; the songs of the merry-go-rounds and the music of the Republican Guard, the garlands of multicolored lights in Cap-de-Laine and the fireworks paid for by the Americans, the school that let out and the parades of children in the cemeteries. It seemed that the entire population communed in the same joy and happiness of finding themselves together."[116] The childhood memories of André Levesque, 7 in 1946, speaking with a profound nostalgia of the times of the first commemorations of June 6, a time when the village gathered around its history and its dead.

Among the memories of the young man, the one concerning visits to the American cemeteries could seem incredible coming from a child.

The Deloeuvre house, rue de Verdun, decorated in the colors of the liberators, and its little Marianne. Collection Airborne Museum

Flowering cemetery n°2, girls to one side and boys to the other. Collection Airborne Museum

We understand that no one, not even the children of the village, remained indifferent to the grand military cemeteries. Of course, the meaning of death for a child of 7 to 10 remained abstract, and the notion of "park" came back often. In the heart of these very particular "parks", children had a prime role. They were active participants in the ceremonies as Geneviève Marie recalls: "We often went to the cemeteries of Sainte-Mère-Église with the school. By the way, I never went to Blosville. In these cemeteries, we were to go deposit bouquets that our parents had made. Starting in June 1945, we began singing "The Star-Spangled Banner" and "The Marseillaise". The rest of the time, our teachers, M. Leblond and Mlle. Burnouf, required an absolute silence in the cemeteries. "Not a word!" they said."[117]

The cover of "Le Monde Illustré" (The World Illustrated) of August 23, 1947, staging a young boy (Maurice Renaud) flowering the grave of Gen. Roosevelt, symbol of the recognition of all of France. Private Collection

M. Leblond, teacher, with his tuning fork, making his children of the class of 1935 sing for the ceremony of June 6, 1946. The children had learned a translated version of the American hymn and "La Marseillaise". On this occasion, M. Leblond, a bit disappointed, said, "Boys, you have sabotaged my Marseillaise!" Collection Airborne Museum

The school-children of Sainte-Mère-Église walking in close ranks in the paths of cemetery n°2, in June 1946, in order to deposit flowers on the graves of American soldiers. Collection Airborne Museum

In the cemetery n°2, American veterans and children of Sainte-Mère-Église attend the ceremonies of June 6, 1947. NARA Film

On June 6, 1945, Huguette Bosvy distributes cookies to the American veterans. Collection Airborne Museum

Near the square of Sainte-Mère-Église, June 6 1945, young Claude Pezeril proudly at the wheel of his jeep. Behind him are Huguette Bosvy (with her traditional bonnet) and Raymonde Endelin. Collection Airborne Museum

Under the influence of the mayor of the village and of his wife, Simone Renaud, the children of Sainte-Mère-Église were integrated into the ceremonies with the idea of establishing a strong symbol: that of a combat against forgetting. By involving the next generation, they were guaranteeing the longevity of local memory. In 1945, the tribute to the heroes of June 6 and to the American veterans was marked by numerous costumed children, proudly sporting military outfits gathered from here and there... but also of objects picked up on the battlefield after the the end of the war. At the request of Mrs Renaud, organizer of the festivities, those who people called "the little paratroopers" paraded in the streets of the town, causing a sensation.

Very early on, Alexandre Renaud realized it would be essential to involve the children of Sainte-Mère-Église in the construction of this great edifice of memory, for which they in their turn would one day be responsible. Because the children of Sainte-Mère had been deprived of everything during the years of the Occupation, at an age when their minds would normally be opening up to the world around them, Mr Renaud organized festive and joyous gatherings – sort of group therapies – aimed at these young people who had just lived through moments which were as brutal as they were inexplicable. For example, in July 1944, an "afternoon performance" was organized in honor of the children of the village. In a document with the overtones of a testament, Alexandre Renaud raised the fear of forgetting this epic story.

"The little paratroopers" of Simone Renaud, featuring the helmets and haversacks found on the battlefield after the combats, but also a Colt 45. From right to left, Yves Cornière, Gaby Besselièvre, Claude Pezeril and, in the background, Lucienne Bodin holding her daughter in her arms.

Gabriel Besselièvre, right,
in the arms of Francis
Lamoureux, veteran of the
508th PIR. Claude Pezeril,
left, shows off his Colt 45.

Collection Airborne Museum

July 1944: in the American camp situated in proximity to the provisional airport of La Londe, east of Sainte-Mère-Église, a show of "son et lumière" (sound and light) was organized in honor of the children of the village. Geneviève Marie would say: "There were candies and jam, everything was there!" In the left picture, the children of Sainte-Mère and the Renaud couple to the right.
Collection Airborne Museum

"TO THE LITTLE CHILDREN OF SAINTE-MÈRE-ÉGLISE

At a party organized for them this summer by the American troops of the aviation camp at La Londe, I told them that they had just lived the most extraordinary fairy tale that anyone had ever dreamed of writing for them. On a soft night of June, delicately lit by the moon, they saw, by the light of a fire and its alarms, men, their faces covered with soot, armed with machine guns and daggers, come down from the sky to grab the first strongholds of the German fortress. They saw all around them, in the crash of the shells and the whistling of tracer bullets, the battle, the killing, the deaths of their parents or beloved others. They saw, finally, on their roofs, the great parachutes of silk, white, red, green and gold, floating in the great sun like immense cocoons emptied of their butterflies, then serving as a shroud to our dead.

I would like them, aided by this little book which will tell them exactly what happened, to guard all their lives this page of History of which Sainte-Mère-Église was the theater.

When we, the adults, have disappeared, I would like these little children, become grandmothers and grandfathers in their turn, to gather their little ones together in June each year to tell them the story of the great drama of Sainte-Mère-Église.

Time will have done its usual work, the real facts will have faded, other stories will have been created from scratch in the course of the years by popular imagination, and the storytellers of that time may embroider their tales, without reducing their plausibility, fantastic and marvelous actions next to which our epic tales will be as faded as the Trojan horse."[118]

The little Renée Catherine in her dress of camouflaged parachute silk. Collection Airborne Museum

THE BEGINNINGS OF MEMORIAL TOURISM

The numerous visitors who flow into the burg of Sainte-Mère-Église today during the summer season, come back again and again to see the famous paratrooper hanging from the bell tower. Here, time has stopped, some will think. Then the visit to this sanctuary of memory will be followed by a little visit to the museum (opened in 1964) dedicated to the airborne troops and situated on the edges of the village square. This is the usual form of the immersive experience that brings visitors from the four corners of the earth. The stalls and the souvenir shops have progressively replaced the small businesses selling basic goods, which pleases the tourists if not the inhabitants.

But, in 1946, none of these attractions were in place for the very first visitors. For it didn't take long to see the curious of the region as well as the occasional American family arrive. Several travel agencies of the Paris region or in the north of France were already offering trips to English and American families to come to see what remained of the battlefield, or, in certain cases, to find the grave of a son or a husband. On May 18, 1946, the travel company, *Westel Père et Fils*, based in Lille, addressed the letter below to the Prefect of La Manche:

« **Grand International Tourism**
WESTEL VOYAGES
in Pullman motor coaches

Monsieur the Prefect,

We have the honor of informing you that our organization, specialized in TOURISM BY MOTOR COACH, is currently establishing the itineraries for voyages whose aim is to facilitate for English and American families a pilgrimage to the graves of those who made the supreme sacrifice on French soil.

These voyages will bring many visitors to your department, and we beg to request, M. the Prefect, that you be so kind as to ask your services to inform us, as soon as possible, of the exact location of the military cemeteries of your region.

This would simplify the task of examining the important matter of hotel accommodation in the vicinity of these burial grounds.

With our thanks in advance." [119]

It is clear that at this time, only the three cemeteries of the county of Sainte-Mère-Église were of notable touristic and historical interest. The document reproduced on the next page thus listed in January 1946, on behalf of the Prefect of the Manche, the sites of the department that would be of particular interest when it came to arranging touristic circuits in the region. Concerning Sainte-Mère-Église and the American cemeteries, it was specified: "The touristic attraction of the localities where the American cemeteries lie consists above all of the enormous memory of the allied landing in Normandy. These localities are all found in the county of Sainte-Mère-Église, the first beachhead of the Americans in Normandy."

If tourism had to come, it would concentrate around the temporary cemeteries of the county. As the last tangible traces of the terrible confrontations of the summer of 1944, the cemeteries would have to constitute the "objects of appeal" of the department of La Manche.

Consequently, a whole series of new infrastructures would have to be built around them which would be capable of receiving future visitors in increasing numbers each year. New services should be developed around these – hotels at first – and new shops able to respond to a demand which was impossible to predict.

In a Normandy battered by the war, it quickly became a case of enhancing the historic wealth of this territory. The touristic and economic potential led the French government, at the highest level, to set up structures capable of responding to the requirements linked to memorial tourism for the departments of La Manche and Calvados. In February 1946, the sub-prefect of Cherbourg addressed a report to the prefect of La Manche in which he drew up an inventory of infrastructure work to be carried out in the department:

"The Allied Road", between Sainte-Marie-du-Mont and Quinéville remained, in certain areas, impassable in 1946. Departmental Archives of La Manche

18 February 1946, the Sub-Prefect of Cherbourg to M. the Prefect of La Manche
Subject: road repair in the county of Sainte-Mère-Église.

The projects developed by the government and by the commission of the Republic in Rouen in relation to the infrastructure for tourism in Lower-Normandy, in order to welcome foreign and especially American visitors who may come to see the battlefields of D-Day, require preparation not only of hotels but also of the roads. [...] I would like to draw your particular attention to the urgency of planning improvements to the roads in the sector between Montebourg and Carentan. In this sector, the Americans will visit:

1. The cemeteries of Sainte-Mère-Église and Blosville
2. The zone Picauville – Chef-du-Pont – Carquebut and Sainte-Mère-Église where the landing of paratroopers of the 82nd division took place.
3. The zone of the beaches of Sainte-Marie-du-Mont to Foucarville where the D-Day Landings took place

The only way of entering these zones is by automobile, using roads which, with the exception of National 13 from Cherbourg to Carentan, are departmental and local. However, the principal roads needed for this tourist activity are barely usable [...].

I believe it will be of the greatest interest to seek by all possible means to plan and implement a concrete program of road repair by intervening with the various ministerial departments concerned in order to ensure that the means be given to the Bridges and Roads Service to carry out this useful task.

The sub-prefect"[120]

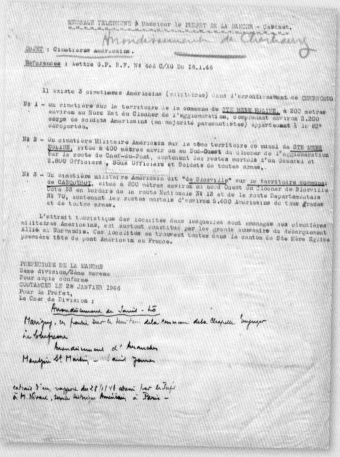

Departmental Archives of La Manche

The French government, through the departmental authorities, was thus involved from the outset in the creation of memorial tourism in Normandy. The aim was to remember D-Day of course, but equally and principally, to launch an economically significant activity, in a little corner of France that had missed the advance of industrialization which had started in the second half of the XIXth century. Earlier, in May 1945, Raymond Triboulet, at the time sub-prefect of Bayeux, had created the D-Day Committee, an association aimed at promoting this recent heritage. All means were put to work to seize this opportunity, and on March 26, 1946, a first report, written by the chief engineer of the Bridges and Roads Service for the department of La Manche, laid out the first sketches of a tourism circuit in the county of Sainte-Mère-Église:

"Creation of tourist circuits in the region of Sainte-Mère-Église

Report of the engineer   Cherbourg, March 26, 1946

I. Tourist circuits organized in the region of Sainte-Mère-Église

If we want to make an effort this year to develop tourism facilities in the region of Sainte-Mère-Église where the landings of D-Day and the parachute landing of the *82nd division* took place, we must limit ourselves in the immediate to a certain number of circuits because all of the roads in this region are in very poor condition. The most we can do, taking into account the possibility of installing a hotel in the former prison camp of Foucarville, would appear to be the creation of two circuits as follows:

1. Circuit A – permitting a visit of the D-Day landing sites (*Utah Beach*) and the numerous remains of German fortifications: Foucarville, D 14 as far as its intersection with D 70, D70 toward the Grande Dune, La Madeleine, the Allied road, D 421 to Quinéville, D 42 until its intersection with D 14, D 14, Foucarville.

2. Circuit B - to visit the sites of the 82nd division's parachute landings and the cemeteries of Blosville and of Sainte-Mère-Église, Foucarville, D 14, D 70, Sainte-Marie-du-Mont, Chef-du-Pont, D 67, Sainte-Mère-Église, National 13, Montebourg, D 42 to its intersection with D 14, D 14, Foucarville.

II. Current state of the circuits

The map, enclosed, shows the current condition of the circuits: red marks those roads in good condition, blue in poor condition, and green those in very bad condition. It appears that only National 13 is in an acceptable condition. Elsewhere, the bomb holes have not been properly filled.

Archives départementales de la Manche.

Region of Sainte-Mère-Église: tourist circuits.
Departmental Archives of La Manche

III. Work to be done.

In order to make these circuits practicable for tourists, circuits for motor coaches will probably be created. Also, the roads must be restored completely and, in particular, must be blacktopped if we wish the traffic to flow comfortably in the summer. [...]

(f) Implementation of the work

Experience shows that installing a company in these underprivileged regions poses problems that the administration will have to resolve. [...] Replenishing the labor force with locals should be considered impossible as they will be busy, in the months to come, with agricultural activities. We will need to bring in workers from outside. Given the changes that are beginning to be felt in the region, we believe that it is not opportune to call on German prisoners of war. French workers will have lodgings in the camp of Foucarville as it seems impossible to find other types of lodgings in this stricken region.

VII. Necessary credits: 37 million."

A hotel project in the former prison camp in Foucarville, repairing the roads of the area, creation – or at least sustainability – of local businesses, all these factors showed the revitalization of the county of Sainte-Mère-Église, until now "under-privileged". One can imagine the enthusiasm of the local officials and the inhabitants for these proposed changes.

Thanks, in particular, to the presence of the American cemeteries, the principal tourism sites of the county along with *Utah Beach*, hope reappeared in the years immediately after the war, marked for example by a poor harvest in 1945 or the continued presence of rationing. The country was slowly recovering from the trauma engendered by the war and, as far as Sainte-Mère-Église was concerned, one could hope because, for a number of reasons, they owed a great deal to the great American military cemeteries.

Except, the idyll suddenly came to an end. The private wish, shared by everyone, to conserve the American cemeteries, was threatened and then destroyed from 1947, when the government of the United States decided to put in place a project of repatriation and of transferring the bodies of American soldiers to two permanent national cemeteries situated in Colleville-sur-Mer (Calvados) and Saint-James (Manche). This generated a profound sadness among the locals who, time after time, had shown their desire to keep their cemeteries, their soldiers, their liberators. They had always tried to forget, deliberately, that these military cemeteries were nevertheless qualified as "TEMPORARY".

Key elements of the future visitors circuit, the American cemeteries (here, n°2) constituted one of the last material testimonies of D-Day. NARA

Sainte-Marie-du-Mont, a stop on the tourist circuit in 1946. NARA

The church (reserved for American military) built in the German prison camp at Foucarville. In 1946, there was a project to convert this giant camp in order to make a hotel complex. NARA

Alexandre Renaud detaching an American parachute from an apple tree. Published August 23, 1947 in Le Monde Illustré, this photo carried the following caption: "And even now, they decorate the room where the wedding meal, or a first communion takes place using carefully conserved parachutes." Private Collection

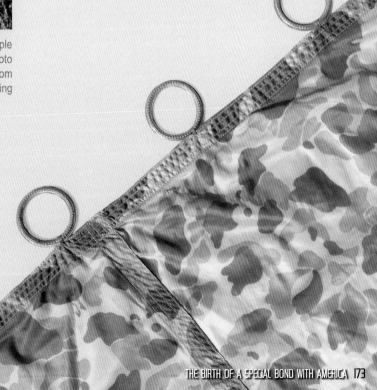

This camouflaged parachute was transformed into a curtain after the war.
Collection M. Rosiers

The repatriation of the bodies of American soldiers to the United States or one of the national cemeteries abroad was started in May 1946. 59% of the bodies initially interred in Normandy were conveyed by boat from Fall 1947 until Winter 1948 in order to repose near their families. This coffin, covered by an American flag, would be sent to the depot of Tourlaville, near Cherbourg, before being loaded on a transport ship, bound for New York. NARA

DON'T TOUCH "OUR DEAD"

LA DISPARITION
DES CIMETIÈRES AMÉRICAINS
DE SAINTE-MÉRE-ÉGLISE

A diverses reprises, la population de Sainte-Mère-Eglise avait
manifesté le désir de conserver
les deux cimetières où sont inhu-
més les corps des nombreux soldats américains tombés pour la
__ la France. En effet,

la côte de la Manche, si un des cimetières militaires américains de Sainte-
Mère-Eglise pourrait être conservé com-
me lieu de sépulture des soldats américains tombés au cours des premiers
combats qui marquèrent la Campagne
de Libération de la France.
    Le Gouvernement des Etats-Unis ap-
précie hautement le sentiment qui a
__ demande. Il ne vous échap-

Toward the closure of the temporary cemeteries

THE REPATRIATION PLAN FOR THE BODIES OF AMERICAN SOLDIERS

During the two world conflicts, America differentiated itself from the other European belligerents in the way it treated its dead. Contrary to the British, German or French who, in principle, remained close to the battlefield where they were killed, the American army wished to bring the bodies of those who died so far from home, back to the soil of the mother country. Even though this young country had suffered severely in 1917 and 1918 and during the Second World War, it remained nonetheless inexperienced in its ability to conceive of death *en masse* on foreign soil. In the aftermath of the First World War, this new situation led the United States government to revise its policy concerning military casualties under the influence of the families of the dead and American society in general. Should they repatriate the bodies of soldiers, sailors and pilots killed on European soil? In 1919, a strong message was sent by Theodore Roosevelt who, on the subject of his own son, Quentin, killed in France on board his fighter plane, had stated in a metaphorical fashion: "Let the tree lie where it has fallen..." Public opinion, in turn, showed signs of a change of attitude, and, in 1919, the Department of War began to ask the 77,091 American families who had lost a son or a husband in WWI whether they wished the deceased to repose in a permanent national cemetery across the ocean. The outcome of this inquiry was that 35% of American families wished to see cemeteries created in Europe.

During the fighting in North Africa, toward the end of 1942, when Tunisia was taken by the American forces, it became necessary once again to respond to the wishes of some of the families who wished their dead to be returned to the United States. Pending the end of hostilities, bodies would be buried in temporary cemeteries, until the question of returning them to their families could be addressed.

On May 16, 1944, the President of the United States, Harry Truman, approved the financing of the repatriation plan to bring back the dead, military and civilian, as well as the project of establishing several permanent cemeteries situated overseas, all of which was the responsibility of the Quartermaster General. As in 1919, America and

The "Request for the Disposition of Remains" sent to the families of soldiers temporarily buried overseas during the Second World War. Here, the copy sent by Ruth Huie, the wife of 1st Lt. Fieldon B. Huie Jr, commander of HQ Co; 2/ IR (*4th Infantry Division*), killed on June 23, 1944 in Digosville and buried at Saint-Mère-Église. Like 41% of American families, she chose to let her husband's remains repose in Norrmandy. NARA

its public powers would take charge of the transfer of bodies, entrusting the Quartermaster Corps of the American Army with the task of setting up the enormous logistics operation. In May 1946, Congress authorized beginning the transfer, thus launching the first phase of the return plan (or non-return plan) of Armed Forces Dead. This first phase consisted of consulting, for each soldier, the legal representative of the deceased, in other words, the widow, the father, the mother or, failing this, a brother or sister, aged 21 or older. Between August 1946 and September 1947, thousands of families received a letter in the post accompanying a form entitled "Request for disposition of remains". Below is presented a letter written by the Quartermaster General to, in this case, Ruth Huie of Conway, Arkansas. Before the war, this young woman, with her husband, Fieldon B. Huie, Jr, ran a shoe shop in town. But, on June 23, 1944, her husband was killed while fighting to take Cherbourg.

« 1st Lt Fieldon B. Huie Jr, 0-338024
Plot P, Row 10, Grave 181)
United States Military Cemetery, Ste-Mère-Eglise n°1, France
Mrs Fieldon B. Huie Jr
Conway, Arkansas   23 September 1947
Dear Mrs. Huie,

The people of the United States, through the Congress have authorized the disinterment and final burial of the heroic dead of World War II. The Quartermaster General of the Army has been entrusted with this sacred responsibility to the honored dead. The records of the War Department indicate that you may be the nearest relative of the above-named deceased, who gave his life in the service of his country.

The enclosed pamphlets, "Disposition of World War II Armed Forces Dead", and "American Cemeteries", explain the disposition, options and services made available to you by your government. If you are the next of kin according to the line of kinship as set forth in the enclosed pamphlet, "Disposition of World War II Armed Forces Dead", you are invited to express your wishes as to the disposition of the remains of the deceased by completing Part 1 of the enclosed form "Request for Disposition of Remains". [...]

Will you please complete the enclosed form, "Request for Disposition of Remains" and mail in the enclosed self-addressed envelope, which requires no postage, within 30 days after its receipt by you? Its prompt return will avoid unnecessary delays.

Sincerely,
Thomas B. Larkin
Major General - The Quartermaster General

"Options to be given next of kin"

Option 1 – The remains be interred in a permanent American military cemetery overseas. The establishment of permanent American military cemeteries overseas in the various areas in which American forces served is contemplated.

Option 2 – The remains be returned to the United States or any possession or territory thereof, for interment by next of kin in a private cemetery. Shipment will be made to the city or town designated by the next of kin.

Option 3 – The remains be shipped within, or returned to a foreign country, the homeland of the deceased or next of kin, for interment by next of kin in a private cemetery. Shipment to a foreign country is dependent on the ability of the United States to obtain entry and reinterment authority therein. If authority can be obtained, shipment will be made tyo the city or town designated by the next of kin.

Option 4 – The remains be returned to the United States for final interment in a national cemetery. When this option is desired, the remains will be transported to the continental United States and interred in a national cemetery selected by the next of kin. Burial in the national cemetery is subject to availability of space therein.

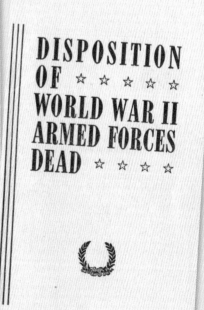

The little booklet entitled "Disposition of World War II Armed Forces Dead", sent systematically to the next of kin of the dead to inform them of the different options of transfer or of repatriation offered to American families. Private Collection.

A PERMANENT CEMETERY IN THE COUNTY OF SAINT-MÈRE-ÉGLISE?

Gen. John J. Pershing (1860-1948). NARA

To put in place a program of repatriation and the transfer of the bodies of American soldiers to the permanent national cemeteries, a partnership was set up at the end of 1945 between the *American Graves Registration Command* (AGRC) and the *American Battle Monuments Commission* (ABMC). Since its creation, in 1923, the prime task of the ABMC[121] had been the mounting and maintenance of American monuments to the First World War, under the presidency of the instigator of this commission, Gen. John J. Pershing, former commander of the American expeditionary forces between 1917 and 1918.

> **"Headquarters**
> **American Graves Registration Command**
> **European Theater of Operations / APO 887 US Army**
>
> Mr. John E. Harbeson / Mssrs. Harbeson, Hough, Livingston
> 1510 Architects Building / Philadelphia 3, PA
>
> Dear Mr. Harbeson,   6 November 1946
>
> You will find in these lines our response to your letter of October 24, addressed to Gen. North [ABMC] in which was joined the sketches and a few notes relative to the different permanent cemeteries proposed for the European theater of operations. [...]
>
> Concerning our discussion and commentaries relative to the previous plans for Sainte-Mère-Église n°2, I am joining to this letter a new proposition for the cemetery which will satisfy your point of view in relation to the "tightness" of the site. I enclose also our first schema concerning the cemetery of Blosville which we have elaborated according to your remarks. To the extent that the new plan for Sainte-Mère-Église n°2 puts aside your preceding objections, we believe we can let Blosville go in favor of Sainte-Mère-Église n°2. Your comments on this possibility will be welcome.
>
> Sincerely,
>
>   I.R. Talbot
>   **Colonel QMC**
>   Head cemetery landscaper [122] »

It was only from May 21, 1934, that the commission was also charged with the maintenance of American cemeteries based abroad. After World War II, a particular responsibility of the ABMC and its secretary, Gen. Thomas North (from April 1946), was to take part in the selection of overseas sites which would host the permanent military cemeteries and to deal with the acquisition of the land in question. Secondly, the commission would be charged with the planning and development of the cemeteries as well as the choice of monuments to be included. While the ABMC were responsible for the caskets, the procedure of re-interment itself fell to the Department of War, represented on site by the Quartermaster and the AGRC.

The repatriation plan, written by the Department of War in September 1945, provided for the construction of 5 cemeteries on French soil. Given the large number of soldiers buried in Normandy (31,886 American soldiers), it was decided that one or even several potential sites capable of accommodating great permanent national cemeteries should be selected. Very rapidly, Maj. Littlejohn, commander of the AGRC in Europe, was attracted to the site of Saint-Laurent-sur-Mer, overlooking *Omaha Beach*. The site combined a breathtaking landscape and, above all, historical significance of prime importance. In this respect, Sainte-Mère-Église was as strong as any other potential sites. In a report dated July 29, 1946, written by the Quartermaster General, three sites were considered: Saint-Laurent-sur-Mer, Sainte-Mère-Église n° 2 and Paris.[123]

"Description and critique of the project to create a permanent cemetery at Sainte-Mère-Église by the architect Harbeson

Ste Mère Eglise n°2. (Retention Priority III) Visited August 29, 1946

"Just off the same road as Blosville Cemetery, Ste Mère Eglise cemetery n°2 was established just eighteen days after the initial landings in France: here are buried many of the men who took part of the Invasion by means of planes, gliders and parachutes. The village is typically Norman, with an interesting old church, the tower of which is in view of this property. The surroundings have natural beauty. There are buried here 4812, among them General Theodore Roosevelt.

The reason that this site is not recommended in preference to that of Blosville is architectural. To develop it, the long pasture on the east side should be included: the main axis would then run approximately north-south, at an angle to the road, the entrance at the north end, the chapel on the higher ground at the south, the burial area somewhat pentagonal in shape, but with arcs at the north and south. It is recommended that it should hold 3500 graves – a few more could be accommodated. This property is smaller than that at Blosville."

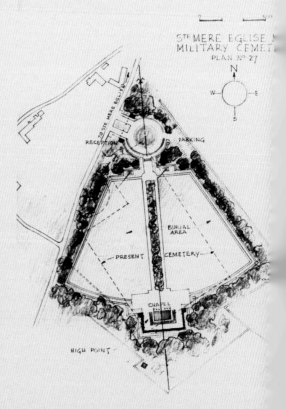

"Description and critique of the project to create a permanent cemetery at Blosville by the architect Harbeson

Blosville Cemetery. (Retention Priority II) Visited August 29, 1946

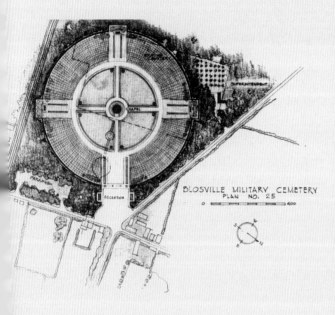

BLOSVILLE MILITARY CEMETERY
PLAN NO. 25

"Blosville Cemetery, twenty miles south of Cherbourg, is in typical hedgerow country surrounding, and is itself surrounded by hedgerows of elm trees clipped of their lower branches, on a main highway. Those living nearby come frequently bringing flowers, 300 to 500 visitors on a Sunday, coming in bus loads from Cherbourg. [...]

It is recommended that the hedgerows character be retained in development. The main axis should be normal to the highway, the chapel on the higher land near the road, the superintendent's house at the eastern end of this northern strip. The two small fields at the east should be included in the property. There are now 5702 buried here: it is proposed to accommodate 3500 in in the new development at the proper spacing."

"Description and critique of the project to create a permanent cemetery at St Laurent sur Mer by the architect Harbeson

St Laurent sur Mer Cemetery. (Retention Priority I) Visited August 29, 1946

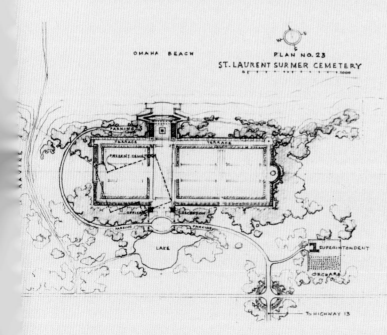

OMAHA BEACH
PLAN NO. 23
ST. LAURENT SUR MER CEMETERY

"This cemetery is on a high bluff directly overlooking the English Channel, Omaha landing beach and a gully used by the American troops making their entry on to the plateau of Normandy. It was inaugurated by the First Army shortly after the D-Day landings: to it were moved the bodies of those who had been buried on the beach itself. Intimately connected with the landing operation, with a magnificent view of the sea and the man-made breakwater, and with vestiges of German fortifications still visible, this site is unique, and is recommended for first consideration for retention."

The village of Sainte-Mère-Église was thus in the running to obtain a permanent military cemetery – for a while. Then, the likelihood of seeing a permanent cemetery built in the county increased, when a few months later the site of Blosville was preselected along with Saint-James (south Manche).

In October 1946, a group of architects based in Philadelphia made a first series of plans to be presented to Gen. Littlejohn, commander of the AGRC. In return, in a letter dated November 6, 1946, Col. Talbot, head landscaper of the AGRC, modified these plans.

A permanent cemetery in Sainte-Mère-Église? Or in Blosville? The idea was seriously considered as shown in the previous pages. However, construction of a second cemetery in Normandy would depend on the actual number of bodies that would remain in place. Procrastination followed during the first half of 1947; nevertheless, it seems that the fate of Sainte-Mère-Église was decided at the beginning of that year, considering the report published after the 49th meeting of the ABMC which was held February 13, 1947. It was reported: "On the recommendation of Mr. Baldwin, the commission has unanimously decided that the permanent cemeteries should be established at St Laurent sur Mer and at Blosville, and that the St. James cemetery should remain open awaiting the confirmation of its eventual utility as a permanent cemetery dependent upon the answers given by its closest members. Mr. Biffle has asked the architect for recommendations regarding choosing Blosville over Sainte Mère Eglise n°2." [124]

Blosville was the final hope for the inhabitants of the county of Sainte-Mère-Église – who knew nothing of these negotiations – to see some of the American bodies remain in place. In other words, remain part of their history... This dream,

harbored by the entire village, finally came to an end with the 50th meeting of the ABMC, May 15, 1947, when the question of the Norman cemeteries was decided: "Saint James or Blosville. For the sector of Normandy, the Quartermaster General parted from 25% of the bodies remaining overseas, the cemetery of St Laurent sur Mer would suffice, however, to commemorate the military operations by a cemetery in place of a monument, then Blosville or St James would be susceptible for establishing a second cemetery in this zone. St James has the preference of the Quartermaster General by the nature of the ground. P.S.: Blosville should be abandoned." [125]

In the end, ten sites were retained in June 1947[126], of which five were French. The total number was raised to fourteen by the end of this same year when the permanent cemeteries were officially named. Two such names were attributed to the cemeteries on Norman soil: *NORMANDY AMERICAN CEMETERY* and *MEMORIAL* (Colleville-sur-Mer) and *BRITTANY AMERICAN CEMETERY* and *MEMORIAL* (Saint-James).

Some would say that Sainte-Mère-Église and its surroundings almost got a great permanent military cemetery. If the opinion of the inhabitants was totally ignored by the different American authorities (AGRC and ABMC), the citizens of Sainte-Mère-Église did everything possible to attempt to conserve at least some of the American graves.

Between 1946 and 1947, Alexandre Renaud and his wife launched several desperate attempts in the direction of the highest American dignitaries, without success. In their various letters, the Renaud couple made a point of emphasizing in every possible way, the very close link which had been established between the soldiers buried in the temporary cemeteries and the inhabitants of Sainte-Mère-Église. There were such strong feelings bound up with these cemeteries that, were they to disappear, it would be synonymous with a profound injustice.

'AS THE TREE FALLS, SO SHALL IT LIE"

Alexandre Renaud first heard the news about the establishment of a permanent American cemetery at the end of 1946, no doubt from the superintendent of the two temporary cemeteries of Sainte-Mère-Église, Sgt. Eitland. The future of these thousands of graves was finally being decided, after months of uncertainty. One can easily imagine the relief of the mayor, who saw in this great news both the long term preservation of the profound bond established with America since 1944 and also opportunities in terms of the economic development of the county. These American cemeteries were now part of the decor, and the mayor longed to know the final verdict.

We now know that no site in the county of Sainte-Mère-Église was selected by the Americans to host a national permanent cemetery. When, during the summer of 1947, the village learned – with stupefaction – the very bad news, one can understand the feeling of injustice that seized everyone and particularly the Renaud couple who had invested so much energy in building the relationship between the American cemeteries and the inhabitants. Alexandre and Simone Renaud had succeeded in giving meaning to these spaces by trying to make the white crosses "speak". Mme Renaud, as usual, took up her pen to describe her profound sadness. In 1947, she wrote a poem which committed to paper her bitterness:

The announcement of the closing of the three cemeteries of Sainte-Mère-Église resounded then like a pure and simple profanation, inconceivable for these highly religious Normans. "It was considered a sacrilege!" says Henri-Jean Renaud, second son

of the mayor of the time. If there were any justice, then the bodies of the American soldiers should legitimately rest eternally at Sainte-Mère-Église; this was the idea with which Alexandre Renaud was

"As the tree falls, so shall it lie

THEY want to tear out the white crosses
And their poor sleeping bodies
From the sacred ground of this country
Where, like the eagles of la Manche

THEY had come, full of pride
Juvenile, and of proud gaiety
They, who one had laid down without a casket
Deepest in this earth.

THEY came from so far
To give peace to our pastures
Ah! Let them have this humble corner
Of the Norman ground – no more -
THEY came from so high
To save the saint Liberty
Leave the little painted crosses

Indicate from Heaven their tombs
SEE these thousands of white crosses
Shoot up from the grass with flowers
Leave their ashes under our branches
As their names are in our hearts

WHO will know them, Who loves them
In the cemetery over there ? ...
Let us keep them! Don't take them away
Softness; the supreme pride

OF watching over these pure remains
And the names whose consonances
Far off should be on
All the lips of France

AND as implored this Mother
Her forehead lined by pain
"Do not disturb their dust
As the tree falls, so shall it lie!"[127]

Simone Renaud

obsessed. With the energy of despair, he threw a bottle into the sea in August 1947 when he wrote a long pamphlet of four pages giving the reasons for which the American cemeteries should remain in this little corner of Normandy. The mayor hoped that those responsible for the AGRC and the ABMC would revise the case of "Sainte-Mère-Église".

Determined, Alexandre Renaud did not hesitate to request the support of influential personalities such as Mrs. Eleanor Roosevelt, the widow of Gen. Theodore Roosevelt Jr (buried in cemetery n°2). A close, visibly sincere bond had been created between the Renaud couple and Mrs. Roosevelt by means of numerous letters since 1944. A veritable spokesperson for the American cemeteries of Sainte-Mère-Église in the United States, Eleanor Roosevelt tried a number of times to convince the members of the AGRC and the ABMC to preserve the cemeteries.

Alexandre and Simone Renaud meditate on the grave of Lt. Joseph Baker, buried in cemetery n°2. Collection H-J. Renaud

Other great ambassadors such as Generals Ridgway and Gavin were called upon before a final letter to the chief of the allied expeditionary forces was finally addressed in June 1944, Gen. Dwight D. Eisenhower. This letter, dated September 1947, restated more concisely the same arguments as those of the preceding month of August. On October 10, 1947, the response came without appeal. Lt. Col. John H. Michaelis, assistant to the general and veteran of D-Day (date at which he was placed at the head of the *502nd PIR*) took pains to respond to the mayor of Sainte-Mère-Église: "St. Laurent was chosen as the premier site for the simple reason that it was the first cemetery established during the invasion of Europe and its location at Omaha Beach lends itself admirably to the creation of a permanent cemetery. Three sites were taken into consideration for the second cemetery in this zone. These were Saint James, Sainte-Mère-Église n°2 and Blosville. Saint-Mère-Église n°2 has no significance, historically speaking, to the extent that is was established to take the overflow of Sainte-Mère-Église n°1. Sainte-Mère-Église n°1 was not taken into account as the sector is small and nearly half the graves belong to the enemy[128]. Sainte-Mère-Église n°1 and Sainte-Mère-Église n°2 are adjacent to the village, which would interfere with satisfactory development. Blosville is considered inappropriate for the same reason. History and the nature of the terrain of the cemetery of Saint-James have determined its selection as the second permanent cemetery in the west of France."[129]

J. H. MICHAELIS
Lt. Colonel, ADC
Aide to General Eisenhower

The dice were thus thrown and the program of transferring the bodies to other places became reality on November 23, 1947. On this date, the American cemetery of Carquebut was officially closed to the public. There remained only a handful of months for the inhabitants of Sainte-Mère-Église to say goodbye to the two remaining cemeteries on either side of the village. They would have to mourn the loss of these two beloved cemeteries. They had to reason that whatever one said, even if there was no tangible trace left of the Landings of June 1944, there remained to the people here two immaterial and precious things: the memory of the events, but also the inalienable bond with the entire nation of the United States. Geneviève Pasquette remembers this period marked by the closing of the American cemeteries: "We were sad, that's for sure. They had taken away a big piece of our beautiful history. For us, the kids, this was a great wrenching ..."[130]

Letter dated September 1947 written by Alexandre Renaud to Gen. Dwight D. Eisenhower. Collection H.-J. Renaud

The local newspaper published, in Fall 1947, an article entitled "The disappearance of the American cemeteries from Sainte-Mère-Église" which recaptured the letter addressed to Paris by the American ambassador in reply to one sent a little earlier by the Deputy (Congressman) of La Manche, M. Lucas. Collection H.-J. Renaud

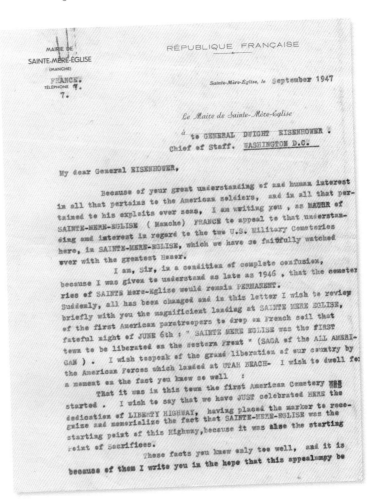

« Sainte-Mère-Église August 1947.

Le Maire de Sainte-Mère-Église

TO WHOM IT MAY CONCERN.
A REQUEST TO MAINTAIN AS PERMANENT THE AMERICAN MILITARY
CEMETERIES 1 and 2 at SAINTE-MERE-EGLISE.

In NORMANDY, there was an unbelievable shock when we learned that the American Cemeteries at SAINT-MERE-EGLISE were not to be permanent, since they had already been placed on a list of American cemeteries which were to remain on the soil of FRANCE with that status. [...]

These cemeteries, which numerically are the most important American cemeteries in NORMANDY are also of great historical significance. They are situated on the peninsula of CHERBOURG, in the heart of UTAH BEACH where the first Divisions of paratroopers and troops came from the sea to meet and give battle- they are placed in the first village of FRANCE to be liberated on the Western Front, and they are the FIRST American cemeteries opened on the soil of FRANCE.

The white crosses appear as a sort of guard of Honor along the National Highway number 13, in the center of the Peninsula, midway between CHERBOURG and SAINT LO, and this in this village of SAINTE-MERE-EGLISE where thousands of American soldiers debarked and which has been called "a Memorial Town".

On the 16th of September, in the presence of Members of the American Legion and Mrs. Theodore ROOSEVELT, Widow of General Theodore ROOSEVELT who rests in our Cemetery number 2, will be solemnly inaugurated here in SAINTE-MERE-EGLISE, the FIRST marker of the LIBERTY-HIGHWAY (SAINTE-MERE-EGLISE) which memorializes the historic place of the beginning of the battles (combats) of this War.

The proximity of this first marker and of the American cemeteries at SAINTE-MERE-EGLISE have a deep significance and at the same time it is a moving spectacle.
We understand very well that the little military cemeteries isolated and far from communication should be regrouped in larger and geographically better located places.

BUT, the cemeteries of SAINTE-MERE-EGLISE are among the most beautiful according to the unanimous opinion of people who have visited the various American cemeteries and they are among those most frequented by visitors from all nations.

Being situated as they are, at the very entrance of SAINTE-MERE-EGLISE, there are many French ceremonials which take place in these cemeteries during the year, and the inhabitants of our little town, because of true devotion and unrecompensed gesture decorate the graves with flowers. A few days ago, even "Les Petits Chanteurs à la Croix de Bois" (The little singers of the wooden crosses) returning from America, stopped here to sing their lovely songs before the plots where the Men and Officers of the first assault divisions sleep.

Mr. de la VASSELAIS, of the HEAD COMMITTEE of the LIBERTY HIGHWAY and I, long ago, took the initiative to ask the land from the French Government for those American cemeteries and in turn it was given to the Government of the United States. Naturally, it is taken as an unfriendly gesture in our eyes, when the WAR DEPARTMENT and the BATTLE MONUMENT COMMISSION definitely decided to disperse those cemeteries of SAINTE-MERE-EGLISE.

Of all the U.S. Military cemeteries, these at Sainte-Mère-Église are the most easily reached from CHERBOURG, the large harbor where the American ships arrive in increasing numbers. This is a great advantage to American families and other voyagers who did not have their own cars with them or access to an automobile. Those, the least favored by fortune, as well as those well off, have every facility for an easy trip to visit those cemeteries. They will find also a direct route by train to PARIS (Gare SAINT-LAZARE)

Consider the respective number of graves: Sainte-Mère-Eglise cemeteries: between 7000 and 7500 graves, Saint Laurent: 3797 graves, Saint James : 4000 graves

One wonders WHY it is wished that the immense necropolis [cemetery] of Sainte-Mère- Église - which the number one cemetery being the very FIRST cemetery established in connection with the invasion of Normandy: June 8th) and in regard with its prominent historical significance- WHY it should be dispersed and taken a number of miles to the cemetery of SAINT LAURENT, much smaller, less accessible and not as well situated geographically.

The plea written in August 1947 by Alexandre Renaud attempting to conserve the American cemeteries of Sainte-Mère-Église.
Collection H.-J. Renaud

Even though there are great disadvantages at Saint Laurent, it is easily understood that Omaha Beach should forever be memorialized because it was the second beach where the Americans debarked, but if that is the case, WHY ignore the first beach, UTAH Beach, where the first waves of the American assault troops came and flanked the entire line of the allied troops?

Many American mothers grieving for a dear Son have written to me such moving letters. So many American families have, up to now, written to me that they have a beloved One: Son, Husband, Brother, lying buried in Sainte-Mère-Église cemetery, and that they hope and wish HE would not be disturbed, [...] and they also beseeched me to do my utmost pleading their cause, and to say they are very much against Sainte-Mère-Église being moved that I promised them to do so, and I certainly will fulfill my duty.

For us, the French people of Sainte-Mère-Eglise and the whole peninsula of CHERBOURG, it is infinitely painful to think that from this sacred earth which was the First to receive the glorious remains, those bodies shall be exhumed and the plough will again cut the earth, the grass will grow, herds of cattle will wander, ...There will be nothing to recall THOSE who, in reality and after their sorrowing families' desires, should always rest there.

In removing the cemeteries from Sainte-Mère-Église one effaces the remembrance of the entire American zone of attack and that, not only without economy for the U.S., but on the contrary, enjoying in new and enormous expenditures, since it will be necessary for Saint Laurent cemetery to make new roads to reach it, build hotels to receive the visitors and buy considerable extra land.

We take as testimony the Parents, Fathers, Mothers, and Widows of the American Heroes entered at SAINTE MERE EGLISE who, in large numbers, have come here to be near their departed loved ones: they have been received in this little town with a deep welcome, they have felt themselves surrounded with true affection and devotedness and respect, and have been able to effect their sejourn with every facility. They ardently desire to maintain these cemeteries.

In consequence, in order to respond to their very legitimate desires and those of the many American families mentioned above, whom I sincerely feel should be listened to, and also in the name of the 4 Divisions which debarked and fought in this sector, I join with the French Deputies of La Manche, and the French Government to ask earnestly the U.S.A. Government, the War DEPARTMENT and the BATTLE MONUMENT COMMISSION again to consider this regrettable decision- to reconsider the question of those cemeteries of Sainte- Mère-Église which are the largest concentration of graves in one place in whole Normandy, in order that they ONCE AGAIN (or at least ONE out of TWO cemeteries) be declared PERMANENT.

Signed: the Mayor
Alexandre Renaud »[131]

Exhumations and transfers

TOWARD THE MOTHER COUNTRY

In the two American cemeteries of Sainte-Mère-Église, the exhumation procedure began the day after their official closure to the public, March 7, 1948. Jean-Baptiste Feuillye recalls the spring of 1948: "Once the families had decided, we installed canvases about 1 m 80 to avoid too much voyeurism and we hired everyone with a shovel from the neighborhood. They had to dig up a grave in the morning, and, if possible, one in the afternoon. They weren't too deep. As soon as the person localized the body, under no circumstances could he touch it.

Teams of Americans coming from the funeral services had been "requisitioned", a contingent of sixty-some civilian grave professionals then took the charge of the body. Between 50% and 60% of the bodies were repatriated. We proceeded from cemetery to cemetery. We had to go really fast. The bodies were exhumed, they were "accommodated" (that's not the term they used but it was really that). Those who were going back to the States, after the procedure of "restoration", were sent to a warehouse in Cherbourg. This site, this depot, was situated in Tourlaville. The transportation of the bodies and their "boxes" was done by a French company ("Soutes et Manutentions of Cherbourg").

The case to which the casket was bolted at the base, in order to avoid any shocks during transportation from Europe to the US. NARA

They had a huge truck that could hold 80 or 90 boxes (I didn't say caskets). There was an entire procedure between digging them up and the departure for Cherbourg. The embalmers (the graves guys) had a pile of documents to fill out. They arranged, they reconstituted the bodies. From Tourlaville, they were taken in hand by civilian funeral directors who directed them toward the *Liberty Ships* which would take them to their final resting place, in the States."[132]

A large number of civilians were employed in the exhumations. The inflow of workers into the village of Sainte-Mère-Église produced a record consumption of cider at Mrs Marie's café, for it was hard work during these few weeks. The job was to dig down 1m 50 in order to collect what was left of these American soldiers, some buried for four years. During this procedure of exhumation, only the employees belonging to the AGRC could handle the remains. The bones were then transferred to a temporary casket, the "boxes" spoken of by Jean-Baptiste Feuillye.

The marker of the grave, the cross, systematically followed the temporary casket to the depot at

The standard casket reserved for the military personnel or civilians who died during the Second World War. NARA

Cherbourg, in Tourlaville, where the body was placed in the final casket. In the morgues of Tourlaville and Saint-Laurent-sur-Mer, several teams composed of an embalmer and two assistants took charge of one body at a time. The remains were placed in a standard coffin made of cast anodized aluminum, accompanied by a transport case. An ID plate was fixed to the handle nearest the head by means of a wire marked with a wax seal "US".

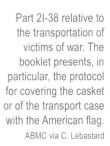

Part 21-38 relative to the transportation of victims of war. The booklet presents, in particular, the protocol for covering the casket or of the transport case with the American flag.
ABMC via C. Lebastard

ALFRED VAN HOLSBECK

The Disinterment Directive (both sides) enabled the body to be traced, from exhumation to handing over to the funeral home in the US. The example presented here is for the soldier Alfred Van Holsbeck, F Company – *505th PIR*, killed on June 6, 1944, after having landed in the flames of the Pommier house near the square of Sainte-Mère-Église. Originally buried in temporary cemetery n°1, the remains of this soldier were exhumed March 31, 1948. On April 2, after having been placed in a temporary casket, the remains were sent to Saint-Laurent-sur-Mer where they were placed in the final coffin. It was only in September 1948 that the coffin was sent to Tourlaville. The coffin was stored from November 16 to 28 in the port of Cherbourg and then embarked aboard the ship *James N. Robinson*. Arrival in New York was on December 6, 1948. The coffin was placed, two days later, at the disposal of the family.

The grave of the soldier Alfred Van Holsbeck in the cemetery of Oakridge, Michigan.
Photo by William Kinney

Repatriation of American soldiers aboard the *Joseph V. Connolly*. September 30, 1947, this ship transported 5,060 caskets from the port of Antwerp to the US. In January 1948, having left the port of New York, it sank in the middle of the Atlantic with a load of empty coffins. NARA

After the various customary verifications, the officer in charge of inspections authorized the closing of the coffin by means of a T-wrench which served to close the 24 points situated around the lid.

The procedure of repatriation to the US was followed thoroughly and recorded on the "Disinterment Directive", a form accompanying the coffin from the morgue to the funeral parlor chosen by the family of the deceased. At each step, the document was initialed by the transporter for maximum monitoring.

From the morgue of Tourlaville, the coffin was transferred to the docks of the port of Cherbourg. The first convoy from the port of la Manche took place November 4, 1947, as the *Robert F. Burns* left Cherbourg with 1,052 coffins on board (coming from Saint-Laurent-sur-Mer) destined for New York. The discharge took place on the quays of Brooklyn and the coffin went to its destination by train. When the funeral involved military honors, the ceremony ended with handing over the flag (which had covered the coffin) to the legal representative.

The transport cases, which contained the caskets, were held in a site in Tourlaville, near Cherbourg, and then sent to the United States. NARA

T-Wrench, used to close the 24 points on the lid of the final coffin. The object comes from the former morgue of Saint-Laurent. Private Collection

JOSEPH CYRIL FITT
UTAH
PVT 505 PRCHT INF 82 ABN DIV
WORLD WAR II
MARCH 23 1922 · JUNE 13 1944

Grave of Joseph Fitt in the cemetery of Taylorsville, in Salt Lake City.
Photo by the author

PFC Joseph Cyril Fitt (C Co -*505th PIR*) photographed in England at the beginning of June 1944. He was killed in combat on June 13 when his unit rejoined the rest of the regiment just installed in Picauville. The flag covered the coffin of the young paratrooper before being given to his mother during a ceremony at Fort Douglas (Utah) in 1948. Private Collection

Insignia of the
66th Infantry Division.
Private collection

John M. Henderson, in
England, in spring 1944.
Private collection

THE FUNERAL OF PFC JOHN M. HENDERSON

On Christmas Eve, 1944, the American transport ship *Leopoldville*, was targeted by the German submarine, *U-486*, off the harbor of Cherbourg. The ship sank in the icy waters of the Channel with 2,235 soldiers of the *252nd and 264th Infantry Regiments* (*66th Infantry Division*) on board.

Among the 763 victims (including 493 lost) of this catastrophe, was PFC John M. Henderson, from Baton-Rouge LA. He was buried until 1948 in the temporary cemetery n° 2 in Sainte-Mère-Église. His body was repatriated at the request of his parents and buried definitively in the Port Hudson National Cemetery in Louisiana.

Anvers – Le S.S. Léopoldville.

The SS Leopoldville. Private collection

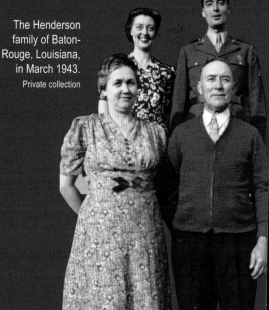

The Henderson
family of Baton-
Rouge, Louisiana,
in March 1943.
Private collection

Funeral of PFC John M. Henderson, Feb 13, 1948. Private collection

A military detachment leaves the funeral parlor carrying the coffin of John Henderson to the national cemetery in Zachary (Port Hudson National Cemetery). Private collection

The coffin of John M. Henderson. Private collection

Military honors are rendered. The American flag, which covered the coffin from France, is deployed then meticulously folded and officially given to the family. Private collection.

THE HOMECOMING OF CHARLES N. DEGLOPPER

In June 1948, the remains of PFC Charles N. DeGlopper (*325th GIR*), hero of the battle of La Fière, killed in action June 9, 1944, were repatriated to the United States. Meanwhile, this farmer of Grand Island (NY) had received the Congressional Medal of Honor, the highest distinction attributed by the American army, posthumously. His coffin was received at the train station of Buffalo by nearly 5000 people come to pay their final respects. Finally, on July 9, 1948, a ceremony was held at the family farm before the coffin went to the cemetery of Maplegrove where military, neighbors and friends came to be present at the funeral of PFC DeGlopper.

Private First Class Charles N. DeGlopper, C Company – 325th GIR, *82nd Airborne Division*. Collection of the family DeGlopper via the Roger family

At the family farm in Grand Island, NY, several military detachments came to pay their respects to PFC Charles N. DeGlopper on July 9, 1948. Collection DeGlopper Family by the Roger family

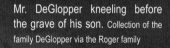

Mr. DeGlopper kneeling before the grave of his son. Collection of the family DeGlopper via the Roger family

Insignia of the *82nd Airborne Division*. Private collection

The coffin is transported to Maplegrove Cemetery. Collection DeGlopper family by Roger family

Before the coffin of PFC DeGlopper, military, neighbors and friends come to pay their respects to the local hero.
Collection DeGlopper family by Roger family

The Congressional Medal of Honor is given to the father of Charles DeGlopper. Collection DeGlopper family by Roger family

The grave of the hero of La Fière in Maplegrove Cemetery.
Collection DeGlopper family by Roger family

TOWARD A NATIONAL CEMETERY: COLLEVILLE-SUR-MER

On Sunday, September 14, 1947, the day of the benediction of the temporary American cemetery of Saint-Laurent-sur-Mer, the program of repatriation was finally implemented. Two days later, the first bodies were exhumed and transferred to the morgue of Saint-Laurent before returning to the US or to the great permanent national cemetery of Colleville-sur-Mer.[133] The historical significance and the spectacular panorama had made Saint-Laurent the number one choice as far as the site for a permanent cemetery in Normandy was concerned. Starting June 7, 1944, a first temporary cemetery was installed on the edge of the beach before being finally transferred to the heights of Saint-Laurent. The site had received 3,797 temporary graves, American, allied and German, up until the end of summer 1947.

"La Mé" (the mother) among the white crosses of the Saint-Laurent cemetery, September 14, 1947. NARA

September 14, 1947; Paul H. Griffith, Commander of the American Legion, converses with Col. Samuel Lowry, commander of the AGRC for the second zone (France). NARA

U.S. MILITARY CEMETERY ST. LAURENT

The day of the closure ceremony, a large number of onlookers and military men came to hear the religious ceremony and the speech of Gen. Peckham, commander in chief of the AGRC, concerning the construction of permanent cemeteries and in particular, the one at Colleville-sur-Mer. Among the prestigious visitors was Eleanor Roosevelt, the widow of Gen. Theodore Roosevelt, who had finally abandoned the idea of one day seeing the body of her husband rest in a permanent cemetery of Sainte-Mère-Église.

Once the bodies were exhumed, and taken to Saint-Laurent-sur-Mer to the morgue (or *Casketing Point B*), the first job was filling the 3,800 holes of the temporary cemetery, then leveling out and marking the boundaries of the future permanent cemetery. The first definitive burials took place toward the beginning of November 1948, in other words more

Brig. Gen. Howard H. Peckham, commander in chief of the AGRC in Europe, announces the main steps of the repatriation plan to the members of the American Legion. NARA

than a year after the closing of the temporary cemetery of Saint-Laurent.

Work in progress on the cemetery of Colleville-sur-Mer in September 1952. NARA

Great trenches, straight and parallel to the shore, were dug and the final coffins accompanied by their transport cases were finally put in place. In a reference work about the American cemetery at Colleville-sur-Mer, Constant Lebastard reviews the principal steps of the burial protocol: "The burials follow a strict protocol: The combination casket/protection case is draped with the colors of the United States and escorted by a military platoon. Following a blessing by a military chaplain, three shots are fired and the bugle call to the dead resounds. Thereafter follows the official folding of the flag and the body is lowered into the grave along with the protection case. The flag is then sent to the next of kin."[134]

The "Disinterment Directive" of 1st Lt. Fieldon B. Huie Jr, initially buried in cemetery n° 1. His disinterment was accomplished on March 17, 1948, and his remains waited for nearly a year at the Saint-Laurent morgue (or *Casketing Point B*). NARA

Aerial view of the cemetery of Colleville-sur-Mer in 1955, a short while before its inauguration. Note the original placement of the temporary cemetery of Saint-Laurent, at the top left. Only plots G and I encroach upon the former temporary cemetery. Collection Museum of Utah Beach

Nearly 41% of the bodies previously buried in the various cemeteries in Normandy were finally buried in the permanent cemetery of Colleville. Once the phase of burials was practically finished at the end of 1949 (9,362 bodies had by then been buried by the personnel of the AGRC), the planning and embellishment of the site was the responsibility of the architects Harbeson, Hough, Livingston & Larson, of Philadelphia.

On this gigantic site, a large number of local companies were put to work for nearly four years. By 1955, although the site had not been inaugurated, the first visitors could come and meditate over the grave of a loved one. The inauguration took place on July 19, 1956, in the presence of the President of the French Republic, René Coty. The question naturally arises of the jurisdictional status of the permanent cemetery of Colleville-sur-Mer. Once again Constant Lebastard will respond with precision to this oft-misunderstood question: "The American cemeteries of the Second World War in France are concessions in perpetuity, exonerated from all charges or taxes but they remain nonetheless subject to French law and they are not American territories."[135]

Three veterans of the *1st Infantry Division* and a British veteran pay their respects to Brig. Gen. Roosevelt, June 6, 1955. NARA

The temporary grave of Quentin Roosevelt (killed on July 14, 1918 in his fighter Nieuport 28 in Chamery), the youngest brother of Theodore Roosevelt Jr. Built by the Germans, the isolated grave of Quentin Roosevelt was maintained for 37 years until it was finally decided by the family to reunite the two brothers in the same place.
On September 22, 1955, Quentin came to join Theodore in the cemetery of Colleville-sur-Mer. This new grave brought the total to 9,386. NARA

On the 10th anniversary of the end of World War II, a large number of pilgrimages were organized by the American Legion to different battlefields of Europe. NARA

THE CASE OF "ROBERT DE LORENZO"

In parallel with the three principal options of repatriation which had been suggested to the American families (repatriation to the United States and burial in a private cemetery, repatriation to the US and burial in a national cemetery, transfer to a national cemetery abroad), there existed a fourth option, much more unusual, which consisted of transferring the remains of the deceased to a foreign country, his birthplace or that of a next of kin, for burial in a private cemetery. This kind of exceptional situation arose in 1948 when the family of Lt. Robert John De Lorenzo (*90th Infantry Division*) killed June 13, 1944, near Gourbesville, decided to leave the remains of their young officer not in Colleville-sur-Mer, but in the village cemetery of Brassac-les-Mines, in Auvergne. Jean-Baptiste Feuillye, still working for the AGRC, was chosen to accompany the coffin of the military man, initially buried at Sainte-Mère-Église, to his final resting place. He tells us this story:

"I accompanied the body of a certain De Lorenzo. His father, of Italian origin, had been engaged in the Battle of Argonne in 1918 by the Americans. He was wounded and fell in love with the nurse who took care of him in Chateau-Thierry. They went home to the United States together. They had a son. And Lt. Robert John De Lorenzo came to his death in Sainte-Mère-Église 20 years later. He was killed June 13. He was a translator (French, Italian and German) in the *90th Infantry Division*. While questioning a German prisoner, he took a shell. He was buried in cemetery n°1, and later, I was assigned to accompany the body to Brassac-les-Mines, in the Puy-de-Dôme. He was to be buried in the family vault next to his grandparents on his mother's side (Ventalon family). We had a jeep with a special trailer, but the coffin was longer than the trailer. This strange convoy drew attention, especially from the hotel owner where we stayed. The next morning, the tarpaulin had been rolled back... We were early at Brassac-les-Mines, but all the Puy-de-Dôme was there; five hundred people were there! Everyone was waiting for us. The Prefect was there for the local hero. His mother was there from the US.

At the moment of burial, the American soldier who accompanied me, Sgt. Bent, was to follow the coffin and never let it leave his sight. I followed him. In the crowd, I heard them say:"Well, well; they take

Insignia of the
90th Infantry Division
Private collection

Lt. Robert J. De Lorenzo, interpreter for the 90th ID during the battle of Sainte-Mère-Église, was the son of an American soldier and a French nurse who met in 1918 in France. In 1948, at the request of his mother, the remains of this Franco-American soldier were buried in the village cemetery of Brassac-les-Mines (Puy-de-Dôme). Collection of the Ventalon family via J.B. Feuillye

In 1948, the whole village was found around the remains of the local hero at his funeral.
Collection of the Ventalon family via J.B. Feuillye

A religious ceremony, in the church of Brassac-les-Mines, preceded the burial in the village cemetery. Jean-Baptiste Feuillye accompanied the coffin to its final resting place. He reassured Mme De Lorenzo by certifying that it was indeed the remains of her son.
Collection of the Ventalon family via J.B. Feuillye

In the family tomb of Brassac-les-Mines, repose the remains of Lt. De Lorenzo, beside his maternal grandparents. The funeral monument has a wealth of information. In addition to a photo of the Franco-American soldier, it also displays his diploma from Camp Richie (Maryland) where he was trained as a translator for the American army. Collection J.-B. Feuillye

In the village church, a stained glass window was erected to the glory of the local hero with this mention: "In memory of Lt. Robert J. De Lorenzo-Ventalon, who died for the liberty of the world on June 13, 1944. Collection J.B. Feuillye

them ever younger!" I was in normal clothes with a badge that read "AGRC 2nd Zone", that was it. Mrs. De Lorenzo came to see me, she had heard there were some little problems with identities at the exhumation... "Is it really my son, sir?" I answered, "Believe me, Madame, I was present when the grave of your son was opened. I give you my word that this is your son." It was obviously very important."[136]

"SAINTE-MÈRE-ÉGLISE: FIRST AMERICAN BRIDGEHEAD IN FRANCE" AND MUCH MORE...

In the morning of June 6 each year, before the bells of the church ring to announce the beginning of the mass commemorating the Landings, a ceremony takes place near the monument which recalls the presence of the American temporary cemetery n°1 of Sainte-Mère-Église. Far from the great popular gatherings, the ceremony is the reunion of a few American veterans, former French employees of the temporary cemeteries, the veterans of Sainte-Mère-Église, a detachment of American military, and a few onlookers. On this occasion, each comes to remember their past glory, the basis of the memorial renown of Sainte-Mère-Église that thousands of visitors discover each year.

Falling little by little into oblivion, the story of these military cemeteries of Sainte-Mère-Église had been obscured and formed a gap in the rich historiography of this Cotentin village.

A commemorative ceremony, June 6, 2012, near the monument commemorating the site of the American temporary cemetery n° 1 of Sainte-Mère-Église. Photo by the author

Elbert Legg, a veteran of the *603rd Quartermaster Graves Registration Company*, returns to Carquebut where he put in place the cemetery of Blosville from June 7, 1944. The text reads "Here reposed from June 1944 to 1948 6000 American soldiers fallen for the liberation of France."
Collection Legg via Y. De La Rüe

Because of the profound impact on the daily lives and world view of the inhabitants of the village, it seems legitimate to shine a light on this singular episode and to include it as a fully independent chapter in the liberation of Sainte-Mère-Église.

Reading the preceding chapters one must admit that the story of Sainte-Mère-Église goes far beyond the jumps of June 6, 1944, over the church square. The battle was long (four days) and deadly. Around the edges of the village, military men and civilians continued to die under the enemy bombardments on the evening of June 7. Finding themselves alone in the world, exhausted by stress and fatigue, the American paratroopers of the *82nd Airborne Division* fought a battle which would be decisive to the success of military operations in the Cotentin peninsula. The intensity and the violence of the fighting experienced by soldiers and civilians contradicts the idea that Sainte-Mère-Église was, in June 1944, "the first village liberated in France". This would be to forget the liberation of Ajaccio, September 9, 1943, or especially Ranville, near Caen, during the early hours of June 6, 1944. For Sainte-Mère-Église, the term "liberation" for the day of June 6, 1944, is inappropriate with regard to the numerous victims, civilian and military, who perished in the following days. In contrast, the expression employed by the mayor of the time, Alexandre Renaud, remains justified:"the first American bridgehead in France."

The battle was not yet over when the first military cemeteries were set up near the beach at *Utah*, at Carquebut, or on the territory of the village of Sainte-Mère-Église.

These places marked the landscape and the hearts of the inhabitants of the county for nearly four years, giving rise to exceptional behavior before the thousands of American bodies were either repatriated to the United States or transferred to the national cemetery at Colleville-sur-Mer.

How were the sites of these American cemeteries restored? In summer 1948, this problem was discussed by the head of rural engineering. In a report dated July 23, he wrote: "SAINTE-MÈRE-ÉGLISE – There are two cemeteries of which one is still occupied. The Americans have informed us that they will restore the other themselves. The mayor, by the way, has requested that the roads and paths be respected in order to transform the space into a sports ground."[137] The fates of the sites, once restored, were surprising, to say the least. In the place of Sainte-Mère-Église cemetery n°1, today you will find a soccer field. At Carquebut, the field of Raymond De La Rüe was returned to pastureland, as was the site of the cemetery n°2 of Sainte-Mère-Église. For the latter, at the end of the seventies, a zone of small industries was set up along the road to Chef-du-Pont, covering all of the ground that once belonged to the military cemetery. In the meantime, in order to commemorate for posterity the presence of these temporary cemeteries, monuments were erected by the D-Day Committee in 1949. They are, today, the only material witnesses of this grand story.

The presence of these American cemeteries, followed by their disappearance, had several consequences for the inhabitants of Sainte-Mère-Église who felt a profound sadness. After the closing of the cemeteries, the era of commemorations, starting in 1945, took over, and in the absence of the cemeteries, a different process of adoration progressively emerged in favor of the survivors, embodied by the veteran paratroopers. Sainte-Mère-Église, with her special bond with the American troops, transferred all her devotion to the veterans of D-Day, raising them to the level of living legends. It is easy to understand that elderly men, seeking recognition and affection, are so fond of coming back each year to this region. For this, the village of Sainte-Mère-Église, this immaterial monument built to the glory of the American paratroopers, has never ceased to be a sacred place. While the military cemeteries have disappeared, the memories of the heroes of June 6, 1944, have made this Norman village an eternal sanctuary to the remembrance of D-Day.

On the road to Chef-du-Pont, another monument recalls the presence of cemetery n°2, today occupied by a supermarket. Photo by the author

Appendix 1

82ND AIRBORNE DIVISION – ORDER OF BATTLE

General: Maj. Gen. Matthew R. Ridgway
Assistant: Brig. Gen. James M. Gavin
Assistant: Brig. Gen George P. Howell

Chief of Staff: Col. Ralph P. Eaton

G1 (Personnel): Lt. Col. Frederick M. Schellhammer
G2 (Intelligence): Lt. Col. Jack Whitfield
G3 (Maps/Plans): Lt. Col. Robert H. Weinicke
G4 (Supplies): Lt. Col. Bennie A. Zinn

505th PARACHUTE INFANTRY REGIMENT : Col. William E. Ekman
    HQ & HQ : Capt. Talton "Woody" Long
1/505th : Maj. Frederick C.A. Kellam
    HQ Co: Lt. Robert D. Keeler
    A Co: Lt. John J. "Red Dog" Dolan
    B Co: Lt. James M. Ervin
    C Co: Capt. Arthur Stefanich
2/505th: Lt. Col. Benjamin H. Vandervoort
    HQ Co: Lt. James Gray
    D Co: Capt. Taylor G. Smith
    E Co: Capt. Clyde Russel
    F Co: Capt. Hubert Bass
3/505th: Lt. Col. Edward C. Krause
    G Co: Capt. Robert Follmer
    H Co: Capt. Walter C. DeLong
    I Co: Capt. Harold H. Swingler

507th PARACHUTIST INFANTRY DIVISION: Col. George V. Millet
    HQ & HQ: Capt. Robert D. Rae
1/507th:: Lt. Col. Edwin J. Ostberg
    A Co: Capt. James R. Nunn
    B Co: Capt. Chester B. Mc Coid
    C Co: Capt. Sanford M. Frank
2/507th:: Lt. Col. Charles J. Timmes
    D Co: Capt. Clarence A. Tolle
    E Co: Capt. Roy E. Creek
    F Co: Capt. Paul F. Smith
3/507th : Lt. Col. Arthutr A. Maloney
    G Co: Capt. Floyd B. Schwarzwalder
    H Co: Capt. Allen W. Raylor
    I Co: Capt. Gordon S. Allyn

508th PARACHUTIST INFANTRY DIVISION: colonel Roy E. Lindquist
       HQ & HQ: Capt. Robert Abraham
1/508th: Capt. Herbert Batcheller
       HQ Co: Capt. Gerald A. Ruddy
       A Co: Capt. Jonathan E. Adams
       B Co: Capt. Royal P. Taylor
       C Co: Capt. Walter Silvers
2/508th : Lt. Col. Thomas J. B. Shanley
       D Co: Capt. Chester E. Graham
       E Co: Capt. Eugene Hetland
       F Co: Capt. Francis E. Flanders
3/508th: Lt. Col. Louis G. Mendez Jr
       G Co: Capt. Frank J. Novak
       H Co: Capt. Hal M. Creary
       I Co: Capt. John J. Daly

325th GLIDER INFANTRY REGIMENT: Col. Harry L. Lewis
1/325th: Lt. Col. Klemm R. Boyd
       HQ Co: Capt. Alex Bishop
       A Co: Lt. James Gayley
       B Co: Capt. Rchard M. Gibson
       C Co: Capt. Dave E. Stokely
2/325th: Lt. Col. John H. "Swede" Swenson
       HQ Co: Capt. Herbert Slaughter
       E Co: Capt. Robert Dickerson
       F Co: Lt. Joe B. Gault
       G Co: Capt. Irvin Bloom
3/325th(2/401st): Lt. Col. Charles A. Carrell
       HQ Co: Capt. Lewis S. Mentlik
       I Co (E-401): Maj. Charles Murphy
       K Co (F-401): Capt. James M. Harney
       L Co (G-401): Capt. John B. Sauls

82nd Airborne Div. Artillery: Col. Francis A. March
319th Glider FA Bn: Lt. Col. James C. Todd
320th Glider FA Bn: Lt. Col. Paul E. Wright
376th Parachutist FA Bn: Lt. Col. Wilbur N. Griffith
456th Parachutist FA Bn: Lt. Col. Wagner J. d'Alessio
80th Airborne AA Bn: Lt. Col. Raymond E. Singleton
307th Airborne Engineer Bn: Lt. Col. Robert S. Palmer
407th Airborne Quartermaster Co: Capt. Samuel H. Mays
782nd Airborne Supply Co: Capt. Jeff Davis Jr
82nd Airborne Signal Co: Lt. Robert B. Nerf
82nd Airborne Reco section: Lt. Joseph V. Demasi
82nd Airborne MP Co: Maj. Frederick G. McCollum
82nd Parachutist Maintenance Co: Capt. James E. Griffith

Major General Matthew R. Ridgway. NARA

Appendix 2

ORGLANDES: THE GERMAN MILITARY CEMETERY OF THE COTENTIN PENINSULA

Even though the German military cemetery of Orglandes is not exactly a part of the county of Sainte-Mère-Église, it is worth briefly returning to the creation of this cemetery which, beginning in 1944, received the German soldiers killed during the Battle of the Cotentin.

While the combats raged around Saint-Sauveur-le-Vicomte, a temporary cemetery was begun on June 19, 1944 by an American unit, the 4th Platoon – 603rd QM Graves Registration Co. Here, more than elsewhere, there was an intensive succession of burials, over 400 per day during the first days. Situated outside the village of Orglandes, the cemetery counted 7,358 graves in 1947.

Following the signature in 1954 of a Franco-German convention relative to military graves, the German Military Graves Maintenance Service undertook the construction of a permanent cemetery on the site of the first. The site was inaugurated on September 20, 1961. It now holds the bodies of 10,152 German soldiers.

A panel indicating the entrance to the German military cemetery, dated September 1, 1944. NARA

The burials and the digging of the graves were done by German prisoners of war. NARA

Various extracts from a film made July 12, 1944, in the cemetery of Orglandes. NARA Film

Aerial view of the German cemetery of Orglandes, taken during the summer of 1947. Far from the rigor of the American temporary cemeteries, the site seems to have grown itself randomly during the years that followed the end of the fighting. This "occupation" – as the mayor of the time called it – of the fields (8 hectares 40) by the bodies of German soldiers was not well appreciated by the owner of the land to the extent that he never received the slightest indemnification for it. NARA

The cemetery at Orglandes today. The site is now managed by a private German association founded in 1919, the Service for the Maintenance of German Military Graves (Volksbund Deutsche Kriegsgräberfürsorge). Photo by author.

Appendix 3

"MY LOVE, JUST COME BACK"

For nearly 65 years, this letter was never opened, never read, until 2009 when the author acquired the document.

Fieldon and Ruth Huie lived in Conway, Arkansas. They ran a shoe shop in the center of town. 1st Lt. Fieldon B. Huie Jr had landed on Utah Beach on June 6, 1944, with the HQ Co, 2/22 Infantry Regiment. He participated in the fighting in the Cotentin to capture Cherbourg. First wounded and missing in action on July 14, 1944 near Quinéville, Fieldon Huie was finally killed June 23, 1944, near Digosville in an assault on a fortified German position. He was buried two days later in cemetery n° 2 of Sainte-Mère-Église.

Monday Aft. July 17th

My Dear,

It seems almost impossible that this month is nearly over. Time passes so quickly it's hard for me to keep up with the date. I don't do anything, especially to make the days fly and yet I don't seem to have much spare time either with working all day in the store. At night I read, go to the show, or play Polly Anna with Doc and that's about all. Maybe an explanation for it could be that I want months to go by faster than possible so you can return. Do you realize we must start a complete new life from than the one we had before? It's fun to think about and wonder if we will live here or somewhere else, if we can have our own home, and what kind of business whether shoes or peanuts. We too will have to start a family before we both are too old and decrepit to enjoy children. But, the thing I like to plan and think about most in that promised six months honey moon - deposited twenty dollars today for that purpose - which you won't be able to get out of. It's a must. Afterward we can settle down to a little peace and quiet and maybe I can eventually learn to cook. Of course you'll growl because the meat will be tough and I'll probably pout for a while then end up by hiring a cook. I still think you are spoiled but I can get you over that and you won't mind at all bringing me a glass of water. In fact think you will like it as I'll reward you with a kissie on the cheekie.

Honey, just come back that's all I'm asking anything else I can take as a soldier's wife should. I'm depending on you so don't fail me. I love you so that these next few months will just be wasted months because you are not around. The one consolation is they can be made up.

All my love,

Ruth »

Knowing nothing of the tragic fate of her husband up until the end of July 1944, Ruth Huie had taken the habit of sending him – once a week – a letter colored with hope and affection. The letter, reproduced below, was written July 17, 1944, in other words four weeks after the death of Fieldon Huie. The letter was unfortunately returned to sender with the note "deceased". In 1948, on the decision of Ruth Huie, the remains of the officer of the *4th Infantry Division* were transported to the American cemetery of Colleville-sur-Mer. Ruth Huie never remarried.

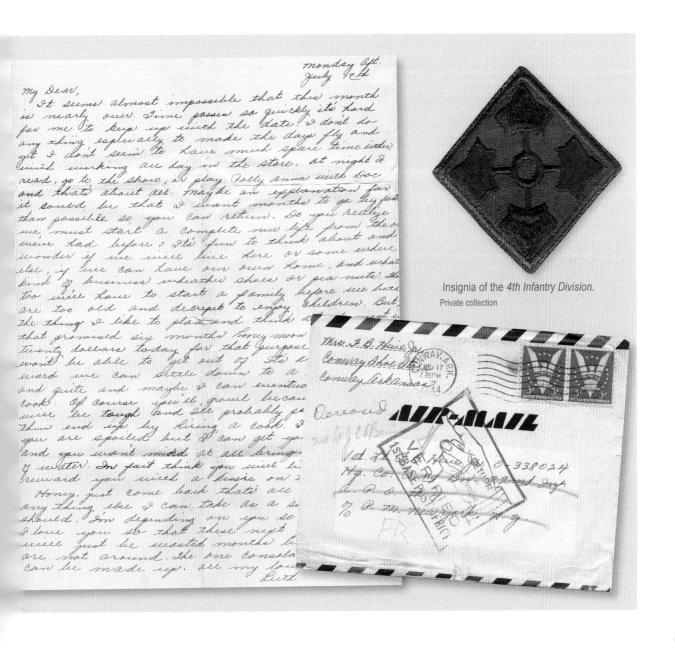

Insignia of the *4th Infantry Division*.
Private collection

Appendix 4

A DRESS UNLIKE OTHERS...

The bell tower at Sainte-Mère-Église and its famous dummy (hung since 1975) representing the paratroopers dropped on the village square in the night of 5 to 6 June, 1944. This substitute for John Steele constitutes – along with the museum of the troops who were dropped – the principal appeal of the village. Thousands of visitors come each year to discover or rediscover this traditional little scene. Note that it was decided to position the dummy on the south side of the church (whereas History would have had the north side) for better visibility from the square. Photo L. Mauduit

This dress of camouflaged parachute silk was made by an inhabitant of Sainte-Mère-Eglise in the days following the Battle of Normandy. Designed to be worn by a young girl, this funny outfit is a good example of the ingenuity of the Normans with regard to recycling the different kinds of material left by the Americans on the battlefield. The dress was undoubtedly worn for special occasions (visits to the temporary cemeteries, commemorations of the Landings, Memorial Day, etc.) Author's collection

Notes

1. See the works of Maurice Lecœur , *Un village du Cotentin: Sainte-Mère-Église (1082-1944)*, Paris, Éditions Fanval, 1988, 195 p.
2. Allied Time (GMT). To obtain French time or "solar time", often employed in the stories of Norman witnesses, it is necessary to subtract two hours.
3. Only 73 C-47 planes out of 808, in other words, 9% of them, dropped their charge correctly over the six theoretical zones in the night of June 6, 1944.
4. The 9 p.m. curfew, established by the German occupier, was raised for certain homes in the town.
5. *Deutsche Dienststelle WASt* was for the information of the next of kin of the ex-*Wehrmacht* dead. This official intelligence office, provided by article 77 of the Geneva Convention of July 27, 1929 relative to the treatment of prisoners of war, was created in Berlin shortly before the beginning of World War II. Linked to the German Army's high command, it came into operation on August 25, 1939 under the name "*Wehrmacht* intelligence service for war losses and prisoners of war". Apart from intelligence communications on captive German prisoners, the *WASt's* principal job was registering the losses of the German army (wounded, sicknesses, deaths and disappearances) and processing this information for civil registration and the official record of war graves. Its localities were, for the duraton of the war, in Thuringe, Saalfeld and Meiningen.
6. Levesque André, *Sainte-Mère-Église, mon été 44. Mémoires d'outres-bombes,* Bordeaux, Éditions des Veys, 2010, p. 42.
7. Mobilization register in the department of La Manche – county of Sainte-Mère-Église, 1939, Departmental Archives of La Manche, 80 ED 2H1.
8. Renaud Alexandre, *Sainte-Mère-Église. Première tête de pont américaine en France. 6 juin 1944,* Paris, Éditions Julliard, 1984, p. 14.
9. Interview with Jacques Pignot, Mont-Saint-Aignan, November 18, 2010.
10. Renaud Alexandre, *Sainte-Mère-Église... op. cit.* p.18.
11. Memoirs of Jacques Pignot, 1994.
12. Renaud Alexandre, *Sainte-Mère-Église... op. cit.* p. 21.
13. Renaud Alexandre, *Sainte-Mère-Église... op. cit.* p. 29.
14. Lecœur Maurice, *Une village du Cotentin: Sainte-Mère-Église. 1082-1944,* Paris, Fanval, 1988, p. 152.
15. Renaud Alexandre, *Sainte-Mère-Église... op. cit.* p. 30.
16. Interview with Yves De La Rüe, Carquebut, June 5, 2012.
17. Memoirs of Jacques Pignot, 1994.
18. *Ibid.*
19. NARA, RG 407, *WWII Combat Interviews, 82nd Airborne Division,* July 1944.
20. *Ibid.*
21. Eisenhower Dwight D., *Report by the Supreme Commander to the Combined Chiefs of Staff on the Operations in Europe of the Allied Expeditionary Force. 6 June, 1944 to 8 May, 1945,* London, H.M. Stationery Office, 1946, p. 6
22. To that, Eisenhower adds: "The airborne landing losses proved only a fraction of what have been feared, amounting in fact to less than 10%."
23. NARA, RG 407, *WWII Operations Reports, 101st Airborne Division,* May 18, 1944.
24. Memoirs of Charles D. Butte, University of Tennessee Special Collections Library, 1940-1948.
25. NARA, RG 407, *WWII Operations Report, 407th Quartermaster Co,* August 14, 1944.
26. NARA, RG 407, *WWII Operations Report, 502nd Parachute Infantry Regiment, May 20, 1944.*
27. Interview with Frederick Morgan Jr, New Orleans, November 19, 2012.
28. NARA, RG 407, *WWII Combat Interviews, 82nd Airborne Division,* July 1944.

29. NARA, RG 407, *WWII Combat Interviews*, *82nd Airborne Division*, July 1944.

30. Shortly before the 505th PIR jumped on DZ "O", a group of scouts was charged with marking the jump zone with seven green Holophane lamps forming the letter T on the ground.

31. NARA, RG 407, *WWII Combat Interviews*, *82nd Airborne Division*, July 1944

32. Interview with Geneviève Pasquette, Chef-du-Pont, January 11, 2012.

33. John P. Ray succumbed to his wounds the following day. He is buried today in the American military cemetery at Colleville-sur-Mer.

34. Recording of Kenneth Russell, *Eisenhower Center, University of New Orleans*.

35. Interview with Raymond Paris, Sainte-Mère-Église, December 23, 2004.

36. Interview with Jacques Pignot, Mont-Saint-Aignan, November 18, 2010.

37. Memoirs of Juliette Brault (born Le Cambaye), Library of the city of Cherbourg.

38. Memoirs of Rudi Escher, Museum of the Airborne troops of Sainte-Mère-Église; 1984.

39. Memoirs of Rudolph May in Murphy Robert, *No better place to die,* Havertown, Casemate Publishers, 2009, p. 205.

40. Interview with Léon Mignot, Chef-du-Pont, March 5, 2011.

41. NARA, RG 407, *WWII Combat Interviews*, *82nd Airborne Division,* July 1944.

42. Country path giving access to isolated parcels.

43. Memoirs of Jacques Pignot, 1994.

44. NARA, RG 407, *WWII Combat Interviews*, *82nd Airborne Division,* July 1944.

45. NARA, RG 407, *WWII Combat Interviews*, *82nd Airborne Division,* July 1944.

46. NARA, RG 247, *Chaplains' reports,* 1944.

47. Turner Turnbull was killed in combat in the morning of June 7, 1944 during a violent German counter-attack north of Sainte-Mère-Église. His body today rests in the American military cemetery in Colleville-sur-Mer.

48. "C" force was composed of elements of the *82nd Airborne Division* that landed on *Utah Beach*.

49. A major event of the Texas war of independence, the American collective memory preserves the memory of the battle of Fort Alamo (1836) as the symbol of a heroic and desperate resistance. For 13 days, the Mexican army (1500 men) laid siege to a fort that had passed into the hands of 200 Americans who resisted relentlessly to the last man.

50. Tucker William H., D-*Day: Thirty-five days in Normandy. Reflections of a Parachutist,* 2002, p. 35.

51. Fred Morgan returned to his little island in Massachusetts in October 1945 and married his girlfriend two months later, finding an engagement unnecessary. They had six children.

52. Interview with Fred Morgan, on May 22, 2013, in Edgartown, MA.

53. In French, "killed in combat" ("tué au combat").

54. Testimony of Cécile Flamand, municipal library of Cherbourg.

55. Bre Gilles, *Un pont en Normandie,* self-published, 2003, p. 162.

56. Fussel Paul, *À la guerre. Psychologie et comportements pendant la second guerre mondiale*, Paris, Seuil, 1992, p. 31.

57. Tucker William H., *D-Day: Thirty-five days in Normandy. Reflections of a Parachutist,* 2002, p. 35.

58. Dahms Joachim, *J'aurais un mot à vous dire,* 2009, Museum of Utah Beach.

59. Interview with Raymond Paris, Sainte-Mère-Église, December 23, 2004.

60. Interview with Henri-Jean Renaud, Sainte-Mère-Église, June 11, 2012.

61. Interview with Jacques Pignot, Mont-Saint-Aignan, November 19, 2010.

62. Renaud Alexandre, *Sainte-Mère-Église... op. cit.* p. 91.

63. Fussel Paul, *À la guerre... op. cit.* p. 151.

64. Audoin-Rouzeau Stéphane, *Combattre. Une anthropologie historique de la guerre moderne*, Paris, Seuil, 2008, p. 29.

65. In Antiquity, one called the body and armor of an enemy a "trophy".

66. NARA, *Individual Deceased Personal File*, George Bailey.

67. Interview with Auguste Dugouchet, Sainte-Marie-du-Mont, June 2, 1999.

68. Interview with Murray Moonhatch, Sainte-Marie-du-Mont, August 2, 2008.

69. NARA, RG 407, *WWII Operations Report, 426th AB QM Co,* July 29, 1944.

70. Documentary "Sainte-Marie-du-Mont, kilometer 0", by Gilles Perrault for the magazine *Cinq colonnes à la une,* in 1964. All rights reserved, INA.

71. NARA, RG 407, *WWII Operations Report, History of the 603 QM GR Co,* May 1945.

72. *Ibid.*

73. Nickname given by the parachutists during their training at camp Toccoa.

74. NARA, RG 407, *WWII Operations Report, History of the 603rd QM GR Co,* May 1945.

75. Interview with Jacques Pignot, Mont-Saint-Aignan, November 19, 2010.

76. 145W 76, Military graves, July 11, 1947, Departmental Archives of La Manche.

77. Interview with Yves De La Rüe, Carquebut, May 12, 2009.

78. Legg Elbert, *Crosses at Normandy, June 1944,* in *Quartermaster Professional Bulletin,* winter, 1994.

79. NARA, RG 407, *WWII Operations Report, History of the 603 QM GR Co,* May 1945.

80. *Ibid.*

81. NARA, RG 92, *Office of the Quartermaster General, Recapitulation of the total remains*, August 1, 1950.

82. "*Negro Service Company*" in the text. The segregation in effect within the American army allowed usage of the term "negro".

83. Butte Charles, *Graves registration during WW II in Europe*, via Jean-Baptiste Feuillye.

84. Interview with Jean-Baptiste Feuillye, Fresville, November 7, 2010.

85. Interview with Léon Mignot, Chef-du-Pont, March 21, 2011.

86. On D-Day, seven American parachutists belonging to the 507th PIR were executed in a field of Hémévez despite their status as prisoners of war. The bodies were buried by the Germans in a common grave in the municipal cemetery. This affair was the object of an inquest to determine those responsible for this war crime.

87. Lecœur Maurice, *Un village du Cotentin: Sainte-Mère-Église. (1082-1944),* Paris, Fanval, 1988, p. 155.

88. Interview with Madeleine Valognes, Sainte-Mère-Église, December 9, 2010.

89. American graves registration command.

90. American graves registration service.

91. NARA, RG 92, *Office of the Quartermaster General, Recapitulation of the total remains*, August 1, 1950.

92. Col. John B. Franks, originally from Kansas, was 55 in 1945 when the camp at Saint-Hilaire-Petitville took his name for this gigantic temporary complex. He was considered by the American Army to be a major figure after spending 25 years in the service of the Quartermaster.

93. Interview with Jacques Pignot, Mont-Saint-Aignan, November 19, 2010.

94. Interview with Jean-Baptiste Feuillye, Fresville, November 29, 2011.

95. *Graves Registration Service, The General Board,* ETO, 1945, p. 9.

96. *Ibid.* p. 10

97. Richardson Eudora R., *Quartermaster supply in the ETO in WWII. Graves Registration,* volume VII, Camp Lee, Virginia, 1948, p. 64.

98. Lebastard Constant, *Le Cimetière américain de Colleville-sur-Mer. Une commision américaine en Normandie.* Bayeux, Éditions OREP, 2012, p. 34.

99. *Graves Registration Service; The general board,* ETO, 1945, p. 27.

100. 145W76; military graves, leaflet of September 19, 1944, Departmental Archives of La Manche.

101. NARA, RG 338, *Records of US Army support organizations, AGRC, Second Zone, Report January 1947.*

102. Interview with Jean-Baptiste Feuillye, Fresville, January 11, 2011.

103. According to Jean-Baptiste Feuillye, given the dangerousness of certain places, these were never explored. "Over the years, nature took hold again. The massive fortifications such as Azeville and Crisbecq became inextricable brambles where lay still winners and losers."

104. The Walls of the Missing in the cemetery of Colleville-sur-Mer carry 1557 names. We must extract from that 24% representing sailors lost at sea and subtract the 307 graves of unknown soldiers in this cemetery. There are thus 876 American soldiers and aviators still buried in the Normandy countryside.

105. The combat manual n° 10-63 (FM 10-63) entitled *"Graves Registration"* nonetheless stipulates that it is strictly forbidden for visitors to photograph the American graves. Furthermore, it is forbidden for visitors to cross the squares of graves: they must remain on the paths of the military cemetery.

106. Collection Renaud family.

107. Sampson Francis L., *Look out below,* Sweetwater, 101st Airborne Association, 1989, p. 78.

108. Collection Richard D. Johnson

109. Interview with Jean-Baptiste Feuillye, Fresville, January 12, 2011.

110. Collection Henri-Jean Renaud.

111. Collection Henri-Jean Renaud via Airborne Museum.

112. Memory is by definition vulnerable and selective. It retains only the events that valorize a group and its past, blocking out the less glorious aspects. The term "duty of history", on the other hand, leads to a rigorous and global approach.

113. Source INSEE, EHESS.

114. From an article which appeared in the magazine *"The Stars and Stripes"* of July 4, 1944. Collection Fitt family, via Richard Johnson.

115. Levesque André, *Sainte-Mère-Église, mon été 44. Mémoires d'outres-bombes,* Bordeaux, Éditions des Veys, 2010, p. 162-163.

116. Levesque André, *Sainte-Mère-Église... op. cit.* p. 171

117. Interview with Geneviève Pasquette, Chef-du-Pont, May 6, 2012.

118. Text by Simone Renaud [unsigned]. Collection Airborne Museum.

119. 145W76, military graves, May 18, 1946, Departmental Archives of La Manche.

120. 1012W341, *Deliberations of the city council of Sainte-Mère-Église, February 18, 1946,* Departmental Archives of La Manche.

121. See on this subject the excellent work of Constant Lebastard, Le *Cimetière américain de Colleville-sur-Mer. Une commission américaine en Normandie.* Bayeux, Éditions OREP, 2012, 328 pages.

122. NARA, RG 92, *Office of the Quartermaster General, Graves Registration, 1946-1948.*

123. NARA, RG 117, *Records of the ABMC, Proceedings of the Commission.*

124. *Ibid.*

125. *Ibid.*

126. The permanent cemetery of Colleville-sur-Mer was decided upon definitively on April 22, 1947.

127. Renaud Simone, *Terroir de Normandie*, 1975, p. 61-62.

128. The German graves in the temporary cemetery of Sainte-Mère-Église n° 1 represented in fact 31%.

129. Letter addressed to Alexandre Renaud, written by Lt. Col. John H. Michaelis, October 10, 1947. Collection Henri-Jean Renaud.

130. Interview with Geneviève Pasquette, Chef-du-Pont, May 5, 2012.

131. Collection Henri-Jean Renaud.

132. Interview with Jean-Baptiste Feuillye, Fresville, January 12, 2011.

133. Although the body of the permanent cemetery is localized on the territory of Saint-Laurent-sur-Mer, the entrance to this new cemetery was situated on the territory of Colleville-sur-Mer.

134. Lebastard Constant, *Le Cimetière américain de Colleville-sur-Mer... op. cit.,* p. 121-123.

135. *Ibid.* p. 95

136. Interview with Jean-Baptiste Feuillye, Fresville, January 12, 2011.

137. 1012W341, *Deliberations of the city council of Sainte-Mère-Église.* Departmental Archives of La Manche.

Bibliography and printed sources

DEATH AND THE COMBATANT EXPERIENCE

Audoin-Rouzeau Stéphane, *Combattre. Une anthropologie historique de la guerre moderne*, Paris, Seuil, 2008, 327 p.

Capdevilla L. et Voldman V., *Nos morts. Les sociétés occidentales face aux tués de la guerre*, Paris, Le Grand Livre du Mois, 2002, 282 p.

Fussell Paul, *À la guerre. Psychologie et comportements pendant la seconde guerre mondiale*, Paris, Seuil, 1992, 415 p.

Overmans Rüdiger, *Deutsche militärische Verluste im Zweiten Weltkrieg*, München, Oldenbourg, 2004, 362 p.

MILITARY CEMETERIES

Biraben Anne, *Les Cimetières militaires en France. Architecture et paysage*, Paris, L'Harmattan, 2005, 213 p.

Gilzmer Mechtild, *Mémoires de pierre. Les monuments commémoratifs en France après 1944*, Paris, Éditions Autrement, 2009, 270 p.

Lebastard Constant, *Le Cimetière américain de Colleville-sur-Mer. Une commission américaine en Normandie*, Bayeux, Éditions OREP, 2012, 328 p.

Ozouf Hugues, *In Memoriam. Les cimetières de guerre de la seconde guerre mondiale en Basse-Normandie. Dimension spatiale et sociale*, Mémoire de master 1, Université de Caen, 1999, 129 p.

HISTORIANS AND SAINT-MÈRE-ÉGLISE

French works

Bernage G. et François D., *Utah Beach. Sainte-Mère-Église. Sainte-Marie-du-Mont*, Bayeux, Heimdal, 2004, 148 p.

Bre Gilles, *Un pont en Normandie. Les combats de l'ouest de Sainte-Mère-Église du 6 au 9 juin 1944*, Publication à compte d'auteur, 2003, 194 p.

De Trez Michel, *Sainte-Mère-Église. 6 June 1944. Photographs of D-Day, Wezembeek-Oppem*, D-Day Publishing, 2004, 303 p.

Jutras Philippe, *Sainte-Mère-Église. Les paras du 6 juin*, Bayeux, Heimdal, 1991, 112 p.

Lecœur Maurice, *Un village du Cotentin. Sainte-Mère-Église. 1082-1944*, Paris, Fanval, 1988, 195 p.

Ryan Cornelius, *Le Jour le plus long*, Paris, Perrin, 1984, 211 p.

English works

Balkoski Joseph, *Utah Beach. The Amphibious Landing and Airborne Operations on D-Day*, Mechanicsburg, Stackpole Books, 2005, 380 p.

Langdon Allen L., *Ready. A World War II History of the 505th PIR*, Édité par le révérend George B. Wood, 1986, 150 p.

Marshall S.L.A, *Night Drop. The American Airborne Invasion of Normandy*, Boston, Atlantic Monthly Press Book, 1962, 425 p.

Nordyke Phil, *Four stars of valor. The combat history of the 505th Parachute Infantry Regiment in World War II*, Minneapolis, Zenith Press, 2006, 480 p.

Stoffer Jeff, *Mother of Normandy. The story of Simone Renaud*, Iron Mike Entertainment Inc., 2010, 117 p.

Tanks of Gen. Leclerc's *2nd Armored Division* crossing Sainte-Mère-Église at the beginning of August 1944. NARA

PRINTED SOURCES (AUTOBIOGRAPHICAL NARRATIVES AND COLLECTIONS OF EYEWITNESS ACCOUNTS)

French works

Levesque André, *Sainte-Mère-Église. Mon été 44. Mémoires d'outre-bombes*, Bordeaux, Éditions des Veys, 2010, 201 p.

Renaud Alexandre, *Sainte-Mère-Église, première tête de pont américaine en France. 6 juin 1944*, Paris, Julliard, 2002, 141 p.

Tucker William H., *Jour J : trente-cinq jours en Normandie. Réflexions d'un parachutiste*, publication à compte d'auteur, traduit de l'anglais par Émile Lacroix, 2002, 147 p.

English works

Murphy Robert M., No better place to die. Sainte-Mère-Église, June 1944. The battle of La Fière Bridge, Boston, Casemate, 2011, 288 p.

Alexander Mark, Jump Commander. In Combat with the 505th and 508th Parachute Infantry Regiments, 82nd Airborne Division in World War II, Boston, Casemate, 2010, 288 p.

Gavin James M., On To Berlin, New York, Bantam, 1992, 165 p.

TABLE OF CONTENTS

June 6, 1944, a lost paratrooper belonging to the 508th PIR (82nd Airborne Division) asks for directions from two children of Ravenoville. NARA

OREP
EDITIONS

Zone tertiaire de Nonant - 14400 BAYEUX
Tel.: 02 31 51 81 31 - Fax: 02 31 51 81 32
Email: info@orepeditions.com - Site: www.orepeditions.com

Editor: Grégory PIQUE
Editorial coordinator: Corine DESPREZ
Graphique design: OREP - **Layout:** Laurent SAND
ISBN: 978-2-8151-252-0 - **Copyright OREP 2015**
Dépôt légal: 2nd quarter 2015